GUIDE TO ICSID
ARBITRATION

GUIDE TO ICSID ARBITRATION

Lucy Reed

Jan Paulsson

Nigel Blackaby

KLUWER LAW INTERNATIONAL
THE HAGUE / LONDON / NEW YORK

A C.I.P. catalogue record for this book is available from the Library of Congress.

ISBN 90 411 2093 9

Published by:
Kluwer Law International
P.O. Box 85889
2508 CN The Hague
The Netherlands

Sold and Distributed in North, Central and South America by:
Aspen Publishers, Inc.
7201 McKinney Circle
Frederick, MD 21704
USA

Sold and distributed in all other countries by:
Extenza-Turpin Distribution Services
Stratton Business Park
Pegasus Drive
Biggleswade
Bedfordshire SG18 8QB
United Kingdom

Printed on acid-free paper.

Contents

Acknowledgments

This Guide proves, once again, that it is a far greater challenge to write a short book than a long one. The challenge is magnified when as here, the goal is, to explain a complex field to newcomers rather than to analyze nuances for fellow experienced practitioners.

We could not have met this challenge without the help of many of our valued colleagues in the Freshfields Bruckhaus Deringer international arbitration group. We thank, in particular, our partners Nigel Rawding and Brian King, and our associates Lise Bosman, Leilah Bruton, Hannah Garry, Stéphanie Giry, Lynn Haaland, Inka Hanefeld, Alison Hayes, Lluis Paradell, Stephanie Rosenkranz, Jonathan Sutcliffe, Stephanie Webster and Alexander Yanos. We also thank our summer associates Donna Lee and Aaron Stonecash, and our assistants Keri Grant, Jo Lipari and Gail Varga.

Preface

One of the chief impediments to foreign investment in developing countries has been the investors' perception that, in the event of disputes with the host State, they would find themselves without an effective legal remedy. Investors may no longer realistically rely on their own governments to espouse their claims, at least promptly and successfully, under traditional avenues of diplomatic protection. If investors proceed alone against the host State, they fear discrimination in the local courts.

To help resolve this quandary, the World Bank conceived a special forum for arbitrating investment disputes. Since its entry into force in 1966, the groundbreaking International Convention on the Settlement of Investment Disputes between States and Nationals of Other States (the *ICSID Convention* or the *Convention*) has offered eligible States and foreign investors the opportunity to bring their investment disputes to neutral ad hoc arbitration tribunals. These tribunals are administered by the World Bank's International Centre for Settlement of Investment Disputes (*ICSID* or the *Centre*) in Washington, DC. These tribunals are entirely self-contained and delocalized, meaning that they function independently of local courts and local procedural law. Most important, ICSID awards – unlike any other international arbitration awards – are immune from any form of national court review, and yet are enforceable in the courts of the more than 135 signatory States as if they were national court judgments.

Nonetheless, because arbitration arising directly under the ICSID Convention is limited to cases in which foreign investors and States have explicitly provided for ICSID arbitration in a contract to which the relevant State (or a specifically designated subdivision of the State) is required to be a party, ICSID arbitration was little used for the first 20 years of its existence. There were isolated cases that did set valuable precedents for investors and States and attracted scholarly interest, but ICSID arbitration remained rather esoteric.

The situation has changed dramatically since the mid-1990s. This is primarily due to the proliferation of bilateral investment treaties (*BITs*) providing for ICSID arbitration of foreign investment disputes. Generally speaking, each State party to a BIT pledges to provide investors from the other State with certain minimum substantive protections, including the right to fair and equitable treatment and the right to be compensated for expropriation, and agrees that such investors may commence ICSID arbitration (or other agreed form of international arbitration) directly against it to obtain redress for violations of the substantive protections of the BIT. Between 1990 and 2003, the number of bilateral investment treaties increased from about 385 to over 2,000. By 2002, some three-quarters of the cases registered with ICSID were BIT arbitrations.

In this dramatic legal development, which we predicted in 1995, bilateral investment treaties have thus generated non-contractual arbitration – or "arbitration without privity."[1] Today, any company considering a new investment in a developing country and any financing entity playing a role in the investment must be aware of ICSID and must be aware of the growing matrix of BITs providing access to ICSID. At the project negotiation and documentation stage, counsel for investors, financiers and government entities must be attuned to possible rights and responsibilities under the ICSID Convention and under available BITs. In sum, advisers to all sides must be at least familiar with the ICSID arbitration regime long before actual disputes might begin to develop.

Similarly, when a dispute arises in connection with an existing foreign investment, counsel for the investor must consider all of the potentially applicable BITs to identify the substantive rights and arbitral mechanisms that may be envisaged under them. This must be done promptly and effectively, because parties that commence litigation or pursue other arbitration remedies may unknowingly waive the essential right of access to ICSID.

It is this fundamental change in the legal context of international investment flows that inspired this Guide.

SCOPE OF THIS GUIDE

We intend this Guide to be true to its purposefully modest title. It is designed to give international investors and their in-house counsel, as well as government legal advisers, an elemental understanding of the ICSID arbitration system and how it may (and may not) be used. For those desiring more detailed and analytical treatment of the ICSID regime, we have included a selective bibliography in Annex 9.

We start with a general introduction to the ICSID regime and the comparative merits of ICSID arbitration (Chapter 1). We then explain:

– the contours of contractual ICSID arbitration and how to draft an ICSID arbitration clause (Chapter 2),
– the growth in bilateral investment treaties and other investment treaties providing for ICSID arbitration and the basics of ICSID treaty arbitration (Chapter 3),
– the ICSID rules and how the ICSID arbitration process works in practice

---

[1]   J. Paulsson, *Arbitration Without Privity*, 10 *ICSID Review* – Foreign Investment Law Journal 232 (1995).

(Chapter 4), and
- the unique "self-contained"regime of annulment, recognition and enforcement of ICSID awards (Chapter 5).

The ICSID Convention, the many sets of ICSID rules (amended as of January 2003) and the ICSID case docket are readily available on the ICSID website at www.worldbank.org/icsid. Nevertheless, for ease of reference, we have annexed the basic ICSID materials most useful for practitioners, as well as illustrative treaty materials and the selective bibliography previously mentioned:

- the ICSID Convention (Annex 1),
  a list of ICSID Contracting States (Annex 2),
- the ICSID Institution Rules (Annex 3),
- the ICSID Arbitration Rules (Annex 4),
- the Model ICSID clauses (Annex 5),
- as an example, the US-Bahrain BIT (Annex 6),
- as an example, the UK Model BIT (Annex 7),
- Chapter 11 of the North America Free Trade Agreement (Annex 8),
- a selective bibliography (Annex 9), and
- an analytical chart of BITs entered into between ICSID Contracting States (Annex 10).

We call particular attention to the chart in Annex 10. Using the public data at our disposal, we have plotted 877 BITs entered into by ICSID Contracting States as of January 2003, with selected industrialized Contracting States on one axis and other Contracting States on the other axis, and the dates of ratification or signature in the body of the chart. This should streamline the surprisingly time-consuming task, when one wants to explore the options for ICSID Convention arbitration of a particular investment dispute, of answering the seemingly simple questions: "Is there a BIT between State X and State Y? If so, effective as of when?"[2]

A primer like this could not possibly be a complete instruction manual for conducting a case. ICSID arbitrations, by definition, involve disputes between States and foreign investors, which typically raise complex issues of public international law including state responsibility and jurisdiction, not to mention the interplay of those issues with local law. The disputes frequently arise in long-term major projects with multiple private and public players, so that the factual and contractual context also tends to be complex. To assume responsibility for such cases calls for experience and learning that cannot be distilled in an introductory guide such as this. Our goal here is much more circumscribed: it is simply to familiarize prospective or first-time users with the ICSID regime.

---

[2] Freshfields Bruckhaus Deringer has also created a more extensive database of the same information for some 2,000 BITs and bilateral trade agreements in force as of January 2003, which is available at < www.kluwerarbitration.com >.

We make the emphatic disclaimer that critical analysis of ICSID case law is beyond the scope of this Guide. ICSID jurisprudence on issues of jurisdiction, merits and damages, as well as on the annulment of awards, is growing and evolving rapidly. In this brief book, our discussion of cases is illustrative only, and therefore necessarily incomplete.

Finally, this Guide assumes basic familiarity with the principles and practice of international commercial arbitration. ICSID arbitration has many distinct procedural and jurisdictional features, but many of its fundamental elements are essentially the same as in other international commercial arbitration proceedings. For those unversed in the basics or wishing a refresher, we recommend *The Freshfields Guide to Arbitration and ADR: Clauses in International Contracts* (***The Freshfields Guide***).[3]

---

[3]   J. Paulsson, N. Rawding, L. Reed & F. Schwartz, *The Freshfields Guide to Arbitration and ADR: Clauses in International Contracts* (2nd ed., Kluwer Law International, 1999).

CHAPTER 1

Introduction to ICSID

The International Centre for the Settlement of Investment Disputes was established under the 1965 ICSID Convention, which came into force in October 1966 (Annex 1). Executed in Washington, DC, the ICSID Convention is also known as the Washington Convention. As of January 2003, 138 States had both signed and ratified the ICSID Convention, including all the major industrialized States with the exception of Canada (***Contracting States***). A list of the Contracting States appears in Annex 2.

HISTORY OF THE ICSID CONVENTION

The International Bank for Reconstruction and Development (the ***IBRD***), more commonly known as the World Bank, sponsored the Convention. Particular credit for the Convention goes to Aron Broches, then General Counsel of the World Bank. As described by Professor Elihu Lauterpacht in his foreword to Professor Christoph Schreuer's detailed commentary on the ICSID Convention,[4] Broches conceived the idea for the Convention in 1961 in the wake of earlier efforts by the Organization for European Economic Co-operation (now the Organization for Economic Co-operation and Development, or ***OECD***) to create a framework for the protection of international investment. The OECD exercise (which led to the OECD Draft Convention on the Protection of Foreign Property) revealed intractable controversy as to the proper level of compensation for expropriation of foreign investments. Broches and others recognized that it would be more productive to strive for multilateral agreement on a *process* for independent resolution of individual investment disputes rather than on actual substantive standards.

Broches effectively conceived and pursued a new strategy for negotiation of the necessary international convention, by convening consultative conferences of legal experts in Africa, the Americas, Asia and Europe to discuss a preliminary draft. On the basis of the reports of these conferences,[5] the World Bank staff prepared a first official draft of the Convention, met with a legal committee representing the

---

[4] C. Schreuer, *The ICSID Convention: A Commentary* xi-xiii (Cambridge University Press, 2001).
[5] The detailed reports of the 1963 and 1964 regional conferences are compiled in *History of the ICSID Convention: Documents Concerning the Origin and Formulation of the Convention on the Settlement of Investment Disputes between States and Nationals of Other States*, Vols. I-IV (ICSID, Washington, D.C., 1970).

Executive Directors of the Bank, and then submitted the final draft to the Executive Directors for approval.

In March 1965, the Executive Directors approved the text of the ICSID Convention, issued a companion report (the **Report**),[6] and directed the President of the Bank to circulate the Convention and Report to all member States. The mandatory minimum 20 States quickly ratified the Convention, and it entered into force on 14 October 1966. Most important, both industrialized and developing countries have signed on over the years, resulting in the remarkably high membership of 138 States (as of January 2003).

GOALS OF THE ICSID CONVENTION

Given the growing body of ICSID jurisprudence and the increasing interest of arbitration practitioners in the ICSID dispute resolution process as a forensic art, it is easy to forget that the primary purpose of the ICSID Convention was (and remains) to promote foreign investment. The Report of the Executive Directors on the Convention, mentioned above, emphasizes the aim of promoting global economic development through private international investment. The theme of partnership and interdependence between industrialized and developing countries, protected by a regime of truly independent dispute resolution, is also emphasized in the Report:

"9. In submitting the attached Convention to governments, the Executive Directors are prompted by the desire to strengthen the partnership between countries in the cause of economic development. The creation of an institution designed to facilitate the settlement of disputes between States and foreign investors can be a major step toward promoting an atmosphere of mutual confidence and thus stimulating a larger flow of private international capital into those countries which wish to attract it.

10. The Executive Directors recognize that investment disputes are as a rule settled through administrative, judicial or arbitral procedures available under the laws of the country in which the investment concerned is made. However, experience shows that disputes may arise which the parties wish to settle by other methods; and investment agreements entered into in recent years show that both States and investors frequently consider that it is in their mutual interest to agree to resort to international methods of settlement.

11. The present Convention would offer international methods of settlement designed to take account of the special characteristics of the dispute covered, as well as of the parties to whom it would apply. It would provide facilities for

---

[6] International Bank for Reconstruction and Development, *Report of the Executive Directors on the Convention on the Settlement of Investment Disputes between States and Nationals of Other States* (18 March 1965), in 1 *ICSID Reports* 23-33 (1993).

conciliation and arbitration by specially qualified persons of independent judgment carried out according to rules known and accepted in advance by the parties concerned. In particular, it would ensure that once a government or investor had given consent to conciliation or arbitration under the auspices of the Centre, such consent could not be unilaterally withdrawn.

12. The Executive Directors believe that private capital will continue to flow to countries offering a favorable climate for attractive and sound investments, even if such countries did not become parties to the Convention or, having joined, did not make use of the facilities of the Centre. On the other hand, adherence to the Convention by a country would provide additional inducement and stimulate a large flow of private international investment into its territories, which is the primary purpose of the Convention.

13. While the broad objective of the Convention is to encourage a larger flow of private international investment, the provisions of the Convention maintain a careful balance between the interests of investors and those of host States. Moreover, the Convention permits the institution of proceedings by host States as well as by investors and the Executive Directors have constantly had in mind that the provisions of the Convention should be equally adapted to the requirements of both cases."[7]

In sum, the Executive Directors of the World Bank emphasized the balance inherent in the Convention: the basic goal of the ICSID system is to promote much-needed international investment by offering a neutral dispute resolution forum both to investors that are (rightly or wrongly) wary of nationalistic decisions by local courts and to host States that are (rightly or wrongly) wary of self-interested actions by foreign investors.

The Preamble of the Convention itself underlines this economic goal and the operational goal of establishing an effective regime for neutral resolution of investment disputes that is attractive to States and investors alike:

"The Contracting States

Considering the need for international cooperation for economic development, and the role of private international investment therein;

Bearing in mind the possibility that from time to time disputes may arise in connection with such investment between Contracting States and nationals of other Contracting States;

Recognizing that while such disputes would usually be subject to national legal processes, international methods of settlement may be appropriate in certain cases;

Attaching particular importance to the availability of facilities for international conciliation or arbitration to which Contracting States and nationals of other Contracting States may submit such disputes if they so desire;

---

[7] *Report of the Executive Directors, supra* note 6, at 25.

Desiring to establish such facilities under the auspices of the International Bank for Reconstruction and Development;

Recognizing that mutual consent by the parties to submit such disputes to conciliation or to arbitration through such facilities constitutes a binding agreement which requires in particular that due consideration be given to any recommendation of conciliators, and that any arbitral award be complied with; and

Declaring that no Contracting State shall by the mere fact of its ratification, acceptance or approval of this Convention and without its consent be deemed to be under any obligation to submit any particular dispute to conciliation or arbitration,

Have agreed as follows:" (emphasis in original).

The Convention then proceeds to its ten chapters and seventy-five articles, with aspirational language giving way to detailed legal procedures.

THE VIEW FROM HERE

How has ICSID measured up against the goals set out in the Preamble and expressed by the Executive Directors in 1965? If this question had been posed in the 1970s or 1980s, the answer would have been qualified. There were few ICSID cases then and scant evidence that ICSID clauses were prevalent in international investment contracts.

The answer today is both clear and positive. This is not just because the number of cases registered with ICSID is at an all-time high. Nor is it because more investors and States are including ICSID clauses in their agreements (as to which there is no reliable statistical data).

The critical difference is the proliferation of bilateral investment treaties, which is an indicator of dramatically increased interest in foreign investment. The fact that many, if not most, BITs include the option of ICSID dispute resolution perhaps confirms the connection between increased foreign investment and the availability of a neutral dispute resolution process, as envisioned by the drafters of the ICSID Convention some forty years ago. The first investment treaty case was registered in 1987 and the case flow has increased steadily since then.

With ICSID now squarely in the international spotlight, the obvious questions are whether and how the actual outcome of the new wave of BIT cases will affect foreign investment (and ICSID itself). As in other fields of dispute resolution, most ICSID cases continue to settle – but some proportion of them will go to awards on the merits and thereby make new investment law. Predictions as to what this law will be are beyond the scope of this Guide. The only certainty is that international investment law will continue to evolve, perhaps in accelerated fashion as a result of the sheer number of cases.

In this context, it is well worth quoting Professor Lauterpacht's observations (again in the foreword to Professor Schreuer's commentary) about the many achievements of the ICSID Convention that are now taken for granted:

"At the time the Convention was concluded, some of its most important features represented significant new developments, though in the light of subsequent advances in international law they now appear almost commonplace. For the first time a system was instituted under which non-State entities – corporations or individuals – could sue States directly; in which State immunity was much restricted; under which international law could be applied directly to the relationship between the investor and the host State; in which the operation of the local remedies rule was excluded; and in which the tribunal's award would be directly enforceable within the territories of the States parties."[8]

ICSID: The Institution

ICSID is one of the five international organizations that make up the World Bank group. It is located at the World Bank headquarters in Washington, DC. The Centre itself does not conduct arbitration proceedings, but administers their initiation and functioning.

ICSID comprises an Administrative Council and a Secretariat. The former is the governing body. It meets in conjunction with the World Bank annual meeting, and is chaired ex officio by the President of the World Bank. It consists of one representative of each Contracting State, usually a finance minister or his or her deputy.

A Secretary-General and a Deputy Secretary-General, who are elected by the Administrative Council, head the Secretariat. The Secretary-General traditionally is the General Counsel of the World Bank. The Secretariat provides institutional support for arbitration by, among other things, keeping lists of possible arbitrators, screening and registering arbitration requests, assisting in the constitution of arbitral tribunals and their operations, administering the funds required to cover the costs of the proceedings, adopting rules and regulations for the conduct of arbitrations, and drafting model arbitration clauses for investment agreements.

The Secretariat staff includes several experienced and multi-lingual counsel, who are generally available for consultations with representatives of the parties who may require clarification as to matters of procedure. Most important, the Secretary-General appoints one of them as the Secretary for each tribunal. The Secretary maintains the file, serves as the official conduit for the transmission of written submissions and evidence, makes the necessary practical arrangements for hearings, keeps minutes of hearings, ensures that adequate funds to cover the costs of the arbitration are in hand, prepares drafts of procedural orders, and generally assists the arbitrators as requested.

The ICSID staff performs substantial professional work beyond case administration, primarily with respect to publication of information and scholarship. The Centre publishes, among other things: (a) the *ICSID Review – Foreign Investment*

---

[8] Schreuer, *supra* note 4, at xi.

Law Journal, a highly regarded journal containing articles, case reports and book reviews (available biannually by subscription); (b) *News from ICSID*, a biannual bulletin (available on the ICSID website); (c) *ICSID Basic Documents*, a bound booklet of the Convention and key rules (the text of which is also available on the website); (d) the *ICSID Annual Report* (also available on the website); and (e) a variety of bibliographies and compilations of bilateral investment treaties and laws. The Centre organizes conferences, and senior Secretariat attorneys make significant spoken and written contributions in the field of investment law.

As noted, the ICSID Secretariat is housed at the World Bank headquarters in Washington, DC. The Bank provides the Centre with office space, general facilities such as hearing rooms and conference space, and administrative services. Pursuant to Convention Article 17, the Bank funds the administrative budget of ICSID.[9] The practical effect is that Contracting States cannot delay proceedings, either in general or in specific cases, by failing to pay separate charges for ICSID membership. Both State and private parties to arbitrations pay only modest usage fees, in addition to the expenses of the particular tribunals constituted to deal with their case.

ICSID: The Rules and Regulations

ICSID has several sets of rules and regulations, designed to serve distinct purposes. All may be found on the ICSID website. The main rules and regulations, amended in January 2003, include:

- the Administrative and Financial Regulations, which govern meetings of the Administrative Council and regulate the Centre's administration of conciliation and arbitration proceedings,
- the Institution Rules, which regulate the initiation of ICSID conciliation and arbitration proceedings (Annex 3),
- the Arbitration Rules, which set out procedures for the conduct of the various phases of arbitration proceedings, including the constitution of the tribunal, the parties' written and oral presentations of their respective cases, and the preparation of the arbitral award (Annex 4), and,
- the Conciliation Rules, which govern the conduct of conciliation proceedings.

The rules and regulations most relevant to ICSID arbitration in practice are discussed in detail in Chapter 4.

---

[9] Article 17 of the Convention provides in full: "If the expenditure of the Centre cannot be met out of charges for the use of its facilities, or out of other receipts, the excess shall be borne by Contracting States which are members of the Bank in proportion to their respective subscriptions to the capital stock of the Bank, and by Contracting States which are not members of the Bank in accordance with rules adopted by the Administrative Council." The Bank and ICSID entered into a Memorandum of Administrative Arrangements on 13 February 1967, under which the Bank pays ICSID staff salaries and administrative expenses.

ARBITRATION UNDER THE ICSID CONVENTION

Essential Criteria

In order for ICSID arbitration to be invoked, three criteria must first be fulfilled (each criterion is examined in detail elsewhere in this Guide):

– First, the parties must have *consented* to their dispute being submitted to ICSID arbitration. Consent must be given in writing. It may refer to either an existing dispute or a defined class of future disputes.

– Second, the dispute must be *between a Contracting State and a national of another Contracting State*. Contracting States may authorize constituent subdivisions or agencies to become parties to ICSID proceedings on their behalf.

– Third, the dispute must be a *legal dispute arising directly out of an investment*. The term "investment" is not defined in the Convention but has been given a broad interpretation by ICSID tribunals.

Contractual versus Non-contractual ICSID Arbitration

ICSID arbitration traditionally arose out of investor-State contracts containing express reference to ICSID for dispute resolution, provided that both the host State and the investor's country of origin were parties to the ICSID Convention and certain other jurisdictional limitations were met. Contractual ICSID arbitration, and the relevant jurisdictional limitations, are discussed in Chapter 2.

ICSID accepts arbitrations that arise not only from a direct agreement to arbitrate between investor and host State, but also arbitrations that arise from indirect consent to ICSID arbitration contained in (a) the host State's national investment legislation, (b) a bilateral investment treaty between the host State and the investor's home State, or (c) a multilateral investment treaty between countries that include the host State and the investor's home State. Three-quarters of the arbitrations pending with ICSID as of 2002 were brought under an instrument other than an arbitration clause in an investor-State contract. Non-contractual ICSID arbitration, which differs in many significant respects from contractual ICSID arbitration, is examined in Chapter 3.

WHY CHOOSE ICSID?

Although counsel to any corporation making a foreign investment in a Contracting State should always carefully evaluate, and often favor, an ICSID arbitration clause, ICSID arbitration is not the best option in every situation. There may well be considerations militating in favor of other dispute resolution options, for example, International Chamber of Commerce (**ICC**) arbitration or ad hoc arbitration under the United Nations Commission on International Trade Law (**UNCITRAL**) arbitration rules.[10] We address some of the main advantages of ICSID arbitration below.

Neutral and Self-contained System

In typical international commercial arbitration, the parties select or the relevant arbitration rules provide a mechanism for determining the place of the arbitration. The place, in turn, determines the procedural law for the conduct of the arbitration. The local courts of the place of arbitration may, depending on the local law, have the opportunity to intervene to (a) designate the arbitral tribunal, (b) grant interim measures, or (c) rule on applications to set aside awards.

By contrast, as detailed in Chapter 5, the ICSID Convention provides that the arbitration law of the place of arbitration, wherever it may be, has no impact whatsoever on the proceedings. The ICSID process is entirely self-contained and hence delocalized. The Centre oversees the appointment of arbitrators to the tribunal, the tribunal handles provisional measures, and an ICSID-appointed ad hoc committee conducts annulment proceedings. ICSID awards are final and binding on the parties. They are not subject to any appeal or review by national courts, but only to the limited remedies provided in the Convention itself: rectification, interpretation, revision and annulment (as discussed in Chapters 4 and 5).

Furthermore, under the Convention, the monetary obligations arising from ICSID awards must be recognized and enforced in Contracting States as if they were final judgments of the local courts. This too is a distinctive feature of ICSID arbitration, as other international arbitration regimes leave enforcement to domestic laws or other applicable treaties such as the 1958 Convention on the Recognition and Enforcement of Foreign Arbitral Awards (the **New York Convention**) and the Inter-American Convention on International Commercial Arbitration (the **Panama Convention**). These domestic laws and treaties typically provide limited grounds for reviewing and setting aside arbitral awards or for refusing to recognize and enforce them.

Privacy with Transparency

Most international arbitral proceedings are private, and some degree of confidentiality may be preserved (although attempts to define the nature of the confidentiality obligation and its exceptions have defeated drafters of legislation and many sets of arbitration rules). As in other international arbitrations, ICSID hearings are private and submissions are confidential.

In contrast to other arbitrations, however, the registers maintained by the ICSID Secretariat (under Administrative and Financial Regulations 22 and 23) – which are

---

[10] For a comparison of the various major international institutional and ad hoc arbitration rules, see *The Freshfields Guide, supra* note 3, at 127-137.

now available not only in the ICSID Annual Reports but also on the ICSID website – ensure that the existence, current status and ultimate disposition of ICSID arbitrations are matters of public record. Article 4 of the Convention allows ICSID to publish awards itself only when both parties consent, but parties also frequently publish unilaterally. In practice, almost all ICSID awards are published and readily available.

This comparative transparency has a strategically important side effect. Because many States want to be considered investment-friendly, the prospect being named – publicly – in an ICSID arbitration may intimidate hosts States more than the threat of other international arbitral proceedings and provide investors with more leverage in early negotiations.

Clear and Reasonable Cost Schedules

Like most major international arbitral institutions, ICSID provides a transparent cost structure. ICSID is unusual, however, in including a fixed rate for the remuneration of arbitrators. This rate was increased from USD1,500 to USD2,000 per day in the July 2002 Schedule of Fees. These fees are modest when compared with those typically charged by leading arbitration professionals in their other work. ICSID's administrative costs are also relatively low.

The "World Bank Factor"

Most, if not all, ICSID awards rendered have been either successfully settled or voluntarily executed by the parties. This is no doubt partly due to ICSID's being an organ of the World Bank and to the perception that failure to respect an ICSID award would have indirect political consequences in terms of credibility with the World Bank. (Whether the World Bank actively promotes respect for ICSID awards is open to question. ICSID claims no special clout and is obviously unlikely to browbeat the very States that constitute its governing Administrative Council. Nevertheless, it is difficult to imagine a World Bank lawyer seriously recommending the use of ICSID clauses in documentation for projects in a country whose government has notoriously ignored an ICSID award.) ICSID's connections to the World Bank also make it popular in contracts involving other multinational lending agencies.

ADDITIONAL SERVICES PROVIDED BY ICSID

The Additional Facility

In the face of demand, the World Bank created the ICSID Additional Facility in 1978 to extend the availability of ICSID arbitration to certain types of proceedings between States and foreign nationals that fall outside the scope of the ICSID Convention. The Additional Facility is not a separate institution or even a physically separate part of ICSID. The same Secretariat serves both.

The arbitrations conducted under the Additional Facility include proceedings where either the State party or the home State of the foreign investor is not a member of ICSID. This possibility is particularly important in the context of cases brought under Chapter 11 of the North American Free Trade Agreement (*NAFTA*), because the United States is an ICSID Contracting State but Canada and Mexico are not. Although ordinary ICSID arbitration under the ICSID Convention is thus not available between NAFTA States, Additional Facility arbitration is available, on the one hand, between US investors and Canada or Mexico and, on the other hand, between Canadian or Mexican investors and the US. (In disputes between Canadian investors and Mexico or between Canada and Mexican investors, only UNCITRAL arbitration is available.) Article 26 of the Energy Charter Treaty also provides for Additional Facility arbitration among other dispute resolution methods.

Under Article 4(3) of the Rules Governing the Additional Facility for the Administration of Proceedings by the Secretariat of the International Centre for Settlement of Investment Disputes (*Additional Facility Rules*), the Secretary-General of ICSID may approve agreements to use the Additional Facility even if they do not arise directly out of an investment, but only if he or she is satisfied that "the underlying transaction has features which distinguish it from an ordinary commercial transaction." This reflects the policy that ICSID is not to be used for commercial disputes of the type routinely handled by other international or national arbitration institutions.

The provisions of the ICSID Convention do not apply to Additional Facility proceedings (although many of the guiding principles are similar). Instead, arbitrations administered under the Additional Facility are subject to: (a) the Additional Facility Rules; (b) the Administrative and Financial Rules (Additional Facility); and (c) the Arbitration (Additional Facility) Rules.

Most important to potential users, these distinctions mean that the ICSID Convention's special self-contained provisions on recognition and enforcement of awards are not applicable to Additional Facility awards. Additional Facility awards should thus be equated with ordinary international commercial arbitration awards such as those rendered under the rules of the ICC, the London Court of Arbitration, the American Arbitration Association and UNCITRAL. This explains why Article 19 of the Arbitration (Additional Facility) Rules provides that arbitral proceedings under the Additional Facility may be held only in countries that are parties to the New York Convention; otherwise, the awards would be unduly vulnerable at the enforcement stage.

Potential users must also be aware that access to Additional Facility arbitration is subject to the Secretary-General's specific consent. According to Article 4 of the Additional Facility Rules, any agreement providing for arbitration proceedings under the auspices of the Additional Facility, whether in respect of existing or future disputes, requires the approval of the Secretary-General. As a practical matter, therefore, it is advisable for the parties to submit the relevant draft agreement to the Secretary-General for approval before the agreement is signed or enters into effect. If the dispute does not "arise directly out of an investment," it is at this stage that the Secretariat may examine whether the transaction nevertheless has "features that distinguish it from an ordinary commercial transaction" under Article 4(3) of the Additional Facility Rules.

ICSID as Appointing Authority

Public and private parties occasionally seek the assistance of the Secretary-General in connection with arbitrations conducted under rules other than those of ICSID, by having the Secretary-General appoint one or more arbitrators in the event the parties fail to do so. As of January 2003, the Secretary-General had acted as appointing authority in ad hoc arbitrations on 15 occasions.

The Secretary-General is not obliged to act as appointing authority and does not always agree to do so. Consequently, parties wishing to utilize this service should obtain the Secretary-General's consent in advance. In practice, parties should submit the appointment provision in draft form to the Secretariat, together with a copy of the relevant arbitration agreement containing the provision. The appointment provision may be bare bones, as illustrated by ICSID Model Clause 22:

> "Any dispute, controversy or claim arising out of or relating to this contract, or the breach, termination or invalidity thereof, shall be settled by arbitration in accordance with the UNCITRAL Arbitration Rules as at present in force. The appointing authority shall be the Secretary-General of the International Centre for Settlement of Investment Disputes. [The number of arbitrators shall be [one]/ [three]. The place of arbitration shall be name of town or country. The languages to be used in the arbitral proceedings shall be name of language(s).]"

Alternative Dispute Resolution

Alternative dispute resolution processes, although rarely used in the ICSID framework, may be valuable in resolution of investor-State disputes. This may particularly be the case where an investor and the host State want to preserve an investment project despite a dispute.

Chapter III (Articles 28 to 35) of the ICSID Convention provides for conciliation as an institutionalized means of resolving investment disputes in a non-binding fashion. Either a Contracting State or a national of a Contracting State may institute conciliation by filing a request with the Secretary-General. As with arbitration, consent to conciliation by both parties is necessary. One or three persons comprise the Conciliation Commission, with the Secretary-General making appointments as necessary.

The heart of the ICSID conciliation process is not fundamentally different than other types of third-party assisted settlement, as illustrated by Convention Articles 34 and 35:

Article 34

"(1) It shall be the duty of the [Conciliation] Commission to clarify the issues in dispute between the parties and to endeavour to bring about agreement between them upon mutually acceptable terms. To that end, the Commission may at any stage of the proceedings and from time to time recommend terms of settlement to the parties. The parties shall cooperate in good faith with the Commission in order to enable the Commission to carry out its functions, and shall give their most serious consideration to its recommendations.

(2) If the parties reach agreement, the Commission shall draw up a report noting the issues in dispute and recording that the parties have reached agreement. If, at any stage of the proceedings, it appears to the Commission that there is no likelihood of agreement between the parties, it shall close the proceedings and shall draw up a report noting the submission of the dispute and recording the failure of the parties to reach agreement. If one party fails to appear or participate in the proceedings, the Commission shall close the proceedings and shall draw up a report noting that party's failure to appear or participate."

Article 35

"Except as the parties to the dispute shall otherwise agree, neither party to a conciliation proceeding shall be entitled in any other proceeding, whether before arbitrators or in a court of law or otherwise, to invoke or rely on any views expressed or statements or admissions or offers of settlement made by the other party in the conciliation proceedings, or the report or any recommendations made by the Commission."

ICSID has reported only three conciliation cases (two involving the same pair of parties). The parties in one case settled before a Conciliation Commission was constituted;[11] the parties in the second case settled with the assistance of a Conciliation Commission;[12] and the parties in the third case did not settle.[13] In light of the limited use of ICSID conciliation services, this Guide will not deal with the topic further.

---

[11] *SEDITEX Engineering Beratungsgesellschaft für die Textilindustrie m.b.H. v. Democratic Republic of Madagascar*, ICSID Case No. CONC/82/1.

[12] *Tesoro Petroleum Corp. v. Trinidad and Tobago*, ICSID Case No. CONC/83/1. *See* L. Nurick and S.J. Schnably, *The First ICSID Conciliation: Tesoro Petroleum Corporation v. Trinidad and Tobago*, 1 *ICSID Review – FILJ* 340 (1986).

[13] *SEDITEX Engineering Beratungsgesellschaft für die Textilindustrie m.b.H. v. Democratic Republic of Madagascar*, ICSID Case No. CONC/94/1.

CHAPTER 2

Contractual ICSID Arbitration

If one were striving for brevity and nothing else, one might devise this ICSID clause:

> "The parties hereto consent to submit to the International Centre for the Settlement of Investment Disputes any dispute relating to or arising out of this Agreement for settlement by arbitration pursuant to the Convention on the Settlement of Investment Disputes between States and Nationals of Other States."[14]

Given the complexity of contractual ICSID arbitration, however, the Centre has published no such succinct multi-purpose model clause. The Centre has instead developed 22 highly sophisticated clauses for various uses (the *Model Clauses*), along with explanatory notes for each. The Model Clauses are tailored to different types of disputes and different circumstances, such as: consent in anticipation of subsequent ratification of the ICSID Convention by a non-Contracting State; contracts signed by government agencies or subdivisions; deemed nationality of the investor; preservation of the rights of the investor after compensation (including by insurers); and exhaustion of local remedies. Annex 5 reproduces the Model Clauses that were current as of 2003; they are updated periodically on the ICSID website (www.worldbank.org/icsid/model-clauses-en/main.htm).

Parties to investment contracts are well advised to consider the Model Clauses when negotiating and drafting an ICSID arbitration agreement. Given that the Convention strictly circumscribes ICSID jurisdiction, however, it would be negligent to cut and paste from the Model Clauses. An ICSID arbitration clause must be adapted to the particular parties, the particular investment contract, and the particular investment disputes most likely to arise. Investors and governments alike should insist upon specialist advice before drafting or agreeing to an ICSID arbitration clause.

This chapter describes traditional ICSID contractual arbitration under the Convention, especially the requirements of ICSID jurisdiction and other considerations relevant to drafting an effective ICSID arbitration agreement.

---

[14] We recommend this as the most basic clause, but with many caveats and drafting suggestions. *See The Freshfields Guide, supra* note 3, at 131.

Lucy Reed, Jan Paulsson and Nigel Blackaby, Guide to ICSID Arbitration, 13–33
© 2004 *Kluwer Law International. Printed in The Netherlands*

THE SCOPE OF ICSID JURISDICTION

Article 25 of the Convention defines the scope of ICSID jurisdiction. In the opening paragraph of that Article, the Contracting States agree:

"(1) The jurisdiction of the Centre shall extend to any legal dispute arising directly out of an investment, between a Contracting State (or any constituent subdivision or agency of a Contracting State designated to the Centre by that State) and a national of another Contracting State, which the parties to the dispute consent in writing to submit to the Centre. When the parties have given their consent, no party may withdraw its consent unilaterally."

Thus, in order for an investment dispute between an investor and a State to be eligible for ICSID arbitration: (a) the dispute must arise out of an investment; (b) the dispute must involve, on the one hand, either a Contracting State (that is, a State that is a signatory to the ICSID Convention) or one of its subdivisions or agencies specifically designated to ICSID and, on the other hand, a national of another Contracting State; and (c) all parties to the dispute must consent in writing to have the investment dispute submitted to ICSID.

These jurisdictional requirements are mandatory. Before concluding their ICSID arbitration clause, parties to an investment contract must ensure that these criteria are met or will be met if and when a dispute arises between them. The parties may not waive these jurisdictional criteria by contractual stipulations. If the jurisdictional requirements are not met, the Centre must and will refuse to administer a dispute, even if the parties have contractually designated ICSID.

What Constitutes an "Investment Dispute?"

The requirement of an investment
The ICSID Convention does not offer a specific definition of the term "investment." This was a deliberate decision by the drafters, who recognized that, given the pivotal role of consent, a definition of the term could prove unhelpfully restrictive.[15] To quote the Report of the Executive Directors on the Convention:

"No attempt was made to define the term 'investment' given the essential requirements of consent by the parties, and the mechanism through which Contracting States can make known in advance, if they so desire, the classes of disputes which they would or would not consider submitting to the Centre (Article 25(4))."[16]

---

[15] *Report of the Executive Directors, supra* note 6, at 28. *See also* A. Broches, *The Convention on the Settlement of Investment Disputes Between States and Nationals of Other States of 1965: Explanatory Notes and Survey of its Application,* 28 Yearbook of Commercial Arbitration 627, 642 (1993).

[16] *Report of the Executive Directors, supra* note 6, at 28. *See also* A. Broches, *supra* note 15, at 642.

Instead the drafters preferred to leave it to the parties to agree upon what constitutes an investment under particular circumstances. As one ICSID tribunal has stated, "[a]s long as the criteria chosen by the parties to define [the] requirements [of an investment] [. . .] are not deprived of their objective significance, there is no reason to discard the parties' choice."[17]

In general, ICSID tribunals have found the project or transaction in question to qualify as an investment for purposes of the Convention where, at a minimum, the project or transaction: (a) had a significant duration; (b) provided a measurable return to the investor; (c) involved an element of risk on both sides; (d) involved a substantial commitment on the part of the investor; and (e) was significant to the State's development. Specific examples of projects and transactions that have been held by ICSID tribunals to qualify as investments under Article 25 range from infrastructure projects to the issuing of promissory notes. Tribunals have found "disputes arising directly out of an investment" to include disputes over capital contributions and other equity investments in companies and joint ventures, as well as non-equity direct investments via service contracts, transfer of technology, natural resource concession agreements, and projects for the construction and operation of production and service facilities in the host State.[18]

Yet, the concept of investment is not infinitely flexible in ICSID practice. For example, as described in Chapter 3, in the arbitration of *Mihaly International v. Sri Lanka* (brought under the bilateral investment treaty between the United States and Sri Lanka) the tribunal declined jurisdiction on grounds that expenses incurred by the claimant before finalization of a power project contract with the government of Sri Lanka did not constitute an investment under the Convention and the bilateral investment treaty.[19]

The requirement of a legal dispute
As with the term "investment," the ICSID Convention does not define the phrase "legal dispute." ICSID tribunals have generally used the phrase to refer either to disputes regarding the existence or scope of a legal right or obligation, or to disputes regarding the nature or extent of the reparation to be made for the breach of a legal obligation.

As the parties obviously cannot anticipate all disputes that might arise in their relationship, particularly in the course of a long-term investment project, they should

---

[17] *Autopista Concesionaria de Venezuela, C.A. v. Bolivarian Republic of Venezuela*, ICSID Case No. ARB/00/5, Decision on Jurisdiction (27 September 2001), 16 *ICSID Review – FILJ* 469, 503 (2001).

[18] *See, e.g., Salini Costruttori S.p.A. and Italstrade S.p.A. v. Kingdom of Morocco*, ICSID Case No. ARB/00/4, Decision on Jurisdiction (23 July 2001), 42 *ILM* 609 (2003); *Fedax N.V. v. Republic of Venezuela*, ICSID Case No. ARB/96/3, Decision on Objections to Jurisdiction (11 July 1997), 5 *ICSID Reports* 183 (2002).

[19] *Mihaly International Corporation v. Democratic Socialist Republic of Sri Lanka*, ICSID Case No. ARB/00/2, Award (15 March 2002), 17 *ICSID Review – FILJ* 142 (2002).

not attempt to include a "laundry list" of potential legal disputes in the arbitration clause. One of the legal disagreements they fail to predict or mention may well be the first to arise.

Who is considered a "national of a Contracting State?"

Article 25(2) of the ICSID Convention provides a specific definition of a "national of a Contracting State," as follows:

> "(a) any natural person who had the nationality of a Contracting State other than the State party to the dispute on the date on which the parties consented to submit such dispute to conciliation or arbitration as well as on the date on which the request was registered pursuant to paragraph (3) of Article 28 or paragraph (3) of Article 36, but does not include any person who on either date also had the nationality of the Contracting State party to the dispute; and
>
> (b) any juridical person which had the nationality of a Contracting State other than the State party to the dispute on the date on which the parties consented to submit such dispute to conciliation or arbitration and any juridical person which had the nationality of the Contracting State party to the dispute on that date and which, because of foreign control, the parties have agreed should be treated as a national of another Contracting State for the purposes of this Convention."

Natural persons

The key issue for natural persons is their country of citizenship. The ICSID Convention permits a person to invoke ICSID arbitration only if he or she was a citizen of a Contracting State from the date he or she made the relevant investment to the date a legal dispute arose over that investment. Thus, a French investor may consent to ICSID arbitration with respect to an investment made in the United States. However, if the French investor were to move to the United States and take US citizenship before a legal dispute arose, ICSID jurisdiction would fail. Similarly, a natural person who is a dual national of the State party to the legal dispute is ineligible for ICSID arbitration, and this ineligibility cannot be waived by the State party. Thus, in the above hypothetical, if the French investor retained his French citizenship and adopted dual US-French citizenship, he or she would also lose the right to commence an ICSID arbitration against the government of the United States – even if the United States agreed to consider him or her only a French citizen for ICSID purposes.

Juridical persons

To qualify as an investor for ICSID jurisdiction purposes, a juridical person must, in general, have the nationality of a Contracting State other than the host State on the date of consent to ICSID arbitration. This is quite straightforward in many investment scenarios.

The ICSID Convention, however, also anticipates the realities of modern investment project structures. Even when the juridical person does not have the requisite nationality on the date of consent, the Centre has jurisdiction if the parties have agreed that "because of foreign control" that juridical person "should be treated as a national of another Contracting State for the purposes of [the] Convention" (Convention Article 25(2)(b)). Essentially, this means that a corporation organized under the laws of the host State, such as a special purpose project company, will be considered a national of another Contracting State if the parties agree that, because such corporation is controlled by a natural or juridical person that has the requisite status as a national of another Contracting State, it should be treated that way. To give a concrete example, if a Dutch company were to incorporate a wholly-owned (or otherwise controlled) Czech company to construct a highway project under an investment contract with the government of the Czech Republic, the affiliate could be treated as a Dutch company for purposes of ICSID jurisdiction.

Again, the ICSID Convention does not define the terms "nationality" or "foreign control." The drafters desired to provide parties with the maximum flexibility.[20] The issues in play are well illustrated by the facts of five prominent cases addressing the question of foreign control.

–   In *Amco v. Indonesia*, the claimant, a United States corporation, formed a special purpose Indonesian company, PT Amco, to carry out the contemplated investment. Amco did so by applying to the Indonesian Foreign Investment Board for permission to incorporate PT Amco as an Indonesian company to build and manage a hotel in Indonesia. In the ensuing ICSID arbitration, Indonesia objected that PT Amco could not be treated as a United States national because, even though it was controlled by a US corporation, the parties had not explicitly agreed to treat PT Amco (an Indonesian corporation) as a national of another State. The tribunal found that by accepting the application to incorporate PT Amco, which expressly stated that PT Amco was a "foreign business," Indonesia had agreed that PT Amco could be treated as a United States company for ICSID purposes.[21]

–   In *SOABI v. Senegal*, the claimant was a Senegalese company owned by a Panamanian joint stock corporation that was, in turn, owned by Belgian nationals. At the time the investment contract was signed, Panama was not an ICSID Contracting State but Belgium was. The relevant arbitration clause

---

[20]   A. Broches, *supra* note 15; *see also* P. Szasz, *A Practical Guide to the Convention on the Settlement of Investment Disputes*, 1 *Cornell Int'l L.J.* 1, 20 (1968) ("The Convention does not specify what constitutes 'control' for this purpose (i.e., must there be a majority of foreign shareholders), and thus it would be difficult to challenge later such a stipulation agreed to by the Contracting State concerned, regardless of the objective situation.").

[21]   *Amco Asia Corporation and others v. Republic of Indonesia*, ICSID Case No. ARB/81/1, Decision on Jurisdiction (25 September 1983), 1 *ICSID Reports* 389 (1993).

provided: "The undersigned expressly agree that arbitration shall be subject to the rules set out in the Convention for the Settlement of Disputes between States and the Nationals of Other States, produced by the 'International Bank of Reconstruction and Development' ('IBRD'). To this end, *the Government agrees that the requirements of nationality set out in Article 25 of the IBRD Convention shall be deemed to be fulfilled.*" (Emphasis added.) The tribunal upheld its jurisdiction over the dispute by interpreting the arbitration clause to mean that the parties had agreed to treat the Senegalese company as a Belgian national for ICSID purposes, and such interpretation would fulfill the nationality requirement of the ICSID Convention.[22]

- In *LETCO v. Liberia*, the claimant, a Liberian company controlled by French nationals, signed a concession agreement with the Liberian government. There was no explicit agreement among the parties as to the nationality of LETCO for the purposes of ICSID arbitration. The tribunal held that it had jurisdiction over the dispute. The tribunal found, among other things, that a Contracting State, in signing an investment agreement containing an ICSID arbitration clause with a foreign controlled juridical person and knowing that it could be subject to ICSID jurisdiction only if it has agreed to treat that juridical person as a national of another Contracting State, should be deemed to have agreed to such treatment by having agreed to the ICSID arbitration clause. The tribunal concluded that this was especially the case when the Contracting State's laws required the foreign investor to establish itself locally as a juridical person in order to carry out the investment.[23]

- In *Vacuum Salt v. Ghana*, the claimant was a Ghanaian company. Ghanaian nationals owned 80 percent of the Vacuum Salt shares and a Greek national owned the remaining 20 percent. The Greek national also sat on the board of directors of the company and served as the company's technical advisor. There was no agreement among the parties as to the nationality of Vacuum Salt. The tribunal held that it did not have jurisdiction over the dispute because the Greek individual's role in the company did not meet any objective criterion of foreign control and hence Vacuum Salt could not be treated as a Greek national for ICSID purposes.[24]

- Finally, in *Autopista v. Venezuela*, a national of a non-Contracting State, Mexico, was the 99 percent shareholder of Autopista Concesionada de Venezuela, C.A. (*Aucoven*), a Venezuelan company, at the time the contract was signed. The relevant concession contract provided for ad hoc arbitration in

---

[22] *Société Ouest Africaine de Bétons Industriels (SOABI) v. State of Senegal*, ICSID Case No. ARB/82/1, Decision on Jurisdiction (1 August 1984), 2 *ICSID Reports* 175, 204 (1994).

[23] *Liberian Eastern Timber Corporation (LETCO) v. Republic of Liberia*, ICSID Case No. ARB/83/2, Decision on Rectification (17 June 1986), 2 *ICSID Reports* 346 (1994).

[24] *Vacuum Salt Products Ltd. v. Republic of Ghana*, ICSID Case No. ARB/92/1, Award (16 February 1994), 4 *ICSID Reports* 329 (1997).

Venezuela. The parties also agreed in the contract, however, that in the event Aucoven's majority shareholder (then Mexican) should come to be a national of a Contracting State, they instead would arbitrate under the ICSID Convention. Eventually, the Mexican shareholder transferred 75 percent of its shares in Aucoven to a corporate affiliate in the United States, with the permission of Venezuela. When Aucoven filed for arbitration, Venezuela challenged jurisdiction on the ground that Aucoven continued to be controlled by the Mexican holding company that owned 100 percent of the stock of the United States affiliate that, in turn, controlled Aucoven. The tribunal upheld its jurisdiction over the dispute. The tribunal relied heavily on the fact that the parties themselves in their agreement had specifically agreed to look to the ownership of a majority of Aucoven's shares, rather than to the entity exercising ultimate effective control over Aucoven, to determine foreign control of Aucoven by a national of another Contracting State for purposes of Convention Article 25(2)(b).[25]

The key issue for all five tribunals was the parties' agreement at the time the investment contract was signed. Potential investors should carefully consider this issue and explicitly record the parties' agreement as to nationality in their arbitration clause. It may be highly advisable for the parties either: (a) to stipulate in the contract that the investor is a national of a Contracting State other than the host State; or (b) to agree that, although the investor is a national of the host State, it is controlled by nationals of another Contracting State and so shall be treated as a national of that other State for purposes of establishing ICSID jurisdiction. These strategies are acceptable to ICSID, as illustrated by its specific Model Clauses 6 and 7:

Clause 6 (Stipulation of Nationality of Investor)
"It is hereby stipulated by the parties that the Investor is a national of [name of another Contracting State]."

Clause 7 (Agreement that a Juridical Person is Under Foreign Control)
"It is hereby agreed that, although the Investor is a national of the Host State, it is controlled by nationals of [name(s) of other Contracting State(s)] and shall be treated as a national of [that]/[those] State[s] for the purposes of the Convention."

As the *Aucoven* case clearly demonstrates, parties may record an enforceable ICSID arbitration agreement even when, for a variety of reasons, ICSID is only prospectively a viable option. This topic is discussed further below in connection with ICSID's recognition that consent to ICSID arbitration may be conditional.

When is a Contract with a "Contracting State"?

In many cases, the question of whether an investor is contracting with a State that is a signatory to the ICSID Convention is easy to answer. When the investor is

---

[25] *Autopista v. Venezuela* (Decision on Jurisdiction), *supra* note 17.

negotiating directly with the State or one of its Ministries, the only issue is whether or not the State has ratified the Convention. This may be ascertained by referring to the list posted on the ICSID website or, in case of doubt, by contacting the ICSID Secretariat directly. (For a list of the 138 Contracting States as of January 2003, see Annex 2.)

The more complicated question under Article 25 is whether a particular government subdivision (i.e., a territorial entity below the level of the State itself) or agency of a Contracting State qualifies as a party under the ICSID Convention. A subdivision or agency of a Contracting State may itself be party to an ICSID dispute if two special requirements are both fulfilled:

- The host State has designated the subdivision or agency to the Centre under Convention Article 25(1) as capable of being a party to an ICSID arbitration; and
- The host State has specifically approved the consent given by the subdivision or agency, or waived this approval right, under Article 25(3).

Under Article 25(1), host States may make such designations for all future disputes involving the subdivision or agency, for specific investment projects involving the subdivision or agency, or for a specific dispute once that dispute has arisen. The Contracting State must communicate the designation to the Centre no later than the day the relevant request for arbitration is made. Under Article 25(3), the host State may notify ICSID that it waives the requirement of specific approval in certain categories of transactions, to which subdivisions or agencies may consent on their own. In all events, the claimant should include in the request for arbitration detailed information on the Contracting State's approval of the relevant subdivision's or agency's consent .

The importance of designation and consent by the host State is illustrated in *Cable Television v. St. Kitts and Nevis*. In this case, the investor entered into an agreement containing an ICSID arbitration clause with the Nevis Island Administration (*NIA*), a subdivision of the Federation of St. Kitts and Nevis (the **Federation**). The Federation had neither designated NIA as a subdivision capable of being a party to an ICSID arbitration nor approved NIA's consent to ICSID arbitration. The tribunal found that it did not have jurisdiction over NIA despite the ICSID arbitration clause in the investment agreement. The tribunal also rejected the investor's attempts to substitute the Federation itself as a party to the ICSID proceeding.[26]

A number of Contracting States, including Australia, Ecuador, Guinea, Kenya, Madagascar, Nigeria, Peru, Portugal, Sudan and the United Kingdom, have designated specific subdivisions and agencies under Article 25 of the ICSID

---

[26] *Cable Television of Nevis, Ltd. v. Federation of St. Kitts and Nevis,* ICSID Case No. ARB/95/2, Award (13 January 1997), 5 *ICSID Reports* 108 (2002).

Convention. Such subdivisions and agencies include: (a) domestic states of a federation, as in the case of Australia; and (b) public sector enterprises, such as State-owned or State-controlled mining, shipping and energy companies (for example, the Consejo Nacional de Electricidad of Ecuador, the Nigerian National Petroleum Corporation, and Perupetro S.A. of Peru). A small number of Contracting States have waived the need to approve consents by subdivisions and agencies, generally by declaring that domestic states or other such subdivisions in federally constituted countries are competent to give autonomous consent to ICSID arbitration.

An investor negotiating a contract with a subdivision or agency of a Contracting State, and wishing to ensure access to ICSID, should address these requirements in the arbitration clause. The clause should identify: (a) the precise name of the relevant subdivision or agency; (b) the details of its ICSID designation by the Contracting State; and (c) the instrument in which the Contracting State has approved the consent to ICSID arbitration by the subdivision or agency, or notified the Centre that no such approval is required. The potential complexities of this situation – but also the roadmap to a drafting solution – are illustrated in ICSID Model Clause 5:

> "The name of constituent subdivision or agency is [a constituent subdivision]/[an agency] of the Host State, which has been designated to the Centre by the Government of that State in accordance with Article 25(1) of the Convention. In accordance with Article 25(3) of the Convention, the Host State [hereby gives its approval to this consent agreement]*/[has given its approval to this consent agreement in citation of instrument in which approval is expressed]/[has notified the Centre that no approval of [this type of consent agreement]/[of consent agreements by the name of constituent subdivision or agency is required]]. [*This alternative can only be used if the government is also a part to the agreement.]"

In the case of a long-term investment project, during the course of which the identity of the designated subdivision or agency involved could change, the investor should seek to obtain a written commitment from the Contracting State to designate any substitute or successor entity.

It is crucial for investors to be aware that a host State's designation of a subdivision or agency as eligible for ICSID arbitration, and its approval of the subdivision's or agency's consent to ICSID jurisdiction, do not represent consent to ICSID jurisdiction by the host State itself. Even if the host State has participated in the events leading to the investment dispute, or has in some way itself interfered with the investment, an investor would need independent consent from the host State (perhaps via a bilateral investment treaty) to bring a claim against it before an ICSID tribunal.

What Constitutes Consent to ICSID Jurisdiction?

Under Article 25 of the ICSID Convention, the parties' consent to submit a dispute to ICSID arbitration is a threshold requirement to establish an ICSID tribunal's jurisdiction over the matter. This requirement is so critical that the Executive

Directors of the World Bank, in their 1965 Report on the ICSID Convention, stated: "Consent of the parties is the cornerstone of the jurisdiction of the Centre."[27]

Consent is the explicit expression of both parties' acceptance of ICSID arbitration. The investor generally consents to arbitrate disputes under a specific investment, while the State may consent to arbitration of a specific dispute or anticipated classes of disputes. In contractual ICSID arbitrations, the State consents in a direct written agreement with the investor or in a letter (as addressed in this chapter); in arbitrations "without privity," in comparison, the State consents in its national legislation or in treaties (as addressed in Chapter 3). As made clear in the Preamble to the ICSID Convention (see Chapter 1), the State never consents solely by having ratified the ICSID Convention.

The form of consent

The only formal requirement for the parties' consent to ICSID arbitration is that it be in writing. The consent may otherwise take many forms. Consent may be given in advance, with respect to a defined class of future disputes, or with respect to an existing dispute. ICSID has Model Clauses for both situations:

Clause 1 (Consent in Respect of Future Disputes)
"The [Government]/[name of constituent subdivision or agency] of name of Contracting State (hereinafter the 'Host State') and name of investor (hereinafter the 'Investor') hereby consent to submit to the International Centre for Settlement of Investment Disputes (hereinafter the 'Centre') any dispute arising out of or relating to this agreement for settlement by [conciliation]/[arbitration]/ [conciliation followed, if the dispute remains unresolved within time limit of the communication of the report of the Conciliation Commission to the parties, by arbitration] pursuant to the Convention on the Settlement of Investment Disputes between States and Nationals of Other States (hereinafter the 'Convention')." (Footnote omitted.)

Clause 2 (Consent in Respect of Existing Disputes)
"The [Government]/[name of constituent subdivision or agency] of name of Contracting State (hereinafter the 'Host State') and name of investor (hereinafter the 'Investor') hereby consent to submit to the International Centre for Settlement of Investment Disputes (hereinafter the 'Centre') for settlement by [conciliation]/ [arbitration]/[conciliation followed, if the dispute remains unresolved within time limit of the communication of the report of the Conciliation Commission to the parties, by arbitration] pursuant to the Convention on the Settlement of Investment Disputes between States and Nationals of Other States, the following dispute arising out of the investment described below: ..."

---

[27] *Report of the Executive Directors, supra* note 6, at 28.

Consent may be encompassed in a single instrument, i.e., an arbitration clause included in the parties' investment contract or in a separate arbitration agreement, or recorded in separate instruments, i.e., by an exchange of letters, telefaxes or other writings. Although the issue apparently has not yet been tested specifically in the ICSID context, consent in the form of an electronic mail exchange (provided receipt is demonstrated or uncontested) presumably meets the writing requirement of Article 25.

Whatever form of writing it takes, consent must have been given for the specific dispute or class of disputes that is submitted for resolution to the Centre. To assume that a State's consent follows automatically from its ratification of the ICSID Convention remains a misconception.

As with any issue of legal authority, the parties must carefully verify the factors relevant to the validity of each other's consent to ICSID arbitration. Special issues arise in connection with State action. It is not uncommon for national laws to restrict a State's ability to enter into arbitration agreements by requiring certain parliamentary approvals or compliance with other legal requirements before the agreement to arbitrate is valid. Some national laws flatly prohibit States from entering into arbitration commitments, either in all transactions or in certain sectors. Each party should consider verifying the validity of the other party's consent, by demanding certification letters, legal opinions and other appropriate evidence before a dispute arises and thereby avoid unnecessary and perhaps extended and unsuccessful litigation. As noted, such due diligence should be a particularly high priority on the private investor's checklist.

The scope of consent
Host States and investors are also free contractually to restrict the scope of their agreement to arbitrate disputes before ICSID. For example, an arbitration clause may stipulate that only certain limited categories of disputes are subject to ICSID jurisdiction.[28] In practice, however, broad consent clauses are thought preferable to avoid eventual disputes over a tribunal's competence.

The ambit of agreements to arbitrate may also be limited under Article 25 of the ICSID Convention, which provides in paragraph 4:

> "Any Contracting State may, at the time of ratification, acceptance or approval of this Convention or at any time thereafter, notify the Centre of the class or classes of disputes which it would or would not consider submitting to the jurisdiction of the Centre. The Secretary-General shall forthwith transmit such notification to all Contracting States. Such notification shall not constitute the consent required by paragraph (1)."

Among the Contracting States that have given such a notification are China, Jamaica, Papua New Guinea, Saudi Arabia and Turkey. The notifications cover, for

---

[28] Model Clause 4 (Annex 5).

example: (a) disputes over compensation resulting from expropriation or nationalization; and (b) certain investments relating to minerals, oil or other natural resources. During contract negotiations, investors should confirm that the host State has not made such a notification, either by checking the ICSID website or by contacting the Secretariat directly.

Consent is irrevocable

Once valid consent to ICSID arbitration is given, neither party may withdraw its consent. This is a fundamental protection within the ICSID regime. The inability to change course by withdrawing a valid consent to ICSID arbitration means that neither party may resort to any other national or international remedy after a dispute arises.

Host States may not use notifications of excepted disputes under Convention Article 25(4) to withdraw consent indirectly, once consent has been validly given. Three cases involving Jamaica, all registered simultaneously and heard by the same ICSID tribunal, have confirmed that valid consent by the host State is irrevocable notwithstanding Article 25(4).[29] In each case, the Jamaican government and the investor had entered into agreements concerning bauxite mining, each containing a "no further tax" clause and a dispute resolution clause providing for ICSID jurisdiction. Jamaica subsequently notified ICSID that it would not submit to ICSID jurisdiction for legal disputes "arising directly out of an investment relating to minerals or other natural resources." Shortly thereafter, Jamaica enacted legislation that provided for an additional tax to be paid on all bauxite extracted in Jamaica. The tribunal held, in each case, that Jamaica could not withdraw the consent given in the agreements with the investors. Jamaica's notification to ICSID under Article 25(4) could operate only prospectively, "by way of information to [ICSID] and potential future investors in undertakings concerning minerals and other natural resources of Jamaica."[30]

Consent is exclusive

In addition to being irrevocable, valid consent to ICSID arbitration creates an exclusive forum unless the parties agree otherwise or the State has required exhaustion of local remedies as a condition of its consent. Under Article 26 of the ICSID Convention:

"Consent of the parties to arbitration under this Convention shall, unless

---

[29] *Kaiser Bauxite Company v. Jamaica*, ICSID Case No. ARB/74/3, Decision on Jurisdiction and Competence (6 July 1975), 1 *ICSID Reports* 296 (1993); *Alcoa Minerals of Jamaica, Inc. v. Jamaica*, ICSID Case No. ARB/74/2, Decision on Jurisdiction and Competence (6 July 1975), 4 *Yearbook Commercial Arbitration* 206 (1979); *Reynolds Jamaica Mines Limited and Reynolds Metals Company v. Jamaica*, ICSID Case No. ARB/74/4 (unpublished).

[30] *Kaiser Bauxite v. Jamaica* (Decision on Jurisdiction and Competence), *supra* note 29, at 304.

otherwise stated, be deemed consent to such arbitration to the exclusion of any other remedy. A Contracting State may require the exhaustion of local administrative or judicial remedies as a condition of its consent to arbitration under this Convention."

Pursuant to this provision, if the parties designate ICSID arbitration as only one of a number of options for dispute resolution in their investment agreement, they may face the complications that may arise from a non-specifically exclusive option. As for an exhaustion of local remedies requirement, ICSID Model Clause 13 suggests how an effective clause might be drafted:

"Before either party hereto institutes an arbitration proceeding under the Convention with respect to a particular dispute, that party must have taken all steps necessary to exhaust the [following] [administrative] [and] [judicial] remedies available under the laws of the Host State with respect to that dispute [list of required remedies], unless the other party hereto waives that requirement in writing."

Conditional consent

Consent to ICSID jurisdiction may be valid even if conditional. This enables parties that do not qualify for access to ICSID nonetheless to agree that their investment disputes will be submitted to ICSID if future events bring the parties' relations within the ambit of ICSID jurisdiction. This is a somewhat complex concept, best illustrated by an actual case.

The very first ICSID arbitration, *Holiday Inns v. Morocco*, affirmed the validity of conditional consent to ICSID arbitration. In that case, the tribunal held that Morocco had validly agreed to ICSID jurisdiction in connection with a contract it had entered into with a Swiss corporation even though, on the date the contract was signed, the company had not yet been incorporated and, once created, was a national of a State that had not yet ratified the ICSID Convention.[31] In particular, the tribunal held that:

"[T]he Convention allows parties to subordinate the entry into force of an arbitration clause to the subsequent fulfilment of certain conditions, such as the adherence of the States concerned to the Convention, or the incorporation of the company envisaged by the agreement. On this assumption, it is the date when the conditions are definitely satisfied, as regards one of the Parties involved, which constitutes in the sense of the Convention the date of consent by that [p]arty."[32]

---

[31] P. Lalive, *The First World Bank Arbitration (Holiday Inns v. Morocco) – Some Legal Problems*, 1 *ICSID Reports* 645 (1993). The *Holiday Inns* case has not been published, but extracts appear in Professor Lalive's article.

[32] *Id.* at 667-668.

Similar facts arose in the *Aucoven* case described above. At the time the parties signed their investment contract, a national of a non-Contracting State (Mexico) owned 99 percent of the Venezuelan project company, Aucoven. The parties, however, agreed that if a national of a Contracting State came to be majority shareholder of Aucoven, any dispute under their contract could be arbitrated under the auspices of ICSID. A United States entity (the United States being an ICSID signatory) did in fact become the majority shareholder, and the tribunal accepted jurisdiction on the basis of this conditional arrangement.[33]

Transfer of consent to successors in interest
Over the life of an investment, an investor may have commercial reasons to want to transfer to another entity all or some of its rights and obligations, including any right to ICSID arbitration. If the successor entity is not a party to the original consent agreement between investor and host State (which is the likely situation), the transfer could provide the host State with grounds to challenge ICSID jurisdiction (for lack of valid consent) in the event of a dispute. Cautious investors should consider the possibility of successors in interest when negotiating an ICSID arbitration clause. Although there is no ICSID Model Clause addressing consent and successors in interest, George Delaume has offered the following possible solution:

> "It is hereby agreed that the consent to the jurisdiction of the Centre shall equally bind any assignee ... to the extent that the Centre can assume jurisdiction over a dispute between such assignee and the other party, and that neither party to this Agreement shall, without written consent of the other, transfer its interest in this Agreement to the assignee with respect to whom the Centre could not exercise such jurisdiction."[34]

Absent a workable contractual clause for successors in interest to ICSID arbitration, the investor could seek a separate consent from the host State. In *Amco v. Indonesia*, noted above, the Indonesian government challenged ICSID jurisdiction on the ground that its consent to arbitration did not extend to a successor in interest to Amco. Amco's original application to the Indonesian Foreign Investment Board, on the basis of which the Indonesian government authorized the incorporation of PT Amco, included consent to ICSID arbitration, but it did not explicitly provide for successors in interest. Subsequently, when Indonesia granted permission to Amco to transfer some of its shares in PT Amco to a successor entity, it did so with no mention of ICSID arbitration. Yet the tribunal held that Indonesia's approval of the share transfer itself constituted agreement that the successor in interest to Amco would acquire all rights attached to those shares, including the right to ICSID

---

[33] *Autopista v. Venezuela* (Decision on Jurisdiction), *supra* note 17.
[34] G. Delaume, *ICSID Arbitration: Practical Considerations*, 1 *Journal of International Arbitration* 101, 116 n. 49 (1984).

arbitration, because the right to ICSID arbitration was not expressly excluded by Indonesia in the approval.[35]

With or without a contractual clause concerning transfer of ICSID arbitration rights, any successor in interest must satisfy the underlying nationality requirements of the Convention for an ICSID tribunal to have jurisdiction of a dispute. In *Holiday Inns v. Morocco*, the original agreement containing consent to ICSID arbitration did in fact generally provide for successors and assigns, but it did not specifically address the rights of any successors and assigns to ICSID arbitration. Holiday Inns subsequently assigned the agreement to four Moroccan subsidiaries. Holiday Inns, the four Moroccan subsidiaries and others claimants commenced an ICSID arbitration against the Moroccan government under the contract. On a challenge made by Morocco, the tribunal dismissed the case with respect to the Moroccan subsidiaries for lack of jurisdiction. The tribunal held that, as Moroccan investors in a claim against the government of Morocco, the four Moroccan successors in interest did not meet the nationality requirements of the ICSID Convention.[36] The parties had not agreed to treat the four Moroccan subsidiaries as "nationals of another Contracting State" under ICSID Convention Article 25(2)(b). The drafting lesson to be learned is that investors should consider addressing nationality, as well as succession in interest, in any investment contract containing an ICSID clause.

Practical Checklist on Jurisdiction

The best practical checklist for ensuring ICSID jurisdiction in contractual ICSID cases under Convention Article 25 is, without question, the text of Rule 2(1) of the ICSID Institution Rules. Rule 2(1), which sets out the minimum requirements for a request for ICSID arbitration, merits full quotation:

"The request shall:
(a) designate precisely each party to the dispute and state the address of each;
(b) state, if one of the parties is a constituent subdivision or agency of a Contracting State, that it has been designated to the Centre by that State pursuant to Article 25(1) of the Convention;
(c) indicate the date of consent and the instruments in which it is recorded, including, if one party is a constituent subdivision or agency of a Contracting State, similar data on the approval of such consent by that State unless it had notified the Centre that no such approval is required;
(d) indicate with respect to the party that is a national of a Contracting State:
    (i)   its nationality on the date of consent; and
    (ii)   if the party is a natural person:
        (A) his nationality on the date of the request; and

---

[35] *Amco Asia v. Indonesia* (Decision on Jurisdiction), *supra* note 21, at 403.
[36] P. Lalive, *supra* note 31.

(B) that he did not have the nationality of the Contracting State party to the dispute either on the date of consent or on the date of the request; or

(iii) if the party is a juridical person which on the date of consent had the nationality of the Contracting State party to the dispute, the agreement of the parties that it should be treated as a national of another Contracting State for the purposes of the Convention;

(e) contain information concerning the issues in dispute indicating that there is, between the parties, a legal dispute arising directly out of an investment;

(f) state, if the requesting party is a juridical person, that it has taken all necessary internal actions to authorize the request."

DRAFTING AN EFFECTIVE ICSID ARBITRATION AGREEMENT

As set out at the opening of the chapter, the simplest possible effective ICSID arbitration clause would be something like the following:

"The parties hereto consent to submit to the International Centre for Settlement of Investment Disputes any dispute relating to or arising out of this Agreement for settlement by arbitration pursuant to the Convention on the Settlement of Investment Disputes between States and Nationals of Other States."

ICSID offers no such simple multipurpose clause but does give guidance on drafting for recurring situations. The ICSID Model Clauses, as illustrated by the several samples quoted throughout this chapter, are extensive and detailed. They provide direction for drafting to cover existing and future disputes, as well as reasonably predictable different subject matters for potential disputes and reasonably predictable casts of characters for potential parties. They also cover important optional provisions for the arbitration clause.

The drafters of any international arbitration clause always face several key decisions during negotiations, for example, determination of the number of arbitrators. Some of these decisions require special consideration in the ICSID context. At the same time, however, some of the most difficult decisions in international commercial arbitration clause drafting – for example, selection of venue and applicable law – are of only minor concern in ICSID clauses. We examine below, from a drafting perspective, the following strategic issues: (a) the method of constituting the tribunal; (b) applicable law; (c) the place of arbitration; (d) the language(s) of the arbitration; (e) provision for a negotiation or "cooling off" period; (f) provisional measures; and (g) waiver of sovereign immunity. Several of these topics are also covered from a procedural perspective in Chapter 4.

Method of constituting the tribunal

The ICSID Convention provides parties with wide latitude to decide how to select their arbitral tribunal. The main relevant article, Article 37(2)(a) of the Convention, provides that an arbitral tribunal "shall consist of a sole arbitrator or any uneven number of arbitrators appointed as the parties shall agree," leaving the parties free to stipulate the number of arbitrators.

ICSID tribunals are almost always comprised of three members rather than a sole arbitrator. (There has never been a five-member tribunal.) It may be that parties prefer the security of having the case evaluated from several perspectives rather than putting their fate in the hands of one person, even if – as is notoriously difficult – they could agree on a sole arbitrator.

Indeed, when the parties have expressed no preference in their arbitration clause as to number, the Convention's default rule, contained in Article 37(2)(b), requires that the tribunal consist of three arbitrators:

"Where the parties do not agree upon the number of arbitrators and the method of their appointment, the Tribunal shall consist of three arbitrators, one arbitrator appointed by each party and the third, who shall be the president of the Tribunal, appointed by agreement of the parties."

If, as is often the case, the parties cannot agree in selecting a president, the Chairman of the Administrative Council makes the appointment after consultation with both parties (Convention Article 38). The parties may, but only occasionally do, stipulate that the Centre appoint all three arbitrators.

Applicable Law

As in any international commercial arbitration, there are potentially four separate questions of applicable law in an ICSID arbitration: (a) what law governs the validity of the arbitration agreement? (b) what law governs the arbitration proceedings themselves? (c) what law applies to the substance of the dispute? and (d) in the event of a conflict regarding the substantive law, under what law is the conflict to be resolved? As compared to the complexities these questions pose in other arbitrations, the ICSID Convention answers all of these questions, should the parties – as is often the case in investor-State contracts – be unable to agree upon the applicable law in their arbitration agreement.[37]

First, as discussed above, Articles 25 and 26 of the Convention and the express terms of the parties' agreement govern the validity of an ICSID arbitration agreement. There is no need for the parties to select a law governing the validity of that agreement; it is governed by the Convention and therefore by international law.

Second, Article 44 of the Convention addresses applicable procedural law. It provides that the proceedings are to be conducted in accordance with the procedural provisions of the Convention (which are found in Articles 41 to 49) "and, except as

---

[37] *See* Model Clause 10 (Annex 5)

the parties otherwise agree, in accordance with the Arbitration Rules in effect on the date on which the parties consented to arbitration." The parties cannot select a national procedural law or other international arbitration procedural rules to govern their ICSID arbitration, and should not attempt to do so. Nor should the parties try to alter the ICSID procedural regime, as there are mandatory provisions in the ICSID Convention and the various sets of ICSID rules. Parties should not invent procedural variations or "improvements" on the ICSID procedural framework in their arbitration agreement.

Third, by contrast and as in any major international agreement, the parties should strive to select one body of national law as the applicable substantive law and set it out plainly in a separate clause in the agreement. This is the single greatest assurance of certainty in the resolution of legal disputes that may arise. Yet, it is often extremely difficult – if not impossible – for the host State to agree to the designation of the investor's home State law or for the investor to agree to adopt the host State's law. Other options (none of them free from difficulty) are to agree on the national law of a third State or on rules or principles of international law (in various permutations), or to remain silent.

Fourth, Article 42(1) of the ICSID Convention anticipates these difficulties, and provides a default choice-of-law rule and conflicts guideline:

> "The Tribunal shall decide a dispute in accordance with such rules of law as may be agreed by the parties. In the absence of such agreement, the Tribunal shall apply the law of the Contracting State party to the dispute (including its rules on the conflict of laws) and such rules of international law as may be applicable."

Despite its apparent simplicity, Article 42(1) has probably generated more debate than any other provision of the ICSID Convention. In extremely simplified and practical terms, Article 42(1) generally – but not without exception or controversy – has been interpreted to mean that, in the absence of agreement by the parties on choice of substantive law, the tribunal should accord supremacy to international law in the event of any inconsistency with the host State's domestic law. As the tribunal in the *Santa Elena v. Costa Rica* case explained, "[t]o the extent that there may be any inconsistency between the two bodies of law, the rules of public international law must prevail."[38] According to the tribunal in *Amco v. Indonesia*, "where there are applicable host-state laws, they must be checked against international laws, which will prevail in case of conflict. Thus international law is fully applicable and to

---

[38] *Compañía del Desarrollo de Santa Elena, S.A. v. Republic of Costa Rica*, ICSID Case No. ARB/96/1, Award (17 February 2000), 15 *ICSID Review – FILJ* 169, 191 (2000). *See also Klöckner Industrie-Anlagen GmbH and others v. United Republic of Cameroon and Société Camerounaise des Engrais, S.A.*, ICSID Case No. ARB/81/2, Decision on Annulment (3 May 1985), 2 *ICSID Reports* 95, 122 (1994) (international law prevails over the host State's law "should the State's law not conform on all points to the principles of international law").

classify its role as 'only' 'supplemental and corrective' seems a distinction without a difference."[39]

The Place of Arbitration

Pursuant to Article 62 of the ICSID Convention, arbitration proceedings are to be held at the seat of the Centre in Washington, DC, unless the parties otherwise agree. Under Article 63(a), the parties may agree to conduct proceedings instead at the seat of the Permanent Court of Arbitration in The Hague or at the seat of another institution with which the Centre has arrangements. The Centre has such arrangements for venues in Cairo, Kuala Lumpur, Melbourne, Singapore and Sydney.[40] Subject to approval by the tribunal after consultation with the ICSID Secretary-General, Article 63(b) also allows the parties to agree to hold hearings elsewhere.

A shift of physical location from Washington, DC, to another venue has no legal effect on the arbitration proceedings. As explained above, the Convention insulates ICSID proceedings from the application of national procedural law. Accordingly, in deciding whether to designate a place of arbitration other than Washington, DC, the parties need only consider practical matters such as comparative cost, efficiency and convenience.

In practice, many, if not most, ICSID arbitration proceedings are conducted at ICSID's headquarters in Washington, DC. Another common venue is the European Office of the World Bank in Paris.

The Language(s) of the Arbitration

The official languages of ICSID are English, French and Spanish. Rule 22(1) of the Arbitration Rules stipulates that the parties may agree on one or two languages for the proceedings. If the parties select a language that is not an official language of the Centre, the tribunal must give its specific approval of the selection following consultation with the Secretary-General. If the parties do not agree on the language or languages for the proceedings, each may select one of the three official ICSID languages.

As in international commercial arbitration in general, it is best for the parties to select the applicable language(s) in the arbitration agreement. Even at the negotiation phase, the drafters of the arbitration clause may often be able to identify the decisive factors for choosing a language or languages for the proceedings, looking, for example, to the choice of the applicable law and the language of the contract, the language of other principal documents, the mother

---

[39] *Amco Asia Corporation and others v. Republic of Indonesia,* ICSID Case No. ARB/81/1, Award in Resubmitted Case (31 May 1990), 1 *ICSID Reports* 569, 580 (1993).

[40] A. Parra, *The Role of the ICSID Secretariat in the Administration of Arbitration Proceedings under the ICSID Convention,* 13 *ICSID Review – FILJ* 85, 93 (1998).

tongue of likely fact and expert witnesses, and the availability of suitable arbitrators and counsel with the necessary language skills.

Selecting two languages inevitably entails complications and expense. In addition to the substantially greater costs of translation and interpretation, the risk of misunderstandings and other problems caused by inexact translation or interpretation of legal concepts increases significantly in bilingual proceedings.

Nevertheless it is not uncommon to conduct bilingual ICSID proceedings. One method to limit translation costs is for the parties to agree to submit documents only in their original language; each party then translates only the documents upon which it intends to rely. In such a procedure, the parties also translate into the other language all memorials, witness statements and expert reports, and use limited interpretation services at the hearings. Of course, if the individual arbitrators themselves are bilingual, the proceedings may be conducted in both languages without translation or interpretation.

Pre-arbitration Negotiation Period

ICSID arbitration clauses often include a mandatory negotiation or "cooling off" period of between 30 and 90 days, during which time a party may not commence arbitration. Such contractually mandated negotiations are aimed at forcing the parties to focus on the advantages of settlement in the initial stages of the dispute rather than on the tactical advantages possibly gained by the early commencement of an arbitration. It may be particularly important for a host State to have the opportunity to investigate and settle a dispute with an investor without the attendant publicity of an ICSID arbitration.

Provisional Measures

Pursuant to Article 47 of the ICSID Convention and Rule 39(5) of the Arbitration Rules, unless they agree otherwise, the parties may seek conservatory or provisional measures (for example, orders to attach assets or preserve evidence) only from the ICSID tribunal, and not from national courts (see Chapter 4).

This unusual restriction applies both before and after the tribunal is constituted; it is a reflection of the intent that the ICSID system be self-contained. Accordingly, parties to ICSID contractual arbitration have the right (if desired) to resort to alternative or additional remedies,[41] and to apply to local courts to secure attachment of assets or other provisional measures. Drafters have the choice of protecting this right for the parties either before or after the tribunal is constituted or, as reflected in ICSID Model Clause 14:

> "Without prejudice to the power of the Arbitral Tribunal to recommend provisional measures, either party hereto may request any judicial or other

---

[41] Model Clause 12 (Annex 5).

authority to order any provisional or conservatory measure, including attachment, prior to the institution of the arbitration proceeding, or during the proceeding, for the preservation of its rights and interests."

This provision is particularly important as it permits (without question) an application to a local court for relief prior to the often lengthy period it takes to constitute an ICSID tribunal.

Sovereign Immunity Waiver

Under Article 25 of the ICSID Convention, consent to arbitration on the part of the host State constitutes an irrevocable waiver of immunity from suit (i.e., arbitration). Bound by its consent, the host State is barred from raising any plea of immunity that would frustrate arbitration proceedings under the ICSID Convention, from the time the case is commenced by the investor up to the tribunal's issuance of the award.

Once the award is issued, however, the Convention does not alter or supersede the applicable national law governing a State's sovereign immunity to the enforcement and execution of the award. In other words, the host State's consent to arbitrate, although a waiver of immunity from suit, does not amount to a waiver of immunity from execution.

It is therefore imperative that foreign investors attempt to obtain from the host State an express waiver of sovereign immunity from execution in the arbitration agreement. ICSID Model Clause 15 provides possible language:

"The Host State hereby waives any right of sovereign immunity as to it and its property in respect of the enforcement and execution of any award rendered by an Arbitral Tribunal constituted pursuant to this agreement."

Without such a waiver – which is unlikely to be readily forthcoming once an investment dispute has arisen – an investor obtaining an award against a host State may be far from certain of achieving practical satisfaction. This important topic is discussed further in Chapter 5.

CHAPTER 3

Non-contractual ICSID Arbitration

Local investment laws and international treaties make it possible for private investors to initiate ICSID arbitration against host governments even when there is no contractual agreement between them. And so they have: in 2000, ICSID reported that two-thirds of the 38 arbitrations pending had been brought under an instrument other than an arbitration clause between investor and host State.[42] Every one of the 16 ICSID proceedings registered in 2002 was based on consent formed outside of contract.[43]

This so-called "arbitration without privity" is possible because Article 25 of the ICSID Convention, which defines the scope of ICSID's jurisdiction, requires only that the parties "consent in writing" to the jurisdiction of the Centre – it does not prescribe how they must do so. So long as the parties' consent is clear, mutual and in writing, it is sufficient to establish ICSID jurisdiction. The Centre has accepted jurisdiction over arbitrations that arise from consent to ICSID arbitration expressed in the host State's national investment legislation, in a bilateral investment treaty (*BIT*) between the host State and the investor's home State, and in a multilateral investment treaty among countries that include the host State and the investor's home State.

The parties express their consent differently in contractual and non-contractual ICSID arbitration. In contract-based ICSID arbitration (as in private international commercial arbitration), the parties generally give their consent simultaneously, in the arbitration clause contained in their investment contract or in a separate submission agreement. In non-contractual arbitration, the parties express their consent in two steps, each in turn. First, the host State consents by including a standing offer to submit to ICSID jurisdiction in its national legislation or in a bilateral or multilateral investment treaty. Second, the investor – which may not have been an investor at the time of the State's offer – consents by accepting that offer later, either in writing to the host State at any time or by filing a request to arbitrate with ICSID. In this way, the parties' agreement to arbitrate is perfected.

---

[42] ICSID *2000 Annual Report*, at < www.worldbank.org/icsid/pubs/2000ar/main-eng.htm >. S*ee also,* E. Obadia, *Current Issues in Investment Disputes: Comments,* 18 *ICSID News* 2 (2001).
[43] ICSID *2002 Annual Report*, at < www.worldbank.org/icsid/pubs/1998ar/2002_ICSID_ar_en.pdf >.

NATIONAL INVESTMENT LEGISLATION

Offer to Consent by the Host State

One basis for non-contractual ICSID arbitration is the national investment legislation of the host State, by which the latter unilaterally offers to submit investment disputes to ICSID jurisdiction. The consent becomes effective when the foreign investor accepts the State's offer to arbitrate, at the latest when the foreign investor files its claim with ICSID. Until then, however, the host State may be at liberty to withdraw its consent to ICSID arbitration by amending or repealing the investment law in which it offered to submit disputes to ICSID (subject to estoppel arguments that may be raised by investors having relied on the offer in the meantime).

Investment protection laws may contain offers to submit to ICSID arbitration in different terms. As a practical matter, therefore, each legislative act needs to be considered individually. Distinctions may seem slight, but they often are significant and warrant close examination.

Some States consent to ICSID jurisdiction by expressly submitting to arbitration under either the ICSID Convention or the Additional Facility Rules. References of this type are usually crafted in the alternative: they point to the ICSID Convention first but also allow investors to resort to the Additional Facility Rules if they are nationals of non-Contracting States. To cite one example, the Côte d'Ivoire's 1996 Investment Code, in establishing the avenue of ICSID arbitration to resolve investment disputes, refers to "the competence of [ICSID] or of the Supplementary Mechanism [Additional Facility], as the case may be, required by the instruments governing them."[44]

In comparison, a State may make a commitment to submit to ICSID jurisdiction by reference only to the Convention. For example, the relevant section of the 1993 Law on Foreign Investment of the Republic of Albania provides:

"If a foreign investment dispute arises between a foreign investor and the Republic of Albania and it cannot be settled amicably, then the foreign investor may choose to submit the dispute for resolution to a competent court or administrative tribunal of the Republic of Albania in accordance with its laws. In addition, if the dispute arises out of or relates to expropriation, compensation for expropriation, or discrimination and also for the transfers in accordance with Article 7, then the foreign investor may submit the dispute for resolution, and the *Republic of Albania hereby consents to the submission thereof, to the International Centre for Settlement of Investment Disputes ('Centre') established by the Convention on the Settlement of Investment Disputes between States and Nationals*

---

[44] Republic of Côte d'Ivoire, Office of the Prime Minister (CEPICI), *The Investment Code*, Law N° 95-620 of 3 August 1996, at Art. 24 (this can be found at www.panapress.com/cepici/law1.asp).

of Other States, done at Washington, March 18, 1965 ('ICSID Convention')."
(Emphasis added.)[45]

It has not yet been decided whether the consent to ICSID jurisdiction as articulated in laws such as this covers only arbitration under the Convention, or also includes, in a case where the foreign investor is from a non-signatory State, arbitration under the Additional Facility Rules.

As a further alternative, a State may consent to ICSID arbitration as one among several dispute resolution methods including, for example, procedures contemplated in applicable BITs or arbitration under related investment contracts. As an example, Egypt's Law No. 43 of 1974 Concerning the Investment of Arab and Foreign Funds and the Free Zone provides that investment disputes may be settled by treaty or ad hoc arbitration or in another manner agreed by the parties:

> "Investment disputes in respect of the implementation of the provisions of this Law shall be settled in a manner to be agreed upon with the investor, or within the framework of the agreements in force between the Arab Republic of Egypt and the investor's home country, or within the framework of the Convention for the Settlement of Investment Disputes between the State and the nationals of other countries to which Egypt has adhered by virtue of Law No. 90 of 1971, where such Convention applies.
>
> Disputes may be settled through arbitration. An Arbitration Board shall be constituted, comprising a member on behalf of each disputing party and a third member acting as chairman to be jointly named by the same two members."[46]

The tribunal in *SPP v. Egypt,* after a detailed linguistic and legal analysis, interpreted Egypt's investment law as providing a hierarchal structure such that a specific agreement between the parties would take precedence, followed by any applicable bilateral investment treaty, and then by the ICSID Convention.[47]

Open offers to ICSID arbitration should be distinguished from those references to ICSID contained in national investment legislation that require the host State to take further steps to forfeit its consent. Some laws, for example, stipulate that the State's offer to submit to ICSID arbitration will be effective only if and when the government other enters into a further agreement with the investor or issues an investment license explicitly referring to ICSID for the resolution of disputes. Such a condition precedent to consent by the State obviously must be satisfied before the investor may pursue ICSID remedies.

---

[45] Quoted *in Tradex Hellas S.A. v. Republic of Albania,* ICSID Case No. ARB/94/2, Decision on Jurisdiction (24 December 1996), 5 *ICSID Reports* 47, 54-55 (2002).

[46] Quoted in *Southern Pacific Properties (Middle East) Ltd. and Southern Pacific Properties Ltd. (Hong Kong) v. Arab Republic of Egypt,* Decision on Jurisdiction (27 November 1985), 3 *ICSID Reports* 112, 126 (1995).

[47] *Id.*

The Investor's Acceptance

A State's offer to submit to ICSID jurisdiction in its national legislation is in itself insufficient to found jurisdiction under Article 25 of the ICSID Convention. The necessary agreement to arbitrate is perfected only when the investor also expresses its consent, in writing, which it may do in different ways.

First, the investor may accept the State's open offer in writing, at any time, by way of a written communication to the State or a formal agreement with the State referring to the relevant national legislation. The investor may also resort to any other method provided for in the legislation itself, such as the filing of a license application with the relevant designated State authorities. In *SPP v. Egypt*, the tribunal found that the investor had perfected its consent to ICSID jurisdiction when, a year before initiating arbitration, it had written to the Egyptian Ministry of Tourism a letter stating: "we hereby notify you that we accept [. . .] the uncontestable jurisdiction of [ICSID] [. . .] which is open to us as a result of Law No. 43 of 1974, Art. 8 of which provides that investment disputes may be settled by ICSID arbitration."[48]

Second, if the investor has not accepted, in writing, the State's offer to arbitrate before it files its request for ICSID arbitration, it will be deemed to have done so under the Convention by virtue of the filing itself. In *Tradex v. Albania*, the tribunal found that a State's unilateral consent to ICSID arbitration "become[s] effective at the latest if and when the foreign investor files its claim with ICSID making use of the respective national law."[49]

Although the necessary agreement to arbitrate may be perfected in the request to arbitrate, investors are on more solid ground by expressing their consent as early as possible because, until they do, the State may be in a position to withdraw its open consent by amending or repealing its national investment legislation. Even more important, an investor should make its acceptance of ICSID jurisdiction unequivocal and should comply with any conditions for acceptance, such as time limits or other formalities required by the investment legislation containing the State's offer. With consent being "the cornerstone" of ICSID jurisdiction, investors cannot expect tribunals to make exceptions to the Convention's requirement of clear and mutual consent by host State and investor alike.

Bilateral Investment Treaties

The first known bilateral investment treaty appears to have been the one entered into in 1959 between Germany and Pakistan. BITs have proliferated since then, their number rising from 385 at the end of the 1980s to some 2000 as of 2003.

The number of ICSID arbitrations under BITs has also risen dramatically in

---

[48] *Id.* at 119.
[49] *Tradex v. Albania* (Decision on Jurisdiction), *supra* note 45, at 63.

recent years. The first ever BIT arbitration under the ICSID regime was filed in 1987. In *AAPL v. Sri Lanka*, the Hong Kong shareholder of a Sri Lankan shrimp farm filed a claim against Sri Lanka under the United Kingdom-Sri Lanka BIT for damage caused by Sri Lankan security forces during a military operation against installations reported to be used by Tamil rebels.[50] The *AAPL* tribunal rendered its award in 1990 requiring Sri Lanka to pay compensation for failing to afford "full protection and security" to AAPL's investment under the UK-Sri Lanka BIT. Since then, bilateral investment treaty arbitrations have transformed the volume and nature of ICSID cases. In April 2002, ICSID registered its hundredth case: of those first 100 cases, 60 had been instituted in the preceding five years and, of those, 45 were brought under investment treaties.

The Basic Nature of a BIT

Bilateral investment treaties establish comprehensive protections under international law, as well as the direct dispute resolution methods for private investors and States that are the subject of this Guide. To illustrate the nature and scope of BITs, Annex 6 contains the full text of the "Treaty between the Government of the United States of America and the Government of the State of Bahrain Concerning the Encouragement and Reciprocal Protection of Investment," signed in 1999 and ratified in 2001. Like most BITs, the US-Bahrain treaty is not long; it consists of 15 articles and fewer than 15 pages. Also included in Annex 6, both for its explanatory value and as an illustration of negotiating history, are the US government's documents transmitting the treaty to the Senate Committee on Foreign Relations for ratification purposes, including the Secretary of State's article-by-article analysis of the treaty text.

Many States have developed model or prototype bilateral investment treaties, which reflect their negotiating goals and hence form the basis for negotiations of new treaties. The United States developed its first prototype BIT in 1983, which has since gone through several iterations. As an example, a copy of the model United Kingdom BIT, entitled "Agreement for the Promotion and Protection of Investments," is included in Annex 7.

The overarching goals of bilateral investment treaties typically appear in the introductory language. The preamble to the US-Bahrain treaty is illustrative:

"The Government of the United States of America and the Government of the State of Bahrain (hereinafter the 'Parties');

Desiring to promote greater economic cooperation between them, with respect to investment by nationals and companies of one Party in the territory of the other Party;

---

[50] *Asian Agricultural Products Ltd (AAPL) v. Republic of Sri Lanka*, ICSID Case No. ARB/87/3, Award (27 June 1990), 4 *ICSID Reports* 245 (1997).

Recognizing that agreement upon the treatment to be accorded such investment will stimulate the flow of private capital and the economic development of the Parties;

Agreeing that a stable framework for investment will maximize effective utilization of economic resources and improve living standards;

Recognizing that the development of economic and business ties can promote respect for internationally recognized worker rights;

Agreeing that these objectives can be achieved without relaxing health, safety and environmental measures of general application; and

Having resolved to conclude a Treaty concerning the encouragement and reciprocal protection of investment;

Have agreed as follows [...]"

The preamble in the model UK BIT is more succinct:

"The Government of the United Kingdom of Great Britain and Northern Ireland and the Government of _____ ;

Desiring to create favourable conditions for greater investment by nationals and companies of one State in the territory of the other State;

Recognising that the encouragement and reciprocal protection under international agreement of such investments will be conducive to the stimulation of individual business initiative and will increase prosperity in both States;

Have agreed as follows [...]"

In general, a bilateral investment treaty affords qualifying investors certain minimum protections in respect of their investments in a State with which the investors' State of nationality or domicile has concluded a BIT. If a host State breaches the substantive protections contained in a BIT in a manner that adversely affects an investor, the latter (subject to any stipulated requirement to exhaust local court remedies) may often commence proceedings directly against that State. Many BITs, in particular, open the way to ICSID arbitration in the event of such a dispute between investor and host State.

Bilateral investment treaties are the product of negotiation between two sovereign States, and the exact scope and content of BITs vary considerably – even among those signed by a single country. The variances reflect the States' different investment approaches and respective bargaining positions. It is therefore necessary, in the event of an investment dispute, to study the exact terms of any applicable bilateral investment treaties with great care.

Most treaties nevertheless do contain recurring provisions, dealing with such matters as: (a) the scope of application of the BIT; (b) the definition of a qualifying investment; (c) the applicable law; (d) substantive investment treaty protections; and (e) access to arbitration and other forms of dispute resolution. These provisions are discussed below by reference to examples of certain bilateral investment treaties, selected because they represent fairly typical host State/investor State relationships – but which contain, nonetheless, several significant substantive and procedural differences (far beyond the scope of this Guide to discuss).

Establishing the Existence of a BIT

The first step in determining whether an investor may enjoy investment treaty protection is to identify whether there is an applicable BIT in force between the host State and the investor's State.

Annex 10 contains a detailed chart of over 850 BITs signed or ratified by ICSID Contracting States, plotted by country and date of entry into force (as of January 2002).[51] (There are also many BITs to which non-Contracting States are party, which could give rise to ICSID Additional Facility arbitration). The ICSID website contains a list of BITs, but it is not necessarily current.[52] The United Nations Conference on Trade and Development (*UNCTAD*) also publishes a list of bilateral investment treaties.[53] Where there is any doubt, the most reliable means of verifying the existence of a BIT is to contact the relevant ministry of foreign affairs or embassy.

Who is Entitled to Rely Upon the BIT?

Where there is a potentially applicable BIT, the next issue is whether it entitles a particular investor to protection as a national of a State party.

Most BITs draw a distinction between two categories of investing entities potentially able to enjoy the protection of the treaty: (a) individuals or natural persons, and (b) companies and other juridical entities. As to the first, the majority of BITs define "individuals" and their nationality by reference to the parties' domestic laws on citizenship. As to the second, many BITs determine the nationality of a company by reference to the domestic law concept of incorporation or constitution, according to which a company is deemed to take its nationality from the State in which it is incorporated regardless of where it actually carries on its economic activities. For example, the US-Bahrain BIT (Annex 6) defines a company as "any entity *constituted or organized under applicable law,* whether or not for profit and whether privately or governmentally owned or controlled, and includes, but is not limited to, a corporation, trust, partnership, sole proprietorship, branch, joint venture, association, or other organization" (emphasis added).

---

[51] As set out in note 2, there is a larger database available at < www.kluwerarbitration.com >.

[52] The bilateral investment treaty list can be found on the ICSID website at < www.worldbank.org/icsid/treaties/treaties.htm >. As of November 2003, it was current only to 1996.

[53] UNCTAD, *Bilateral Investment Treaties 1959-1999*, UNCTAD/ITE/IIA/2 (15 December 2000), at < www.unctad.org >.

Other bilateral investment treaties use the concept of the seat of company management, according to which the actual place of management of the company determines nationality; this is general German BIT practice. In still other BITs, including most of the recent Swiss treaties, the critical concept is control, according to which the nationality of the company is based on the nationality of dominant shareholders of the company.

Most BITs may be relied upon either by (a) the entity that makes the investment directly or (b) where this is a host State entity, such as a locally-incorporated investment vehicle, by the foreign individual or company that directly or indirectly controls that entity. For example, the US-Kazakhstan BIT states that " 'investment' means every kind of investment in the territory of one Party *owned or controlled directly or indirectly* by nationals or companies of the other Party" (emphasis added).[54] In this manner, the obligation frequently imposed by host States on a foreign investor to incorporate a local entity as a special purpose vehicle for the investment does not prevent the controlling foreign investor from relying on the treaty.

Some bilateral investment treaties go further to encompass and protect investing entities, wherever located, that are directly or indirectly controlled by investors of a State party to the treaty.[55] Control, under international law, is a flexible and broad concept that may refer not only to the rights of majority shareholders but also to other "reasonable" criteria such as management responsibility, voting rights and nationality of board members. The ICSID tribunal in the *Vacuum Salt v. Ghana* award, while finding that the 20 percent Greek shareholder could not be considered as exercising control over a local company so as to be able to confer Greek nationality on the company, stated that acting or being "materially influential in a truly managerial rather than technical or supervisory vein" or being "in a position to steer, through either positive or negative action, the fortunes" of the company would suffice to demonstrate control.[56]

A related question is whether a national of one Contracting State that owns a minority (or other non-controlling) shareholding interest in a corporation that is a national of the other Contracting State may bring a claim – independent of the corporation – against the host State. The tribunal in *CMS Gas Transmission v. Argentina*, after canvassing relevant sources of international law, answered this

---

[54] Treaty Between the United States of America and the Republic of Kazakhstan Concerning the Encouragement and Reciprocal Protection of Investment, 12 January 1994, Art I(1)(a), available at < www.export.gov/tcc >.

[55] *See, e.g.,* Agreement on Encouragement and Reciprocal Protection of Investments Between the Kingdom of the Netherlands and the Argentine Republic, 1 October 1994 (International Centre for Settlement of Investment Disputes, *Investment Promotion and Protection Treaties—Argentina/Netherlands* ed., Oceana Publications, Inc., July 1993).

[56] *Vacuum Salt Products Ltd. v. Republic of Ghana* (Award), *supra* note 24, at 350. *See also Autopista v. Venezuela* (Decision on Jurisdiction), *supra* note 17.

question in the affirmative. In that case, the government of Argentina, ultimately unsuccessfully, challenged the jurisdiction of the tribunal on a variety of grounds, most of which focused on CMS Gas Transmission's status as a minority shareholder in an Argentine corporation (Transportadora de Gas del Norte or *TGN*) that held a government license for gas transportation. The tribunal first described the trend in general international law to recognize the independence of shareholders:

"The Tribunal therefore finds no bar in current international law to the concept of allowing claims by shareholders independently from those of the corporation concerned, not even if those shareholders are minority or non-controlling shareholders. Although it is true, as argued by the Republic of Argentina, that this is mostly the result of *lex specialis* and specific treaty arrangements that have so allowed, the fact is that *lex specialis* in this respect is so prevalent that it can now be considered the general rule, certainly in respect of foreign investments and increasingly in respect of other matters."[57]

The tribunal went on to find, after detailed review, that "there is no bar to the exercise of jurisdiction in light of the 1965 Convention and its interpretation as reflected in its drafting history, the opinion of distinguished legal writers and the jurisprudence of ICSID tribunals."[58] The tribunal also found that CMS Gas Transmission's minority shareholding interest was an investment under the US-Argentina BIT (see the discussion immediately below) even though CMS Gas Transmission was not a party to TGN's license with the government:

"[T]he Tribunal concludes that jurisdiction can be established under the terms of the specific provisions of the BIT. Whether the protected investor is in addition a party to a concession agreement or a license agreement with the host State is immaterial for the purpose of finding jurisdiction under those treaty provisions, since there is a direct right of action of shareholders. It follows that the Claimant has *jus standi* before this Tribunal under international law, the 1965 Convention and the Argentina-United States Bilateral Investment Treaty."[59]

Given the growing importance of BIT protections, it is now imperative for international investors, just as they routinely structure their investments to take advantage of available tax benefits, to consider structuring investments in ways that enable them to benefit from BIT protections. Investors and their counsel should be familiar with the substantive protections and dispute resolution methods offered by various host jurisdictions. Specifically, along with other factors, an investor should consider selecting the nationality of its investing company or companies in order to

---

[57] *CMS Gas Transmission Company v. The Republic of Argentina*, Decision of the Tribunal on Objections to Jurisdiction (17 July 2003), 42 *ILM* 788, 795 (2003) (footnote omitted).

[58] *Id.* at 796 (The tribunal relied heavily on *Lanco International, Inc. v. Argentine Republic*, Preliminary Decision of the ICSID Tribunal (8 December 1998), 40 *ILM* 457 (2001).).

[59] *Id.* at 798.

take advantage of the most favorable regimes from among perhaps many potentially applicable BITs.

What Constitutes an "Investment"?

For a qualifying investor to be able to rely on the substantive protections and procedural safeguards of a BIT, it must have made an investment protected by the treaty.

Most BITs define the term "investment" in a broad, open-ended way that ensures a high degree of flexibility in application. Definitions often include general language referring to "every kind of asset"[60] or "every kind of investment in the territory."[61] Treaty definitions often provide specific and non-exhaustive examples, such as:

(a) "movable and immovable property" (UK-Russia BIT); "tangible and intangible property" (US-Argentina BIT);
(b) "shares in, and stock, bonds and debentures of, and any other form of participation in a company or business enterprise" (UK-Russia BIT); "company or shares of stock or other interests in a company or interests in the assets thereof" (US-Argentina BIT);
(c) "claims to money, and claims to performance under contract having a financial value" (UK-Russia BIT); "a claim to money or a claim to performance having economic value and directly related to an investment" (US-Argentina BIT); and
(d) "intellectual property" (US-Argentina BIT); "intellectual property rights, technical processes, know-how and any other benefit or advantage attached to a business" (UK-Russia BIT).

Some BITs explicitly apply only to investments made after the conclusion of the treaty. Others are broader in scope in terms of time. For example, Article 1(a) of the UK-Turkmenistan BIT states that "the term 'investment' includes all investments, whether made before or after the date of entry into force of this Agreement."[62]

In some BITs the term "investment" is linked to specified criteria. For example, the Sweden-Argentina BIT provides that "the term 'investment' shall comprise every kind of asset, invested by an investor of one Contracting Party in the territory of the

---

[60] *See, e.g.*, Agreement Between the Government of the United Kingdom of Great Britain and Northern Ireland and the Government of the Union of Soviet Socialist Republics for the Promotion and Reciprocal Protection of Investments, 3 July 1991, Art. 1(a). (International Centre for Settlement of Investment Disputes, *Investment Promotion and Protection Treaties – Soviet Union/United Kingdom* ed., Oceana Publications, Inc., October 1993).

[61] *See, e.g.,* Treaty Between the United States of America and the Argentine Republic Concerning the Reciprocal Encouragement and Protection of Investment, 20 October 1994, Art. I(1)(a), available at < www.export.gov/tcc > .

[62] Agreement Between the Government of the United Kingdom of Great Britain and Northern Ireland and the Government of Turkmenistan for the Promotion and Protection of Investments, 9 February 1995 (International Centre for Settlement of Investment Disputes, *Investment Promotion and Protection Treaties – Turkmenistan/United Kingdom* ed., Oceana Publications, Inc., March 1996).

other Contracting Party, *provided that the investment has been made in accordance with the laws and regulations of the other Contracting Party*" (emphasis added).[63] In *Gruslin v. Malaysia*, the ICSID tribunal held that Malaysia had not consented to ICSID jurisdiction under the criteria set out in the Belgium-Malaysia BIT, which provided for protection of "approved projects" only. The investment in question, an investment by Gruslin in shares listed on the Malaysian stock market, was not of the type that could be considered an "approved project."[64]

The broad nature of the definition of investment has been confirmed by the decisions of many ICSID tribunals in BIT arbitrations. In *Fedax v. Venezuela*, for example, the tribunal held that promissory notes issued by Venezuela and acquired by the claimant from the original holder in the secondary market, through endorsement, constituted an investment under the Netherlands-Venezuela BIT.[65] The tribunal extensively analyzed the notion of investment under bilateral and multilateral investment treaties and refused to limit it to the classic forms of direct investment, i.e., "the laying out of money or property in business ventures, so that it may produce a revenue or income," as argued by Venezuela.[66] Another ICSID tribunal has held that transactions that, taken in isolation, might not qualify as investments may nevertheless be considered as investments if the overall operation of which they are part ("composed of various interrelated transactions") constitutes an investment.[67]

Although flexible and broad, the notion of investment is not without limitation in ICSID practice. In 1985, for example, the ICSID Secretary-General refused to register a case on the basis that the alleged dispute related to a mere commercial sale and thus could not be considered as arising out of an investment.[68] Another example is the award declining jurisdiction in the case of *Mihaly International v. Sri Lanka* in 2002.[69] There the tribunal held that expenses incurred by the claimant following execution of a letter of intent with Sri Lanka to construct a proposed power project, including substantial sums spent in planning the financial and economic modeling necessary for the negotiation and (unsuccessful) finalization of a contract, were not an investment under the applicable BIT. The tribunal emphasized the care taken by the government of Sri Lanka to point out to Mihaly, throughout the negotiations, that the preliminary evaluation activities created no rights and obligations between

---

[63] Agreement Between the Government of the Kingdom of Sweden and the Government of the Republic of Argentina on the Promotion and Reciprocal Protection of Investments, 28 September 1992, Art. 1(1) (International Centre for Settlement of Investment Disputes, *Investment Promotion and Protection Treaties – Argentina/Sweden* ed., Oceana Publications, Inc., March 1993).

[64] *Phillipe Gruslin v. Malaysia,* ICSID Case No. ARB/99/3, Award (27 November 2000), 5 *ICSID Reports* 484 (2002).

[65] *Fedax v. Venezuela* (Decision on Objections to Jurisdiction), *supra* note 18.

[66] *Id.* at 190.

[67] *Ceskoslovenska Obchodni Banka, A.S. v. The Slovak Republic,* ICSID Case No. ARB/97/4, Decision on Objections to Jurisdiction (24 May 1999), 5 *ICSID Reports* 335, 352 (2002).

[68] ICSID *1985 Annual Report* at 6.

[69] *Mihaly v. Sri Lanka* (Award), *supra* note 19.

the parties. Thus, the tribunal found that the claimant had not acquired any asset, right or interest that could fall within the notion of investment. The *Mihaly International* tribunal summarized the necessity of determining the existence of an "investment" on a case-by-case basis:

> "The Tribunal has not been asked to and cannot consider in a vacuum whether or not in other circumstances expenditure of moneys might constitute an 'investment'. A crucial and essential feature of what occurred between the Claimant and the Respondent in this case was that first, the Respondent took great care in the documentation relied upon by the Claimant to point out that none of the documents, in conferring exclusivity upon the Claimant, created a contractual obligation for the building, ownership and operation of the power station. Second, the grant of exclusivity never matured into a contract. To put it rhetorically, what else could the Respondent have said to exclude any obligations which might otherwise have attached to interpret the expenditure of the moneys as an admitted investment?"[70]

Many BITs exclude from coverage investments in certain industries or other sectors. For example, the 1992 model US BIT is drafted to reserve the right of the United States to make exceptions to the "national treatment" protection (see below) in a number of sectors including banking, insurance, ownership of real property, use of land and natural resources, and mining on the public domain. It also reserves the right to make exceptions to "most favored nation" treatment (see below) in the following sectors: ownership of real property, mining on the public domain, maritime services and maritime-related services, and primary dealership in US government securities. These exceptions have been introduced in a number of individual BITs, for example in the US-Kazakhstan BIT.

The Choice of Law Applicable to BIT Claims

Some bilateral investment treaties recite that an arbitration tribunal shall apply some combination of the law of the relevant Contracting State, the provisions of the treaty and other agreements, general principles of international law and/or such rules of law as the parties may have agreed.

Most bilateral investment treaties, however, do not explicitly refer to the law that tribunals must apply in arbitrating disputes between investors and the host State. As noted above in Chapter 2, Article 42(1) of the ICSID Convention provides that, where the parties have not agreed upon applicable law, the tribunal should apply "the law of the Contracting State party to the dispute (including its rules on the conflict of laws) and such rules of international law as may be applicable." In practice, Tribunals in BIT arbitrations generally apply the substantive provisions of the relevant treaty itself and other sources of international law rather than national law.

---

[70] *Id.* at 155.

The ICSID tribunals in the *Maffezini* and *Vivendi* cases, even in the face of applicable law clauses in the relevant BITs referencing national law, looked to the treaties and to international law.[71] In the words of the ad hoc annulment committee in the *Vivendi* case:

"in respect of a claim based upon a substantive provision of that BIT ... the inquiry which the ICSID tribunal is required to undertake is one governed by the ICSID Convention, by the BIT and by applicable international law. Such an inquiry is neither in principle determined, nor precluded, by any issue of municipal law."[72]

Professor Prosper Weil, referring to the *Maffezini* and *Vivendi* cases, among others, has stated:

"[these] cases are noteworthy illustrations of the trend – which can only grow stronger – toward ICSID arbitration governed by international law by virtue of the fact that the BIT implicitly or explicitly provides that disputes must be settled not only on the basis of the provisions of the treaty itself, but also, and more generally, on the basis of the principles and rules of international law."[73]

Given that BITs grant foreign investors direct access to arbitration to claim the substantive protections of the treaty itself, it is entirely logical that the substantive standards of the treaty are the primary source of applicable law. As BITs are international law instruments, international law is also applicable by virtue of the Vienna Convention on the Law of Treaties, which provides that treaties are "governed by international law" and must be interpreted in light of "any relevant rules of international law applicable."[74] Further, Article 3 of the International Law Commission's Articles on State Responsibility provides:

"The characterization of an act of a State as internationally wrongful is governed by international law. Such characterization is not affected by the characterization of the same act as lawful by internal law."[75]

---

[71] *Emilio Agustín Maffezini v. The Kingdom of Spain*, ICSID Case No. ARB/97/7, Decision on Jurisdiction (25 January 2000), 5 *ICSID Reports* 396 (2002); *Compañía de Aguas del Aconquija S.A. and Compagnie Générale des Eaux v. Argentine Republic* (hereinafter *Vivendi*), ICSID Case No. ARB/97/3, Award (21 November 2000), 5 *ICSID* Reports 296 (2002). *See also American Manufacturing and Trading, Inc. v. Democratic Republic of the Congo*, ICSID Case No. ARB/93/1, Award (21 February 1997), 5 *ICSID Reports* 14 (2002); *Wena Hotels Ltd. v. Arab Republic of Egypt*, ICSID Case No. ARB/98/4, Decision on Annulment (5 February 2002), 41 *ILM* 933 (2002).

[72] *Compañía de Aguas del Aconquija S.A. and Compagnie Générale des Eaux v. Argentine Republic*, ICSID Case No. ARB/97/3, Decision on Annulment (3 July 2002), 41 *ILM* 1135, 1156 (2002).

[73] P. Weil, *The State, the Foreign Investor, and International Law: The No Longer Stormy Relationship of a Ménage à Trois*, 15 *ICSID Review – FILJ* 401, 412 (2000).

[74] Vienna Convention on the Law of Treaties, Articles 2(1)(a) and 31(3)(c).

[75] Articles on Responsibility of States for Internationally Wrongful Acts, adopted by the International Law Commission (2001), Article 3.

ICSID tribunals frequently refer to international case law, including the extensive jurisprudence of the Iran-United States Claims Tribunal, on disputes relating to illegal expropriation and nationalization, other takings and measures affecting property rights, as well as breach of contract. As is reflected even in the brief descriptions in this Guide, substantive ICSID case law is itself emerging rapidly.

What Substantive Rights do BITS Afford Investors?

Although the precise scope and content of individual bilateral investment treaties vary considerably, BITs in general grant investors certain minimum protections for their investments in foreign States with which their home State has concluded treaties. Many of the substantive protections described in summary form below are derived from longstanding principles of customary international law on the protection of alien property. Detailed discussion is beyond the scope of this Guide. The main principles may nevertheless be introduced by reference to some key features.

Fair and equitable treatment

Nearly all BITs require host States to accord "fair and equitable treatment" to investors of the other State party. For example, the Argentina-Netherlands BIT provides:

> "Each Contracting Party shall ensure fair and equitable treatment to investments of investors of the other Contracting Party and shall not impair, by unreasonable or discriminatory measures, the operation, management, maintenance, use, enjoyment or disposal thereof by those investors."[76]

The notion of fair and equitable treatment cannot readily be reduced to a precise statement of an exact legal obligation. Rather, the principle leaves considerable room for judgment and appreciation to tribunals charged with reviewing the "fairness" and "equity" of the host State's actions in light of all the circumstances of the case and without necessarily embarking upon deliberations on the requirements of either municipal or international law.[77]

Overall, the fair and equitable treatment standard requires States to maintain stable and predictable investment environments consistent with reasonable investor expectations. This is best illustrated by examples. One ICSID tribunal, in *Maffezini*

---

[76] Netherlands-Argentina BIT, *supra* note 55, at Art. 3(1).

[77] *See, e.g.,* C. Brower, *Investor-State Disputes under NAFTA: the Empire Strikes Back*, 40 *Columbia Journal of Transnational Law* 43, 56 (2001); S. Vasciannie, *The Fair and Equitable Treatment Standard in International Investment Law and Practice*, 70 *British Yearbook of International Law* 99, 163 (1999); F.A. Mann, *British Treaties for the Promotion and Protection of Investments,* 52 *British Yearbook of International Law* 241, 244 (1981) (an arbitral tribunal must "decide whether in all the circumstances the conduct in issue is fair and equitable or unfair and inequitable").

v. Spain, held that the government's failure to ensure transparency in the workings of public authorities constituted a breach of the fair and equitable treatment standard in the Argentina-Spain BIT.[78] The tribunal in the *CME v. Czech Republic* case found that the Czech Republic had breached the fair and equitable treatment standard by failing to provide a predictable framework for investment, contrary to the investor's legitimate expectations and its reliance on the State's earlier commitments.[79]

Full protection and security

As with "fair and equitable treatment," it is difficult to give an exact meaning to the notion of "full protection and security" in the abstract. Indeed, the two concepts are often linked, as for example in Article 2(2) of the model UK BIT (Annex 7):

> "Investments of nationals or companies of each Contracting Party shall at all times be accorded fair and equitable treatment and shall enjoy full protection and security in the territory of the other Contracting Party."

ICSID tribunals have found breaches of the full protection and security obligation in situations where the host State failed to take reasonably expected protective measures to prevent the physical destruction of the investor's property, in particular, measures that fell within the normal exercise of governmental functions. The investor is not required to establish either negligence or bad faith.[80] For example, in *AAPL v. Sri Lanka,* Sri Lankan security forces destroyed the investor's shrimp farm and killed more than 20 of its employees in efforts to try to curb Tamil insurgents. On the basis of the full protection and security clause in the UK-Sri Lanka BIT, the tribunal found that the Sri Lankan government would be held to a standard of due diligence. On the basis of this standard, the tribunal held that Sri Lanka had violated its obligation of full protection and security by not taking all possible measures to prevent the killings and the destruction of investment property.[81]

Although this standard has found application primarily in situations of physical protection of real and tangible property, its coverage also extends to other circumstances. In the *Goetz v. Burundi* case, the ICSID tribunal held, for example, that the withdrawal of a government authorization vital for the operation of the

---

[78] *Maffezini v. Spain* (Decision on Jurisdiction), *supra* note 71.

[79] *CME Czech Republic B.V. (The Netherlands) v. The Czech Republic,* Partial Award (13 September 2001), at para. 611 available at < www.mfcr.cz > . (Note, however, that a different tribunal in a related arbitration found, after examining the same facts, that the State had not breached the fair and equitable treatment standard even though it too held that under the fair and equitable treatment standard a State is required to maintain a predictable investment framework. *Ronald S. Lauder v. The Czech Republic,* Final Award (3 September 2001), at paras. 289-304 available at < www.mfcr.cz > .)

[80] *See AAPL v. Sri Lanka* (Award), *supra* note 50; *American Manufacturing & Trading v. Congo* (Award), *supra* note 71.

[81] *See AAPL v. Sri Lanka* (Award), *supra* note 50.

investment may amount to a breach of the investor's right to full protection and security.[82]

No arbitrary or discriminatory measures impairing the investment

Treaties usually impose a legal obligation on the host State not to impair the management or operation of the investment by "arbitrary or discriminatory measures." For example, the Sweden-Estonia Treaty provides:

> "Each Contracting Party [...] shall not impair the management, maintenance, use, enjoyment or disposal [of the investments by investors of the other Contracting Party] as well as the acquisition of goods and services and the sale of their production, through unreasonable or discriminatory measures."[83]

The notion of what constitutes "arbitrary" or "discriminatory" measures is not defined in the treaties. The International Court of Justice has, however, formulated a test of arbitrariness in the context of investment protection in the well-known *ELSI* case. The Court explained:

> "Arbitrariness is not so much something opposed to a rule of law, as something opposed to the rule of law. ... It is a willful disregard of due process of law, an act which shocks, or at least surprises, a sense of juridical propriety."[84]

In general, a measure is discriminatory in effect if it results in treatment of an investor that is different than that accorded to other investors in a similar or comparable situation.[85] As might be expected, whether a measure is arbitrary or discriminatory is a question of fact, to be determined in the light of the circumstances of each case.

National and "most favored nation" treatment

Investment treaties typically define the treatment required for the investment in relation to the treatment accorded other investments. Under the "national treatment" standard, the host State must treat foreign investments no less favorably than the investments of its own nationals and companies. Under the "most favored nation" (*MFN*) standard, the host State may not treat one foreigner's investment less favorably than that of an investor from another foreign country. The two standards,

---

[82] *Antoine Goetz and others v. République du Burundi,* ICSID Case No. ARB/95/3, Award (10 February 1999), 15 *ICSID Review – FILJ* 457 (2000).

[83] Agreement Between the Government of the Kingdom of Sweden and the Government of the Republic of Estonia on the Promotion and Reciprocal Protection of Investments, 2 May 1992, Art. 2(2) (International Centre for Settlement of Investment Disputes, *Investment Promotion and Protection Treaties – Estonia/Sweden* ed., Oceana Publications, Inc., March 1993).

[84] *Case Concerning Elettronica Sicula S.p.A. (ELSI) (United States v. Italy),* Judgment (20 July 1989), 1989 ICJ *Reports* 15, 76.

[85] *Goetz v. Burundi* (Award), *supra* note 82.

which are usually combined, are illustrated in the MFN clause (Article 2(1)) of the US-Bahrain BIT (Annex 6):

"With respect to the establishment, acquisition, expansion, management, conduct, operation and sale or other disposition of covered investments, each Party shall accord treatment no less favorable than that it accords, in like situations, to investments in its territory of its own nationals or companies (hereinafter 'national treatment') or to investments in its territory of nationals or companies of a third country (hereinafter 'most favored nation treatment'), whichever is most favorable (hereinafter 'national most favored nation treatment'). Each Party shall ensure that its state enterprises, in the provision of their goods or services, accord national and most favored nation treatment to covered investments."

Exceptions to national and MFN treatment, e.g., atomic energy, broadcast licenses, fisheries and initial privatization of oil exploration, are set out in the Annex to the US-Bahrain BIT (also in Annex 6). Article 7 of the model United Kingdom BIT (Annex 7) reflects the preference of the UK to except from the treaty protections of national treatment and MFN treatment any benefits under "customs union or similar international agreement" and under "any international agreement or arrangement relating wholly or mainly to taxation or any domestic legislation relating wholly or mainly to taxation."

As MFN treatment is a relative standard, its scope by definition varies according to the circumstances of each case. Foreign investors traditionally rely on the MFN clause in the context of substantive rights. For example, if the host State provides tax concessions to Italian investors in the oil industry but not to UK investors, a UK investor could rely on an MFN clause in an applicable BIT to demand the same treatment or to claim compensation for loss suffered as a result of being denied the same treatment.

Based on the ICSID award in the *Maffezini* case, there is nevertheless room for MFN treatment to be extended beyond substantive rights to certain procedural rights concerning the dispute resolution mechanism between host States and investors. In *Maffezini*, an Argentine investor filed an ICSID claim against Spain, although he had not previously submitted the dispute to the Spanish courts as required by the Argentina-Spain BIT. The investor argued, however, that he could by-pass this precondition to ICSID arbitration by invoking the most favored nation clause of the Argentina-Spain BIT to claim a benefit under Spain's BIT with Chile, which does not require investors to make prior recourse to local courts. The ICSID tribunal agreed, holding that, on the basis of the MFN clause in the Argentina-Spain treaty, the Argentine investor could rely on the less stringent procedural provisions of the Chile-Spain BIT.[86]

---

[86] *Maffezini v. Spain* (Decision on Jurisdiction), *supra* note 71.

Following *Maffezini*, a foreign investor considering a claim under a BIT containing an MFN clause should systematically review other treaties concluded by the relevant host State for more beneficial dispute resolution procedures. This is particularly the case for any foreign investor facing potential jurisdictional hurdles under the BIT (or BITs) underlying its claim. Equally, legal advisers to States should be familiar with the variations in the MFN landscape created by the States' investment treaties.

Free transfer of funds related to investments

Many treaties provide that the host State must "permit all transfers related to an investment to be made freely and without delay into and out of its territory."[87] Foreign investors are entitled to compensation if they are affected by currency control regulations or other acts of the host State that effectively freeze investor funds maintained in the host State.

Free transfer provisions are usually broad in scope and are not restricted to certain types of funds, but instead cover any amounts derived from or associated with an investment. These would include profits, dividends, interest, capital gains, royalty payments, management, technical assistance or other fees, or returns in kind. Some BITs reserve the possibility for the host State to restrict transfers of funds during periods of limited availability of foreign exchange, or due to balance of payments problems.

No expropriation without compensation

Perhaps the most critical protection offered by bilateral investment treaties is the host State's obligation to compensate foreign investors in the event of expropriation. Indeed, expropriation provisions appear to be the ones most frequently relied upon by foreign investors in treaty arbitration.

The notion of expropriation is expansive in nature. It is a well-accepted principle of public international law that expropriation may result from either (a) a direct and deliberate formal act of taking, such as an outright nationalization, or (b) from an indirect taking that substantially deprives the investor of the use or enjoyment of its investment, including deprivation of the whole or a significant part of the economic benefit of property, even if the legal and beneficial title of the asset remains with the investor. Government measures may amount to expropriation regardless of their form and purpose. An expropriation may also be "creeping" or "constructive;" it need not be immediate, but may unfold through a series of acts, the cumulative effect of which is substantial deprivation of the use or value of an investment. Government measures such as tax increases, environmental regulations or the revocation of a license may, in certain circumstances, amount to an expropriation.

---

[87] *See, e.g.,* US-Argentina BIT, *supra* note 61, at Art. V(1).

International law does not prohibit expropriation as such. Rather, it requires that expropriation be for a public purpose and non-discriminatory, and that the State pay adequate compensation to the investors. The provisions setting out the acceptable parameters for expropriation vary from BIT to BIT. The expropriation clause in the US-Bahrain BIT (Annex 6, Article 3) is comparatively detailed:

"1. Neither Party shall expropriate or nationalize a covered investment either directly or indirectly through measures tantamount to expropriation or nationalization ('expropriation') except for a public purpose; in a non-discriminatory manner; upon payment of prompt, adequate and effective compensation; and in accordance with due process of law and the general principles of treatment provided for in Article 2, paragraph 3.

2. Compensation shall be paid without delay; be equivalent to the fair market value of the expropriated investment immediately before the expropriatory action was taken ('the date of expropriation'); and be fully realizable and freely transferable. The fair market value shall not reflect any change in value occurring because the expropriatory action had become known before the date of expropriation.

3. If the fair market value is denominated in a freely usable currency, the compensation paid shall be no less than the fair market value on the date of expropriation, plus interest at a commercially reasonable rate for that currency, accrued from the date of expropriation until the date of payment.

4. If the fair market value is denominated in a currency that is not freely usable, the compensation paid – converted into the currency of payment at the market rate of exchange prevailing on the date of payment – shall be no less than:
   (a) the fair market value on the date of expropriation, converted into a freely usable currency at the market rate of exchange prevailing on that date, plus
   (b) interest, at a commercially reasonable rate for that freely usable currency, accrued from the date of expropriation until the date of payment."

Focusing just on examples of compensation standards, Article 5(1) of the UK-Russia BIT requires that compensation amount to "the real value of the investment expropriated immediately before the expropriation or before the impending expropriation became public knowledge, whichever is the earlier [to be paid] within two months of the date of expropriation, after which interest at a normal commercial rate shall accrue until the date of payment."[88] The US-Kazakhstan BIT speaks, at Article III(1), of "compensation [...] equivalent to the fair market value of the expropriated investment" with similar provisions as to interest, although without a grace period for payment.[89]

---

[88] United Kingdom – Russia BIT, *supra* note 60.
[89] US-Kazakhstan BIT, *supra* note 54.

These BIT protections against uncompensated expropriation are not new. They reflect the evolving rules of customary international law on the protection of what historically was referred to as alien property, included those set out in many treaties of friendship, commerce and navigation of an earlier vintage. What is new in the BITs is the opportunity for investors themselves, under ICSID or other dispute resolution mechanisms in the treaties, to proceed directly – without espousal of their claims by their home governments – against the expropriating State for compensation in an international forum.

There is developing BIT case law on expropriation. The tribunal in the *CME* case considered the expropriation claim of an investor in a joint venture in the Czech Republic. The investor alleged that the joint venture collapsed after the official Czech broadcasting authority forced it to give up its exclusive licensing rights and changed other key terms of the joint venture agreement. The tribunal held that the acts of the Czech regulatory authority interfered with the "economic and legal basis of CME's investment" and "destroy[ed] the legal basis ('the safety net') of the claimant's investment," which ruined the "commercial value of the investment" and, thus, amounted to expropriation.[90]

The ICSID tribunal in the *Santa Elena v. Costa Rica* case found expropriation despite the environmental purposes underlying the relevant takings:

"Whilst an expropriation or taking for environmental reasons may be classified as taking for a public purpose, and thus may be legitimate, the fact that the Property was taken for this reason does not affect either the nature or the measure of the compensation to be paid for the taking. That is, the purpose of protecting the environment for which the Property was taken does not alter the legal character of the taking for which adequate compensation must be paid. The international source of the obligation to protect the environment makes no difference.

Expropriatory environmental measures – no matter how laudable and beneficial to society as a whole – are, in this respect, similar to any other expropriatory measures that a state may take in order to implement its policies: where property is expropriated, even for environmental purposes, whether domestic or international, the state's obligation to pay compensation remains."[91]

Observance of specific investment undertakings
Treaties may also contain blanket provisions obligating the host State to observe, or guarantee the observance of, specific undertakings towards investors. An example of such a clause appears in Article 2(2) of the model UK BIT (Annex 7):

"Each Contracting Party shall observe any obligation it may have entered into with regard to investments of nationals or companies of the other Contracting Party."

---

[90]   *CME v. Czech Republic* (Partial Award), *supra* note 79.
[91]   *Santa Elena v. Costa Rica* (Award), *supra* note 38, at paras. 71-72.

Such clauses are sometimes referred to as "umbrella clauses," the idea being that they are meant to cover every conceivable commitment with respect to investments flowing between the two States. An immediate issue is the interrelationship between such a clause and any relevant investor-State contract.[92]

The ICSID tribunal in *SGS v. Pakistan* was the first international arbitration tribunal to rule on the legal effect of such a clause in a jurisdictional context.[93] SGS brought a claim against Pakistan for alleged breaches of both a contract for customs-related pre-shipment inspection services and the Switzerland-Pakistan bilateral investment treaty. Pakistan challenged the tribunal's jurisdiction of SGS's claims for breach of the contract on the ground, among others, that such claims were subject exclusively to the arbitration clause in the contract. In response (again on one among many grounds), SGS relied on Article 11 of the BIT, which provided:

> "Either Contracting Party shall constantly guarantee the observance of the commitments it has entered into with respect to the investments of the investors of the other Contracting Party."

SGS argued that Article 11 was a clause "that takes breaches of contract under municipal law and elevates them immediately to the level of a breach of an international treaty,"[94] and hence that the tribunal automatically had jurisdiction under the BIT of all of SGS's claims for breach of the pre-inspection services contract.

Applying the traditional tools of treaty interpretation, and thus examining the language of Article 11 and the object and purpose of the BIT, the tribunal refused to adopt the investor's far-reaching characterization of Article 11. The tribunal based its decision in part on burden of proof:

> "Considering the widely accepted principle with which we started, namely, that under general international law, a violation of a contract entered into by a State with an investor of another State, is not, by itself, a violation of international law, and considering further that the legal consequences that the Claimant would have us attribute to Article 11 of the BIT are so far-reaching in scope, and so automatic and unqualified and sweeping in their operation, so burdensome in their potential impact upon a Contracting Party, we believe that clear and convincing evidence must be adduced by the Claimant. Clear and convincing evidence of what? Clear and convincing evidence that such was indeed the shared intent of the Contracting Parties to the Swiss-Pakistan Investment Protection Treaty in incorporating Article 11 in the BIT. We do not find such evidence in the text itself of Article 11.

---

[92] *See, e.g., The World Bank in a Changing World: Selected Essays and Lectures* (I. Shihata, ed., Martinus Nijhoff, 1995).

[93] *SGS Société Générale de Surveillance S.A. v. Islamic Republic of Pakistan*, ICSID Case No. ARB/01/13, Decision on Jurisdiction (6 August 2003), *ASIL International Law in Brief* (17 September 2003).

[94] *Id.* at para. 163.

We have not been pointed to any other evidence of the putative common intent of the Contracting Parties by the Claimant."[95]

The tribunal noted that the investor's reading of Article 11 would tend to make substantive BIT standards (such as fair and equitable treatment) superfluous, because a claimant would not have to prove a violation of those standards if a simple contract breach sufficed as a treaty claim. The third consequence would be that "an investor may, at will, nullify any freely negotiated dispute settlement clause in a State contract," leaving the benefits of such a dispute resolution clause to flow only to the investor.[96]

Enforcement of Rights Under a BIT

Assuming that the investor believes that one or more of the substantive protections of the applicable bilateral investment treaty has been breached, the investor must next check that the treaty grants direct rights to investors to commence arbitration proceedings or to invoke some other means of recourse against the host State.

Negotiation period

BITs typically include a negotiation or consultation period, sometimes described as a "cooling off" period, before a claim may be brought. The period is usually between three and six months from the date when the dispute arose or was formally notified by the investor to the host State, at the end of which an arbitration may be commenced. For example, Article 8(1) of the model UK BIT (Annex 7) provides:

> "Disputes between a national or company of one Contracting Party and the other Contracting Party concerning an obligation of the latter under this Agreement in relation to an investment of the former which have not been amicably settled shall, after a period of three months from written notification of a claim, be submitted to international arbitration if the national or company concerned so wishes."

The practical purpose of the "cooling off period" is to facilitate settlement out of the public eye before positions become entrenched. This objective assumes added importance for a sovereign State dealing with disaffected foreign investors.

As a matter of practice, the foreign investor typically starts the negotiation period by sending a letter – commonly referred to as a "trigger letter" – to the most senior central authorities of the host State (such as the Head of State and the Minister in charge of foreign investment) notifying them of the existence of a dispute under the relevant BIT. It should be noted that notification to a subdivision of a State, such as a provincial governor, may not be sufficient, even if the underlying investment

---

[95] *Id.* at para. 167.
[96] *Id.*

agreement was with the province. The trigger letter typically provides a basic summary of the background and nature of the dispute and then requests negotiations. If negotiations do not ensue, the invitation may be periodically repeated. Upon expiry of the negotiation period, absent a meeting of the minds, either side may institute the arbitration.

ICSID tribunals have generally considered such consultation period clauses to be procedural rather than jurisdictional in nature. The tribunal in the *Lauder v. Czech Republic* case, for example, rejected the Czech Republic's jurisdictional objections based on the claimant's alleged failure to observe the six-month negotiation period under the relevant BIT:

> "the Arbitral Tribunal considers that this requirement of a six-month waiting period of [the BIT] is not a jurisdictional provision, i.e. a limit set to the authority of the Arbitral Tribunal to decide on the merits of the dispute, but a procedural rule that must be satisfied by the Claimant ... As stated above, the purpose of this rule is to allow the parties to engage in good-faith negotiations before initiating the arbitration."[97]

Among the factors that ICSID tribunals, including the *Lauder v. Czech Republic* tribunal, examine in interpreting negotiation clauses is whether the parties have actually commenced consultations and, if not, whether the host State has indicated a willingness to negotiate.

Prior reference to local courts

Some BITs also require that the foreign investor first present disputes to the courts of the host State. If those courts do not issue a decision within a specified period of time, the investor is then entitled to resort to arbitration irrespective of whether a judicial decision has resulted. For example, the Argentina-Netherlands BIT requires both a negotiation period and the submission to local courts before arbitration may be commenced:

> "1. Disputes between one Contracting Party and an investor of the other Contracting Party regarding issues covered by this agreement shall, if possible, be settled amicably.
>
> 2. If such disputes cannot be settled according to the provisions of paragraph (1) of this article within a period of three months from the date on which either party to the dispute requested amicable settlement, either party may submit the dispute to the administrative or judicial organs of the Contracting party in the territory of which the investment has been made.
>
> 3. If within a period of eighteen months from submissions of the dispute to the

---

[97] *Lauder v. Czech Republic* (Final Award), *supra* note 79, at para. 187. *See also SGS v. Pakistan* (Decision on Jurisdiction), *supra* note 93; *Ethyl Corporation v. The Government of Canada*, Award on Jurisdiction (24 June 1998), 38 *ILM* 708, 724 (1999).

competent organs mentioned in paragraph (2) above, these organs have not given a final decision or if the decision of the aforementioned organs has been given but the parties are still in dispute, then the investor concerned may resort to international arbitration or conciliation. Each Contracting Party hereby consents to the submission of a dispute referred to in paragraph (1) of this Article to international arbitration."[98]

However, a virtually identical provision in the Argentina-Spain BIT was successfully bypassed by relying on the most favored nation clause (see the discussion of the *Maffezini* case above).

"Fork in the road" provisions

Generally speaking, the procedural dispute resolution mechanisms in BITs present both parties, or sometimes the investor alone, with a series of options ranging from pursuing the claim in the local courts of the host State, to bringing ICSID arbitration, to resorting to another form of international arbitration. Some BITs contain a stipulation that if the investor chooses to submit a dispute to the local courts of the host State, or to any other agreed dispute resolution procedure (for example, to ICC arbitration under the dispute resolution clause in the investor-State contract), the investor forever loses the right to submit the same claims to the international arbitration procedure in the BIT. Such a mechanism is commonly called a "fork in the road" provision.

As an illustration of a "fork in the road" provision, the US-Kazakhstan BIT provides at Article VI(2) and (3):

"2. In the event of an [investor/State] investment dispute, the parties to the dispute should initially seek a resolution through consultation and negotiation. If the dispute cannot be settled amicably, the national or company concerned may choose to submit the dispute for resolution: (a) to the courts or administrative tribunals of the Party that is a party to the dispute; or (b) in accordance with any applicable, previously agreed dispute-settlement procedures; or (c) in accordance with the terms of paragraph 3 [below].

3(a). *Provided that the national or company concerned has not submitted the dispute for resolution under paragraph 2(a) or (b)* [above] and that six months have elapsed from the date on which the dispute arose, the national or company concerned may choose to consent in writing to the submission of the dispute for settlement by binding arbitration:
  (i) to the International Centre for the Settlement of Investment Disputes ('Centre') established by the [Convention], provided that the Party is a Party to such Convention; or
  (ii) to the Additional Facility for the Centre, if the Centre is not available; or

---

[98] Argentina-Netherlands BIT, *supra* note 55, at Art.10.

(iii) in accordance with the Arbitration Rules of [UNCITRAL]; or

(iv) to any other arbitration institution, or in accordance with any other arbitration rules, as may be mutually agreed between the parties to the dispute." (Emphasis added).[99]

An investor must therefore evaluate carefully any inclination to proceed with claims before a domestic tribunal if the possibility of ICSID arbitration under a BIT also exists – lest the investor inadvertently, and irrevocably, take the wrong fork in the road.

The Vivendi *"Essential Basis of Claim" Test*

"Fork in the road" issues, and the impact of contractual dispute resolution clauses, may be particularly complex in cases where an investor is pursuing both contract breach claims and BIT breach claims in the same proceeding. This is illustrated in the landmark *Vivendi* ICSID arbitration, which resulted in a first award,[100] which was subsequently annulled in part.[101] The case arose from a dispute under a concession contract entered into by a French company and its Argentine affiliate, on the one hand, and Tucumán, a province of Argentina, on the other, for the operation of the Tucumán water and sewage system. Although the concession contract provided that the parties would submit disputes to the local administrative courts, the claimants did not bring their dispute before the local courts. They instead filed claims against Argentina under the France-Argentina BIT, seeking damages for breaches of the concession contract that they alleged amounted to breach of the BIT.

The first tribunal found that it had jurisdiction, but refused to consider the treaty breach claims on grounds that they were inextricably linked with questions of interpretation of the concession contract, which were reserved for the local Argentine courts under the dispute resolution clause of that contract. The ad hoc committee convened for the annulment proceeding, set aside this part of the first *Vivendi* award. The ad hoc committee found that, among other things, the tribunal had exceeded its authority by refusing to rule on the merits of the treaty claims over which it had jurisdiction, even if there was an overlap between the contract and treaty claims. The committee emphasized the legal distinction between the two categories of claims:

"95. [As to the relation between breach of contract and breach of treaty in the present case, it must be stressed that Articles 3 [fair and equitable treatment] and 5 [expropriation] of the BIT do not relate directly to breach of a municipal contract. Rather they set an independent standard. A state may breach a treaty without breaching a contract, and *vice versa*, and this is certainly true of these provisions of

---

[99] US-Kazakhstan BIT, *supra* note 54, at Art. VI.

[100] *Vivendi v. Argentina* (Award), *supra* note 71.

[101] *Compañía de Aguas del Aconquija S.A. and Compagnie Générale des Eaux v. Argentine Republic*, ICSID Case No. ARB/97/3, Decision on Annulment (26 June 2002), 41 *ILM* 1135 (September 2002).

the BIT. The point is made clear in Article 3 of the ILC Articles, which is entitled 'Characterization of an act of a State as internationally wrongful':

> The characterization of an act of a State as internationally wrongful is governed by international law. Such characterization is not affected by the characterization of the same act as lawful by internal law.

96. In accordance with this general principle (which is undoubtedly declaratory of general international law), whether there has been a breach of the BIT and whether there has been a breach of contract are different questions. Each of these claims will be determined by reference to its own proper or applicable law – in the case of the BIT, by international law; in the case of the Concession Contract, by the proper law of the contract, in other words, the law of Tucumán."[102]

The *Vivendi* ad hoc committee proceeded to develop an "essential" or "fundamental basis of the claim" test:

> "98. In a case where the essential basis of a claim brought before an international tribunal is a breach of contract, the tribunal will give effect to any valid choice of forum clause in the contract.
>
> .
>
> 101. On the other hand, where 'the fundamental basis of the claim' is a treaty laying down an independent standard by which the conduct of the parties is to be judged, the existence of an exclusive jurisdiction clause in a contract between the claimant and the respondent state or one of its subdivisions cannot operate as a bar to the application of the treaty standard. At most, it might be relevant – as municipal law will often be relevant – in assessing whether there has been a breach of the treaty." Footnotes omitted[103]

In a subsequent ICSID decision, the *SGS v. Pakistan* tribunal applied the *Vivendi* "essential basis" test to dismiss certain of SGS's claims for lack of jurisdiction. The tribunal found the dispute resolution clause in the parties' pre-inspection services contract, which called for arbitration in Pakistan, to be "a valid forum selection clause *so far as it concerns the Claimant's contract claims which do not also amount to BIT claims.*"[104]

Common Arbitral Mechanisms

Once all of the preconditions for exercising treaty causes of action are satisfied, BITs usually present the investor with a choice of actual dispute resolution mechanisms. This choice typically includes more than one type of international arbitration, alongside local court litigation and any contractually agreed dispute settlement

---

[102] *Id.* at 1154, paras. 95-96.
[103] *Id.* at 1155-1156, paras 98, 101.
[104] *SGS v. Pakistan* (Decision on Jurisdiction), *supra* note 93, at para. 161.

procedures. the most frequently designated international arbitration institution is ICSID, but reference to ad hoc arbitration under the UNCITRAL Arbitration Rules is also common. Occasionally there are options to refer disputes to the ICC or the Stockholm Chamber of Commerce.

Two broadly typical examples may be taken from the US-Bahrain and UK-Turkmenistan BITs:

(a) The US-Bahrain BIT (see Annex 6) provides that, after the negotiation period, an investor may choose to submit a dispute to: ICSID, if it is available, or the Additional Facility; arbitration in accordance with the UNCITRAL Rules; or any other arbitration institution or in accordance with any other arbitration rules agreed between the parties to the dispute.
(b) The UK-Turkmenistan BIT provides that the investor and the host State "may agree to refer the dispute" to: ICSID or the Additional Facility; the ICC; or an international arbitrator or ad hoc tribunal to be appointed by a special agreement or established under the UNCITRAL Rules.[105]

Duration of Bilateral Investment Treaties

The typical duration of a bilateral investment treaty is ten years, with the term automatically extended thereafter unless and until one party terminates the treaty with notice. In light of the long-term nature of major foreign investment projects, a critical extra protection is a lengthy extension of treaty coverage after termination for investments made before termination. The model UK BIT (see Article 14, Annex 7) envisions a sunset period of 20 years:

> "This Agreement shall remain in force for a period of ten years. Thereafter it shall continue in force until the expiration of twelve months from the date on which either Contracting Party shall have given written notice of termination to the other. Provided that in respect of investments made whilst the Agreement is in force, its provisions shall continue in effect with respect to such investments for a period of twenty years after the date of termination and without prejudice to the application thereafter of the rules of general international law."

The US-Bahrain BIT (see Article 16, Annex 6) provides for ten years of post-termination protection:

> "2. A Party may terminate this Treaty at the end of the initial ten year period or at any time thereafter by giving one year's written notice to the other Party.
> 3. For ten years from the date of termination, all other Articles shall continue to apply to covered investments established or acquired prior to the date of termination, except insofar as those articles extend to the establishment or acquisition of covered investments."

---

[105] UK-Turkmenistan BIT, *supra* note 62, at Art. 8.

The recent vintage of most bilateral investment treaties – the real boom having started less than ten years ago – means that there is little experience with termination and expiry of BITs. In the wake of the recent spike of the number of BIT arbitrations filed with ICSID, and the perception in some circles that jurisdiction is being stretched too far, there has been speculation as to whether some developing countries may choose to exercise their option to terminate BITs as the (typically) ten year term comes to an end. While this seems unlikely, in light of the importance of foreign investment to industrialized and developing countries alike, it is entirely possible that there may be adjustments to substantive protections in the next generation of bilateral investment treaties.

Multilateral Investment Treaties

The acceptance in BITs of protective standards of treatment for foreign investment and investor-State arbitration has led to the adoption of similar provisions in the "investment chapters" of multilateral economic cooperation treaties and free trade agreements. Among these are Chapter 11 of the North American Free Trade Agreement (*NAFTA*) and Part III and Article 26 of the 1994 Energy Charter Treaty (*ECT*), both described below. Others include the 1987 ASEAN Agreement for the Promotion and Protection of Investments, the 1994 Colonia and Buenos Aires Investment Protocols of Mercosur, and Chapter 17 of the 1990 Group of Three Agreements.

With the exception of NAFTA, there have been very few investment arbitrations under these multilateral investment treaty arrangements.

NAFTA Arbitration

In 1992, Canada, Mexico and the United States concluded the North American Free Trade Agreement establishing the North American Free Trade Area. NAFTA, which came into force on 1 January 1994, removes trade barriers and is intended to promote economic cooperation between the three participating States and increase investment opportunities in their territories. The investment chapter of NAFTA, Chapter 11, implements these objectives by identifying the standards for treatment of investors and establishing a dispute resolution mechanism for arbitration of investor-State disputes, similar to that contained in most BITs.

The NAFTA Chapter 11 dispute resolution mechanism may be invoked by any investor of a NAFTA State that has invested in the territory of another NAFTA State and incurred loss or damage as a result of measures adopted or maintained by the host State. In order to form the basis for a claim, the measures in question must have been in breach of the substantive obligations contained in Chapter 11. The full text of NAFTA Chapter 11, which includes both the treaty's substantive investment protections (Section A) and the available dispute resolution mechanisms (Section B), is set out in Annex 8.

The jurisprudence developing from NAFTA Chapter 11 tribunals affects the interests of more than Canada, Mexico, the United States and their respective investors. This is because many of the provisions of Chapter 11 are similar to the most common substantive and procedural BIT provisions. Although a full account of NAFTA Chapter 11 is beyond the parameters of this Guide, certain key points are described below.

Procedural framework

Articles 1118 to 1120 of NAFTA Chapter 11 authorize an investor to initiate arbitration against a host State for the alleged breach of one of the investment protections contained in NAFTA after (a) the passage of a negotiation period of six months, which runs from the date of the events giving rise to the claim, and (b) a 90-days written notice of the intent to submit a claim. A claim is allowed only within three years from the date on which the investor knew or should have known of the treaty breach and resulting damage (Article 1113(2)).

A special feature of NAFTA Chapter 11 is that, under Article 1121(1), an investor must waive its rights "to initiate or continue before any administrative tribunal or court under the law of any Party, or other dispute settlement procedures, any proceedings with respect to the measure of the disputing Party" alleged to be a NAFTA breach (other than certain applications for non-monetary interim relief). The operation of this waiver requirement is illustrated in the *Waste Management v. Mexico* case. In 1998, Waste Management, a US company, filed a claim against Mexico alleging various breaches of NAFTA Chapter 11. The ICSID (Additional Facility) tribunal constituted to hear the case declined jurisdiction on the ground that Waste Management, in pursuing remedies in Mexico while also taking part in the NAFTA Chapter 11 proceedings, had failed to waive its rights to initiate or continue non-NAFTA legal actions relating to the measures adopted.[106] The case, therefore, was dismissed. Waste Management then resubmitted its claim in 2000, having concluded or discontinued all claims before Mexican courts that involved breaches also alleged to be breaches of Chapter 11. The tribunal ruled that the dismissal of the earlier claim for lack of a proper waiver did not preclude Waste Management from resubmitting the same case, provided that it subsequently had made a proper waiver.[107]

Under Article 1201 of NAFTA Chapter 11, the investor has the option of bringing its arbitration claim either under the ICSID Convention, the Additional Facility Rules of ICSID, or the UNCITRAL Rules. Subject to the specific

---

[106] *Waste Management, Inc. v. United Mexican States*, ICSID Case No. ARB/98/2, Award (2 June 2000), 5 *ICSID Reports* 443 (2002).
[107] *Waste Management, Inc. v. United Mexican States*, ICSID Case No. ARB(AF)/00/3, Decision of the Tribunal (26 June 2002), 41 *ILM* 1315 (2002). (The text of this decision is also available at <www.state.gov/documents/organizations/12244.pdf>.)

mandatory provisions of NAFTA, the procedural rules chosen by the investor govern the arbitration.

Although NAFTA Chapter 11 provides for ICSID arbitration as one of the options open to an aggrieved investor, the ICSID Convention proper is still of limited relevance to NAFTA claims. As of 2003, the only NAFTA State to have ratified the ICSID Convention was the United States. Consequently, unless and until Canada or Mexico becomes a party to the ICSID Convention, the ICSID Centre may not administer NAFTA arbitrations under the ICSID Convention. Instead, the Centre administers arbitrations involving the United States and either Mexico or Canada under the Additional Facility Rules. UNCITRAL arbitration is also available for disputes involving Canada and Mexico, with the Secretary-General of ICSID available to assist as appointing authority (Article 1124).

Except where the parties agree otherwise, a NAFTA tribunal is comprised of three arbitrators, one appointed by each party and the third, the "presiding arbitrator," by agreement between the parties (Article 1123). Unless there is an agreement to the contrary, the Secretary-General of ICSID is the appointing authority in the event of default by a party in making its appointment or the parties' failure to agree upon the presiding arbitrator of the tribunal (Article 1124).

NAFTA Article 1131(1) addresses applicable law:

> "A Tribunal established under this Section shall decide the issues in dispute in accordance with this Article and applicable rules of international law."

This reflects a different approach than that found in the ICSID Convention. As compared to ICSID Convention Article 42, NAFTA Article 1131(1) makes no provision for application of the law of the NAFTA State party to the arbitration.

NAFTA contains consolidation avenues not available in the ICSID Convention or in bilateral investment treaty arbitration provisions. Where several claims arise from the same measures taken by a NAFTA State, Article 1126 allows a disputing party, whether the NAFTA State or the investor, to request the Secretary-General of ICSID to establish a special three-member tribunal pursuant to the UNCITRAL Rules to hear a request to consolidate the claims. In the event the special tribunal determines that the claims "have a question of law or fact in common" and that the "interests of fair and efficient resolution of the claims" favor consolidation, the special tribunal may either (a) assume jurisdiction over all or part of the claims or (b) assume jurisdiction over one or more of the claims to assist in the resolution of the others. The special tribunal may also order that the proceedings of a previously established Chapter 11 tribunal be stayed.

These consolidation provisions of NAFTA Chapter 11 are designed to avoid inconsistent results in cases arising from the same State measures and similar facts. However, parties inclined to try to take advantage of consolidation must be aware that the consolidation process is complex, brings with it the mandatory application of the UNCITRAL Rules, and involves special provisions governing constitution of the tribunal.

A NAFTA Chapter 11 tribunal may order interim measures, including orders to protect its jurisdiction or to preserve evidence in the possession or control of a party but it cannot "order attachment or enjoin the application of the measure alleged to constitute a breach" of Chapter 11 (Article 1134). As alluded to above, as an exception to the strict waiver of alternative remedies provision of Article 1121(1), NAFTA also provides for the right to request provisional measures including "injunctive, declaratory or other extraordinary relief, not involving the payment of damages" before the competent domestic courts.

Article 1135 explicitly circumscribes the final relief that a NAFTA tribunal may award – monetary damages plus applicable interest, or restitution of property. In respect of the latter, the award must provide that the State may choose to pay monetary damages and applicable interest in lieu of restitution of property. Article 1135(3) specifically prohibits any award of punitive damages. In terms of remedies, therefore, NAFTA Chapter 11 leaves only the issue of costs to the arbitration rules chosen by the investor.

NAFTA awards are binding as "between the disputing parties and in respect of the particular case" (Article 1136(1)). NAFTA Chapter 11 does not deal with the questions of review of awards or recourse against awards; this crucial matter is left to the rules selected by the investor. Therefore, unless and until Mexico or Canada ratify the ICSID Convention and NAFTA arbitrations are conducted under the ICSID Arbitration Rules (with their special annulment procedures, as discussed in Chapter 5), NAFTA awards will remain open to review by the national courts at the place of arbitration. To cite a leading example, an application for judicial review of the *Metalclad* award was made in Vancouver, the place of arbitration, on several grounds including alleged violation of "public policy." The Canadian court set aside the award in part and suggested that the matter be remitted to the NAFTA tribunal if the parties were unable to agree on the issues at stake.[108]

NAFTA has mandatory and automatic waiting periods for enforcement of awards (Article 1136(3)). In the (still theoretical) case of a final NAFTA award made under the ICSID Convention, a disputing party may not seek enforcement until either (a) 120 days have elapsed from the date the award was rendered and no disputing party has requested revision or annulment of the award or (b) any revision or annulment proceedings that were initiated have been completed. In the case of an award rendered under the ICSID Additional Facility Rules or the UNCITRAL Rules, the comparable waiting period is (a) three months from the date the award was rendered if no party has commenced proceedings to revise, set aside or annul the award or (b) the date the relevant court has dismissed or allowed an application to revise, set aside or annul the award if there is no further appeal.

---

[108] *United Mexican States v. Metalclad Corporation,* Judicial Review, Supreme Court of British Columbia (2001 BCSC 664), 5 *ICSID Review – FILJ* 236 (1990).

Given that the United States is the only NAFTA State to have ratified the ICSID Convention, NAFTA awards rendered under the auspices of ICSID do not benefit from the self-contained Convention enforcement regime and hence are not enforceable as if they were final court judgments of the country of enforcement (see Chapter 5). Instead, NAFTA awards must be enforced under the New York Convention. Indeed, under Article 1130 of NAFTA, the tribunal is required to hold the arbitration in the territory of a State party to the New York Convention unless the parties agree otherwise – which they would be ill-advised to do, except in highly unusual circumstances.

NAFTA Article 1136(4) directs each State party to "provide for the enforcement of an award in its territory." If a NAFTA State fails to comply with a final award, the investor's home State may request the formation of a dispute resolution panel under NAFTA Chapter 20. The complaining NAFTA State may seek a determination from that panel that the responding State's failure to comply with the award is inconsistent with NAFTA and a recommendation in favor of compliance.

Jurisdiction

Only an investor of a State party – Canada, Mexico or the United States – has the right to bring a claim under NAFTA Chapter 11. The term "investor" includes an "enterprise," which is broadly defined to include any corporation, trust or other association, whether privately or governmentally owned (Article 1139).

NAFTA Article 1117 provides that an investor may submit to arbitration a claim against the host State on behalf of an enterprise constituted or organized under the host State's law, which the investor owns or controls directly or indirectly. In *S.D. Myers v. Canada*, the claimant S.D. Myers was a US-based private company owned by an individual who also owned a company incorporated in Canada. The Canadian government argued that S.D. Myers lacked standing as an investor because it held no shares in the Canadian company and there was no joint venture agreement between the two companies. The tribunal found jurisdiction on the ground that the same individual effectively controlled the two entities.[109] In so doing, the tribunal refused to allow technical arguments regarding corporate structure to defeat the claim.

Subject to prior notification, a NAFTA State may deny the benefits of Chapter 11 to an enterprise of another NAFTA State if non-NAFTA State investors own or control the enterprise and the enterprise has no substantial business activities in the territory of the NAFTA State under the laws of which it is organized. The practical effect of this provision is to prevent non-NAFTA parties from creating a legal entity in one of the NAFTA States solely to benefit from the investment protections and dispute resolution mechanism of NAFTA Chapter 11.

---

[109] *S.D. Myers, Inc. v. Government of Canada*, Partial Award (13 November 2000), available at < www.dfait-maeci.gc.ca/tna-nac/disp/SDM_archive-en.asp.com >.

The Chapter 11 definition of "investment" is also broad. It includes not only traditional concepts like enterprises, securities, and tangible and intangible property, but also interests under construction contracts, concessions or other "contracts where remuneration depends substantially on the production, revenues or profits of an enterprise" (Article 1139). Claims to money under simple sales contracts or trade credits are, however, excluded.

An investor may bring a claim in relation to any "measure" – any law, regulation, procedure, requirement or practice, with no specific requirement that the measure have legal force – that is adopted or maintained by a State party and that causes damage to an investor or the enterprise of an investor. The measure must constitute a breach of one of the substantive obligations set out in NAFTA Chapter 11.

Substantive obligations
Section A of NAFTA Chapter 11 establishes the following investment protection obligations: (a) national and MFN standards of treatment (Articles 1102 and 1103); (b) minimum standards of treatment, including fair and equitable treatment and full protection and security (Article 1105); (c) freedom from performance obligations (e.g., obligations to export, to favor domestic suppliers or to transfer technology) (Article 1106); (d) the right to control investments using senior managers of any nationality (Article 1107); (e) the right to repatriate without delay and in a freely usable currency all profits, fees or other proceeds resulting from investments (Article 1109); and (f) conditions of expropriation (notably non-discrimination and compensation at "fair market value of the expropriated investment immediately before the expropriation took place") (Article 1110).

In three significant Chapter 11 cases, NAFTA tribunals have found that the respondent State breached the fair and equitable treatment standard set out in Article 1105. The tribunals found that certain acts of public authorities – i.e., the lack of a "transparent predictable framework" and of an "orderly process and timely disposition" of the investor's permit applications, as well as threats, denial of reasonable demands and information requests requiring the investor to incur necessary expenses and offer unnecessary disruption – violated the fair and equitable treatment standard and amounted to effective discrimination in favor of domestic entities.[110]

NAFTA Chapter 11 disputes, not surprisingly, have fueled the long-simmering legal debate as to whether the fair and equitable treatment standard is tantamount to the minimum standard required by customary international law or instead represents an independent concept affording greater protection. In the wake of the refusal of

---

[110] *See S.D. Myers v. Canada* (Partial Award), *supra* note 109, at 64-67; *Metalclad Corporation v. The United Mexican States*, ICSID Case No. ARB (AF)/97/1, Award (30 August 2000), 5 *ICSID Reports* 209 (2002); *Pope & Talbot, Inc. v. Government of Canada*, Award on the Merits of Phase 2 (10 April 2001), available at < www.dfait-maeci.gc.ca/tna-nac/phases-en.asp#comm >.

NAFTA tribunals to adopt a restrictive interpretation of the principle, the NAFTA States effectively sought to impose it by issuing a binding interpretative statement of NAFTA Article 1105 in the "Notes of Interpretation" of the NAFTA Free Trade Commission.[111] The statement provides that fair and equitable treatment "does not require treatment in addition to or beyond that which is required by the customary international law minimum standard of treatment of aliens."[112] This process of interpretation, and the interpretation, have provoked controversy. The *Pope & Talbot* tribunal had occasion to reevaluate its award on the merits, in which it had found Canada had violated the fair and equitable treatment standard, against the Notes of Interpretation. The tribunal, effectively, made findings concerning customary international law and interpreted the Notes of Interpretation as not warranting a more restrictive interpretation of the NAFTA fair and equitable treatment standard than the tribunal had originally applied.[113]

NAFTA tribunals have also developed jurisprudence on expropriation in claims brought by investors under Chapter 11. In *Metalclad,* for example, the tribunal defined the test of indirect or "de facto" expropriation under Chapter 11 as follows:

"Expropriation under NAFTA includes not only open, deliberate and acknowledged takings of property, such as outright seizure or formal or obligatory transfer of title in favor of the host State, but also covert or incidental interference with the use of property which has the effect of depriving the owner, in whole or in significant part, of the use or reasonably-to-be-expected economic benefit of property even if not necessarily to the obvious benefit of the host State."[114]

The Energy Charter Treaty

In 1994, in Lisbon, 49 States plus the European Communities signed the Energy Charter Treaty (*ECT*).[115] The signatories include major energy producing or purchasing powers, including France, Germany, Italy, Japan, Kazakhstan, the Netherlands, Russia, Spain and the United Kingdom. The United States has declined to sign.

The ECT provides a comprehensive international legal framework for cross-border economic cooperation in the energy sector. The treaty's primary aim is to promote a climate of legal stability and predictability to attract investment and stimulate business activity in the energy sectors of member States. To this end, it includes wide-ranging provisions designed to ensure the opening up of the energy sector, including: (a) non-discriminatory treatment of foreign investors; (b) free

---

[111] The Notes of Interpretation are available at < www.dfait-maeci.gc.ca/tna-nac/nafta-interpr-en.asp >.

[112] *Id.* at para. B(2).

[113] *Pope & Talbot Inc. v. Government of Canada,* Award on Damages (31 May 2002), 41 *ILM* 1347 (2002), also available at < www.dfait-maeci.gc.ca/tna-nac/phase-en.asp#comm >.

[114] *See Metalclad v. Mexico* (Award), *supra* note 110, at 230.

[115] *Energy Charter Treaty,* opened for signature Dec. 17, 1994, 34 *ILM* 381 (1995).

transit of energy products; (c) transfer of investment capital and returns; and (d) measures aimed at eliminating anti-competitive practices in the energy sector. Article 26 of the ECT grants foreign investors of State parties the right to bring legal proceedings against all other State parties for breach of Part III of the Treaty, which contains the provisions relating to investment promotion and protection.

Jurisdiction

The definitions in Article 1 of the ECT are very broad. "Investment" includes the now-familiar generic language seen in NAFTA and in many BITs and also, more broadly, "claims to money and claims to performance pursuant to a contract having an economic value and associated with an Investment." The definition includes "returns," defined as "the amounts derived from or associated with an Investment, irrespective of the form in which they are paid, including profits, dividends, interest, capital gains, royalty payments, management, technical assistance or other fees and payments in kind."[116]

Procedural Framework

As stated above, a foreign investor of a State party may invoke Article 26 of the ECT in relation to any alleged breach of an obligation under Part III of the treaty. There is no requirement that the investor exhaust local remedies or, indeed, that the investor exhaust any other form of dispute resolution that may have been agreed upon with the host State. Article 26 does not apply to other disputes in which a foreign investor may be involved. For example, if a country fails to promote the conditions for access of foreign investors to its capital markets, such investors may not bring claims under the ECT, because the relevant provision is not contained in Part III.

Following a three-month negotiation period, the foreign investor may choose to submit the dispute for resolution (a) to the domestic courts or administrative tribunals of the host State, (b) to any previously agreed dispute resolution procedure (for example, under an arbitration clause in a contract) or (c) to international arbitration. If a foreign investor chooses to submit a dispute to international arbitration, it then has to make a further choice between ICSID (including the ICSID Additional Facility Rules), the UNCITRAL Rules or the Stockholm Chamber of Commerce Rules. Factors affecting the choice include the amount in dispute, the legal issues raised, the nationalities of the parties, the arbitration venue thought desirable, and the effect of the choice of rules on the composition of the arbitral tribunal.

Where a local company is subject to foreign control, ECT Article 26(7) provides that a company with the nationality of a Contracting State party to the dispute

---

[116] *Id.* at Art. 1

that was under the control of investors of another Contracting State before the dispute arose is to be treated as a national of another Contracting State for the purposes of the ICSID Convention and the ICSID Additional Facility Rules. In a separate understanding adopted together with the ECT, control is defined as meaning "control in fact, determined after an examination of the actual circumstances in each situation."[117] Relevant factors to be considered include the investor's: (a) financial interest, including equity interest in the investment; (b) ability to exercise substantial influence over the management and operation of the investment; and (c) ability to exercise substantial influence over the selection of the board of directors or any other managing body. Where there is any doubt, the burden of proof is on the investor to demonstrate control over the entity in question.

Under the ECT, each Contracting State is deemed to have given its unconditional consent to the submission to international arbitration of a dispute under Part III, subject to two exceptions:

(a) Contracting States are permitted to decline giving unconditional consent to international arbitration where the investor has previously submitted to another dispute resolution forum; and

(b) Certain Contracting States have not given unconditional consent to international arbitration in respect of disputes relating to the obligations under an individual investment contract between a Contracting State and an investor or investment of any other Contracting State.

Regardless of the type of arbitration or other dispute resolution mechanism chosen, Article 26 requires the dispute to be decided in accordance with the Energy Charter Treaty itself and with applicable rules and principles of international law. The ECT limits remedies against a State found to be in breach of the treaty to monetary damages. Therefore, ECT tribunals may not order specific performance, order restitution of property or "annul governmental acts."

The ECT dispute resolution mechanism was invoked for the first time in 2001. In *AES Summit Generation v. Hungary*, the claimant, a subsidiary of the AES Corporation (US), brought a case under the treaty before ICSID against Hungary. AES Summit claimed that Hungary had expropriated it in violation of Article 13 of the ECT by mishandling a privatization contract.[118] The case settled, and so the tribunal did not have occasion to rule on several issues of first impression, including the legal basis of the claim in the face of Hungary's having exercised its right to opt out of the ECT provision allowing treaty arbitration of a State's contractual obligations.

---

[117] *Id.* at Art. 26(7).

[118] *AES Summit Generation v. Hungary*, ICSID Case No. ARB/01/4, Order of Discontinuance (3 January 2002).

Third-Party Participation: A Developing Phenomenon

In investor-State arbitrations, and in particular in NAFTA arbitrations, the traditionally private nature of international commercial arbitration is evolving to take account of the public issues that often arise in treaty disputes. For example, in *Methanex v. United States*, the NAFTA tribunal concluded that it could be appropriate to allow third-party environmental and public interest groups to submit amicus briefs, relying on Article 15(1) of the applicable UNCITRAL Rules, which confers procedural flexibility on the tribunal. The tribunal indicated it was "minded" to allow the amicus filings, but found it premature to decide the issue.[119] The tribunal, however, went on to find that the flexibility of Article 15(1) is limited by UNCITRAL Rule 25(4), which requires hearings to be private unless otherwise agreed by the parties, and refused requests by the amicus groups to attend the merits hearing and obtain copies of filings. The NAFTA tribunal in *UPS v. Canada* took a similar approach, emphasizing that the flexibility conferred by UNCITRAL Rule 15(1) could be used to facilitate its inquiry into the dispute before it but not to convert the dispute into a different one, for example by adding a new party.[120] In comparison (in terms of outcome), in yet another NAFTA case, *S.D. Myers v. Canada*, the tribunal refused to allow an environmental group to intervene, finding that the proposed intervention would not facilitate its mandate to make an interpretation of the terms of the NAFTA treaty.[121]

It is clear, from the vantage point of 2003, that the pressure from public interest groups and other third parties to make ICSID and other investor-State arbitrations more open and transparent will not abate. Transparency has potential benefits for States as well as private parties:

> "Transparency is not merely aimed at ensuring that third parties get their say on issues of public importance. It also encourages good government."[122]

This is an issue that investors and States alike will increasingly have to take into account as they initiate and pursue treaty arbitration.

---

[119] *Methanex v. United States of America*, Decision on Petition from Third Persons to Intervene as Amici Curiae (15 January 2001), available at < www.state.gov/s/l/c5821.htm >.

[120] *UPS v. Canada*, Decision of the Tribunal on Petitions for Intervention and Participation as Amici Curiae, available at < www.dfait-maeci.gc.ca/tna-nac/disp/parcel-en.asp >.

[121] *Attorney General of Canada v. S.D. Myers, Inc.*, 2001 F.C.T. 317 (11 April 2001); *Attorney General of Canada v. S.D. Myers, Inc.*, 2002 F.C.A. 39 (28 January 2002).

[122] N. Blackaby, *Public Interest and Investment Treaty Arbitration*, Swiss Arbitration Association Special Series No. 19, *Investment Treaties and Arbitration* (August 2002).

CHAPTER 4

ICSID Arbitration Procedure

The purpose of this chapter is to describe the basic process of arbitration under the auspices of ICSID, from the filing of a request to the issuance of final awards.

In addition to the parameters defined in the ICSID Convention itself, ICSID arbitration procedure is governed by the Rules of Procedure for the Institution of Conciliation and Arbitration Proceedings (the *Institution Rules*) (see Annex 3); the Rules of Procedure for Arbitration Proceedings (the *Arbitration Rules*) (see Annex 4); and the Administrative and Financial Regulations (the *Regulations*). The requirements of the Convention are few in number, but are for the most part mandatory. There is more flexibility with respect to the Rules and Regulations. The parties may modify provisions of the Arbitration Rules by agreement, and depart from the Regulations to the extent expressly provided therein.

Arbitrations under the aegis of the ICSID Additional Facility are governed by the Additional Facility Rules and the Arbitration (Additional Facility) Rules (the *Additional Facility Arbitration Rules*).[123] Most of the provisions that apply to Additional Facility arbitrations are identical or very similar to those that apply to ICSID Convention arbitrations. This chapter singles out only those Additional Facility Rules that differ.

Amendments to ICSID's rules and regulations took effect on 1 January 2003. The prior rules may still be relevant in certain arbitrations, however, because Article 44 of the Convention specifies that arbitration proceedings are governed by the rules in force at the time the parties consent to ICSID arbitration.[124] When ICSID arbitrations are based on bilateral investment treaties, the applicable Arbitration Rules are likely to be those in force when the investor consents to arbitration by accepting the State's offer to arbitrate contained in the BIT – usually when the investor files its request for arbitration with ICSID (see Chapter 3).

---

[123] The Additional Facility Arbitration Rules in effect as of 1 January 2003 are available on the ICSID website at < www.worldbank.org/icsid/amend.htm >.

[124] The prior Arbitration Rules adopted by the ICSID Administrative Council, which were effective 26 September 1984, are available at 1 *ICSID Reports* 157 (1993).

COMMENCING AN ICSID ARBITRATION

Initiating Arbitration under the ICSID Convention

The Rules of Procedure for the Institution of Conciliation and Arbitration Proceedings, as the title suggests, govern the claimant's commencement of an ICSID arbitration (or conciliation) under the Convention. (The Institution Rules, like the other ICSID rules, identify the two parties with the terms "requesting party" and "other party." This Guide uses the terms "claimant" and "respondent," which are more common in international arbitration.)

Institution Rule 1 provides that a Contracting State or a national of a Contracting State wishing to institute an arbitration must send a written request to the Secretary-General at ICSID headquarters in Washington, DC (together with five additional signed copies, under Institution Rule 4). The request must be in one of ICSID's official languages (English, French and Spanish), signed by the claimant or its duly authorized representative, and dated. The rule envisions that the parties to the dispute (State and investor) may in theory file a joint request, although this is unknown in practice.

Convention Article 59 and Regulation 16 require the claimant to pay a non-refundable "lodging fee" (filing fee), set at USD7,000 in the July 2002 Schedule of Fees.

The request for arbitration

Article 36(2) of the ICSID Convention requires the request for arbitration to "contain information concerning the issues in dispute, the identity of the parties and their consent to arbitration." Accordingly, Institution Rule 2(1) (which is set out as a jurisdiction checklist in Chapter 2, and is quoted again for convenience) provides:

"The request shall:

(a) designate precisely each party to the dispute and state the address of each;

(b) state, if one of the parties is a constituent subdivision or agency of a Contracting State, that it has been designated to the Centre by that State pursuant to Article 25(1) of the Convention;

(c) indicate the date of consent and the instruments in which it is recorded, including, if one party is a constituent subdivision or agency of a Contracting State, similar data on the approval of such consent by that State unless it had notified the Centre that no such approval is required;

(d) indicate with respect to the party that is a national of a Contracting State:

    (i)   its nationality on the date of consent; and

    (ii)   if the party is a natural person:

        (A) his nationality on the date of the request; and

        (B) that he did not have the nationality of the Contracting State party to the dispute either on the date of consent or on the date of the request; or

(iii) if the party is a juridical person which on the date of consent had the nationality of the Contracting State party to the dispute, the agreement of the parties that it should be treated as a national of another Contracting State for the purposes of the Convention;

(e) contain information concerning the issues in dispute indicating that there is, between the parties, a legal dispute arising directly out of an investment; and

(f) state, if the requesting party is a juridical person, that it has taken all necessary internal actions to authorize the request."

Institution Rule 2(2) requires that the request be accompanied by documentation supporting the information called for under Rules 2(1)(c), 2(1)(d)(iii) and 2(1)(f) (above). Rule 2(1)(c), which deals with consent, and Rule 2(d)(iii), which deals with nationality, are critical to ICSID jurisdiction and are discussed at length in Chapter 2. Rule 2(1)(f), which requires juridical entities to affirm their authorization to commence arbitration, is a new feature of the 2003 amendments to the rules, although in practice the Centre has required such documentation for some time. One purpose of this requirement for proof of authorization is to ensure that shareholders do not bring ICSID cases as claimants on behalf of a corporation without express authorization from the corporation.

Under Institution Rule 3, if the parties have previously agreed on the number of arbitrators and/or the method of their appointment (i.e., in their investment contract or in the applicable treaty), this information should be recited in the request.

Experienced ICSID practitioners include a brief summary of the facts and the substantive breaches of the relevant treaty or investment contract in the request, because the request is likely to be the first substantive document to be studied by the respondent and, later, by the tribunal. Practitioners may consult the Secretariat about the form and scope of the request, in order to clarify technical issues before they seek registration.

The Convention does not set any time limitations for the filing of a request, but there may well be such limits in the parties' arbitration agreement or in the applicable legislation or treaty authorizing ICSID arbitration. As noted previously, such instruments often also mandate negotiation or "cooling off" periods before the parties may institute arbitration.

Acknowledgment and registration of the request
Under Institution Rule 5, the ICSID Secretary-General first sends an acknowledgment of receipt of the request to the claimant. Provided the claimant has paid the lodging fee, the Secretary-General also forwards a copy of the request and supporting documentation to the respondent.

The Secretary-General either registers the request or refuses it (Convention Article 36(3) and Institution Rule 6(1)). The Secretary-General may refuse to register the request only "if he finds, on the basis of information contained in the request, that the dispute is manifestly outside the jurisdiction of the Centre" (Institution Rule

6(1)(b)). This threshold test is purposefully lenient, as the drafters of the Convention intended to prevent registration only of cases patently lacking a jurisdictional foundation.[125] This would be the case, for example, where one party is neither a Contracting State nor a national of a Contracting State, or where the claimant had provided no evidence of written consent to ICSID jurisdiction.

If there is any doubt whether the request meets ICSID jurisdictional requirements, or whether it is otherwise complete, it is common for the Secretariat to contact the claimant's representative and provide an opportunity to correct or supplement the request before deciding on registration. Even if the Secretary-General refuses registration based on a technical deficiency, the claimant may subsequently file a new request based on the same claim once the technical deficiency has been cured.

In practice, requests are seldom so deficient as to warrant refusal of registration. The Secretary-General's decision to register a request, of course, in no way prejudges the ICSID tribunal's subsequent determination of its own competence and the Centre's jurisdiction.[126]

Institution Rule 6(2) establishes that an ICSID arbitration "shall be deemed to have been instituted on the date of the registration of the request." The registration date is important in several respects.

Under Institution Rules 6(1)(a) and 7, the Secretary-General sends a notice of registration to both parties on the registration date. The notice of registration, among other things, invites the parties to inform the Secretary-General of any agreement regarding the number and method of appointment of the arbitrators and directs the parties to proceed to constitute the tribunal as soon as possible. A claimant may unilaterally withdraw its request only up to the registration date; thereafter, the proceedings may be discontinued only with the respondent's consent (Institution Rule 8).

Initiating Arbitration Under the Additional Facility Rules

A party's access to the ICSID Additional Facility is conditional on the Secretary-General's specific approval. Under Additional Facility Rule 2, the Additional Facility may administer three categories of proceedings:

> "(a) conciliation and arbitration proceedings for the settlement of legal disputes arising directly out of an investment which are not within the jurisdiction of the Centre because either the State party to the dispute or the State whose national is a party to the dispute is not a Contracting State;

---

[125] *Executive Directors Report, supra* note 6, at 28-30.

[126] *See Holiday Inns S.A. and others v. Morocco,* ICSID Case No. ARB/72/1, Decision on Jurisdiction (1 July 1973), *as cited in* P. Lalive, *supra* note 31 (finding that registration of the proceeding by the Secretary-General did not preclude a finding by the tribunal that the dispute lay outside the jurisdiction of the Centre); *see also American Manufacturing & Trading v. Congo* (Award), *supra* note 71, at 22 (noting the "extremely light control" conferred upon the Secretary-General by Convention Article 36(3)).

(b) conciliation and arbitration proceedings for the settlement of legal disputes which are not within the jurisdiction of the Centre because they do not arise directly out of an investment, provided that either the State party to the dispute or the State whose national is a party to the dispute is a Contracting State; and

(c) fact-finding proceedings."

Where one of the parties is neither a Contracting State nor a national of a Contracting State, the Secretary-General's approval is dependent on whether the parties have consented to jurisdiction under the Convention in the event the non-Contracting State party does become a party to the Convention by the time arbitration proceedings are actually instituted (Additional Facility Rule 4(2)). Where the relevant dispute does not arise directly out of an investment, the Secretary-General's approval depends on whether the underlying transaction has "features which distinguish it from an ordinary commercial transaction" (Additional Facility Rule 4(3)). The Secretary-General's approval may also be made conditional on the parties' undertaking to submit their dispute to arbitration under the Convention proper if the Secretary-General deems it "likely" that a tribunal will decide that the dispute does in fact arise directly out of an investment (Additional Facility Rule 4(4)).

Pursuant to Additional Facility Arbitration Rule 4, the Secretary-General will register the request if he or she is satisfied that it "conforms in form and substance to the provisions of Article 3." Article 3 requires that an Additional Facility request:

"(a) designate precisely each party to the dispute and state the address of each;

(b) set forth the relevant provisions embodying the agreement of the parties to refer the dispute to arbitration;

(c) indicate the date of approval by the Secretary-General pursuant to Article 4 of the Additional Facility Rules of the agreement of the parties providing for access to the Additional Facility;

(d) contain information concerning the issues in dispute and an indication of the amount involved, if any; and

(e) state, if the requesting party is a juridical person, that it has taken all necessary internal actions to authorize the request."

Under the January 2003 Schedule of Fees, the claimant is assessed USD7,000, which includes the fee for requesting approval for access to the Additional Facility and the fee for lodging the request itself.

CONSTITUTION OF AN ICSID TRIBUNAL

Tribunals under the ICSID Convention

Articles 37 to 40 of the Convention and Arbitration Rules 1 to 6 deal with the constitution of arbitration tribunals. Among other things, these provisions encourage the parties to establish the tribunal "as soon as possible" and "with all possible dispatch" after the Secretary-General has registered the request. "Dispatch" is a relative term in practice; constitution of an ICSID tribunal very seldom takes less than three months.

The Panel of Arbitrators

As envisioned in Article 12 of the Convention, ICSID maintains a Panel of Arbitrators. The Panel is not exclusive; the parties may appoint arbitrators from this Panel, but are not obliged to do so.

Under Article 13 of the Convention, each Contracting State may designate four individuals – who need not be its nationals – to the Panel of Arbitrators. In addition, the Chairman of the Administrative Council may designate ten individuals to the Panel of Arbitrators, each of a different nationality. Each Panel designee serves for a renewable six-year term and is not remunerated unless and until appointed to a tribunal. Not all Contracting States designate their full complement of four individuals to the Panel of Arbitrators; nor may it be said that all designees are experienced international arbitrators.

Appointment of arbitrators by the parties

The Convention and the Arbitration Rules contain few limitations on the parties' freedom to select their tribunal, both as to the number and as to the specific arbitrators. First, Article 37(2)(a) of the Convention provides that a tribunal "shall consist of a sole arbitrator or any uneven number of arbitrators." Second, pursuant to Article 39 of the Convention and Arbitration Rule 1(3), the tribunal may not consist of a majority of arbitrators with the same nationality as either party, unless the parties have appointed the arbitrators by agreement. This means that, for the most common composition of a three-member tribunal, one party may not appoint a national of either State involved unless the other party agrees. Third, a person who previously acted as either a conciliator or an arbitrator in proceedings to settle the same dispute brought to arbitration may not be appointed to the tribunal (Arbitration Rule 1(4)).

If the parties have not previously agreed on the number of arbitrators or the method of their appointment, Arbitration Rule 2 establishes a procedure under which the parties exchange proposals regarding constitution of the tribunal. The parties have 60 days from registration of the request in which to reach an agreement. This time limit may be, and often is, extended by agreement. If the parties cannot agree within the deadline on constituting a tribunal, Arbitration Rule 3 provides that either party may invoke the default formula for a three-member panel set out in Article 37(2)(b) of the Convention: each party names one arbitrator and the two parties then agree on the third arbitrator, who becomes president of the tribunal. This default mechanism prevents one party from frustrating the constitution process.

If one party refuses to appoint its arbitrator or cooperate in selecting the president, the Chairman of the Administrative Council takes action under Article 38 of the Convention (see below).

Under Arbitration Rule 5, the parties must notify the Secretary-General of the name and method of appointment of each arbitrator, and the Secretary-General then asks the appointee if he or she accepts the appointment. If the appointee does not accept the position within 15 days, the Secretary-General invites the relevant party to appoint another arbitrator. Until the date of the Secretary-General's notification that the tribunal has been constituted, each party may unilaterally replace its own appointee and the parties together, by agreement, may replace any arbitrator (Arbitration Rule 7).

Appointment of arbitrators by the Centre

If the parties have failed to constitute the tribunal within 90 days of the notice of registration, or within such further time as they have agreed, either party may invoke Article 38 of the Convention and request the Centre's assistance. Acting under Arbitration Rule 4(4), the Chairman of the Administrative Council will appoint any remaining arbitrators from the Panel of Arbitrators, after consultation with both parties, using his or her "best efforts" to do so within 30 days. Again, none of the arbitrators appointed by the Chairman of the Administrative Council from the Panel may be of the same nationality as either of the parties. This fallback procedure ensures that an uncooperative party cannot prevent the constitution of the tribunal and thereby frustrate the arbitration process. At this stage, the ICSID Secretariat may informally propose certain names outside of the Panel of Arbitrators, which take into account the specific needs of the case. Such candidates require the express consent of both parties before appointment can be made. If no agreement is reached, the formal fallback procedure is used.

Notification of final constitution of an ICSID tribunal

Once all of the arbitrators have accepted their appointments, the Secretary-General sends a formal notice to the parties. The tribunal is then deemed constituted under Arbitration Rule 6, and the arbitration proceedings officially begin.

Tribunals Under the Additional Facility Rules

Arbitrators for Additional Facility tribunals are selected in largely the same manner as arbitrators for ICSID tribunals (Additional Facility Arbitration Rules 6 to 11). One significant exception is that the Chairman of the Administrative Council, if called upon to assist in constituting the tribunal, need not appoint Additional Facility arbitrators from the Panel of Arbitrators.

ARBITRATOR QUALIFICATIONS AND CHALLENGES

Tribunals Constituted Under the ICSID Convention

Whether ICSID arbitrators are appointed by the parties or by the Chairman of the Administrative Council, and whether they are selected from the Panel of Arbitrators or otherwise, Articles 14(1) and 40(2) of the Convention mandate that all ICSID arbitrators "be persons of high moral character and recognized competence in the fields of law, commerce, industry or finance, who may be relied upon to exercise independent judgment." Article 14 specifies that "[c]ompetence in the field of law shall be of particular importance in the case of persons on the Panel of Arbitrators," and in practice, most ICSID arbitrators are international lawyers. Either before or at the tribunal's first session, each ICSID arbitrator must sign a declaration affirming his or her independence and agreement to respect the confidentiality of the proceedings (Arbitration Rule 6).

Article 57 of the Convention sets an extremely high bar for challenging an arbitrator (or a member of an ad hoc annulment committee (see Chapter 5)). The challenge application must establish that the arbitrator has exhibited "a manifest lack of the qualities" required by Article 14(1) of the Convention. As stated in the Decision on the Challenge to the President of the ad hoc Committee in *Compañia de Aguas del Aconquija S.A. & Vivendi Universal v. Argentine Republic*:

> "[I]n cases where [...] the facts are established and no further inference of impropriety is sought to be derived from them, the question seems to us to be whether a real risk of lack of impartiality based upon those facts (and not of any mere speculation or inference) could reasonably be apprehended by either party."[127]

A party must base a challenge on facts, rather than inference, proving the arbitrator's manifest lack of high moral character, manifest lack of recognized competence in his or her field, or manifest lack of ability to exercise independent judgment.

In principle, an arbitrator may also be removed under Convention Article 57 on grounds of ineligibility for appointment to the tribunal under the requirements in the Convention regarding nationality and/or membership on the Panel of Arbitrators. This is unlikely to occur in practice, given the detailed scrutiny necessarily undertaken by the parties and by the Centre during the appointment process.

Under Article 58 of the Convention and, specifically, under Arbitration Rule 9, a party must make a proposal to disqualify an arbitrator "promptly, and in any event before the proceeding is declared closed," through a filing with the Secretary-

---

[127] See *Compañia de Aguas del Aconquija S.A. & Vivendi Universal v. Argentine Republic*, ICSID Case No. ARB/97/3, Decision on the Challenge to the President of the Committee (3 October 2001), 17 *ICSID Review – FILJ* 168, 180 (2002).

General stating the reasons for disqualification. A challenge to a single member of a tribunal must be "promptly" decided by the other members of the tribunal; if they cannot agree, the Chairman of the Administrative Council will use "best efforts" to make a decision on the application within 30 days. It is also the Chairman of the Administrative Council who decides a challenge to a sole arbitrator or to a majority of the arbitrators on a multi-arbitrator tribunal, again within a "best efforts" 30-day time period.

The ICSID Convention does not allow truncated tribunals, meaning tribunals operating with less than a full complement of members. Under Article 56 of the Convention and Arbitration Rules 10 to 12, if a vacancy occurs on the tribunal due to the disqualification, death, incapacity or resignation of an arbitrator, the proceedings must be suspended until the vacancy is filled. The vacant position is usually filled by the same process used to appoint the original arbitrator. However, if the vacancy occurred because an arbitrator resigned without the consent of the tribunal (as could theoretically happen if an unscrupulous party-appointed arbitrator resigned for tactical purposes) or if the vacancy has not been filled within 45 days and the parties so request, the Chairman of the Administrative Council appoints a replacement from the Panel of Arbitrators. The proceedings then resume, with the possibility of any hearing being repeated if required by the newly appointed arbitrator.

Additional Facility Tribunals

Arbitrators in ICSID Additional Facility proceedings are appointed and challenged through processes largely similar to those in Convention arbitrations. They must meet the same basic personal qualifications (Additional Facility Arbitration Rules 8 and 15) and make the same declaration (Additional Facility Arbitration Rule 13) as arbitrators selected under the Convention. Identical provisions also govern the procedures for filling vacancies on tribunals (Additional Facility Arbitration Rules 16 to 18), with the exception that the Chairman of the Administrative Council is not limited to the Panel of Arbitrators if he or she must appoint a replacement arbitrator.

CONDUCT OF PROCEEDINGS

Arbitration Proceedings Under the ICSID Convention

Articles 41 to 47 of the Convention, as well Arbitration Rules 13 to 38, regulate the conduct of ICSID proceedings from the constitution of the tribunal through issuance of the award.

The tribunal's first session(s) and basic procedure
The tribunal must hold its first session within 60 days of its official constitution, or

within such other time period as agreed by the parties (Arbitration Rule 13). The session takes place at ICSID headquarters in Washington, DC, unless the parties have agreed to, and the tribunal and Secretary-General have approved, an alternative location. (As noted in Chapter 2, the choice of the location for an ICSID Convention arbitration has no legal significance because it has no impact on the applicable procedural law or on the enforceability of the ultimate award. If the parties choose a location other than Washington, DC, it is for reasons of economy and efficiency).

The first session typically is the "preliminary procedural consultation" described in Arbitration Rule 20. Under that rule, the president of the tribunal is mandated to ascertain the parties' views on issues of procedure. Questions to be resolved include: (a) the number of arbitrators necessary for a quorum (Arbitration Rule 14 requires a majority unless the parties agree otherwise); (b) the language(s) of the proceedings; (c) the number, sequence and timing of written pleadings; (d) the number of copies of filings; (e) whether to dispense with either the oral or the written procedure; (f) the manner of apportioning the costs of the proceedings; and (g) the manner of keeping the record. These procedural goals aside, the first session takes on particular importance because it is not only the parties' first opportunity to meet the tribunal but, given the nature of treaty disputes, also often their first opportunity to interact with each other. Experienced arbitrators are aware that the tone for the entire proceeding may be set at the first session.

Arbitration Rule 21 envisions an additional pre-hearing conference to allow an exchange of information and a stipulation of uncontested facts among the parties, with a view to reaching an amicable settlement. In practice, given the logistical complexity and expense of convening arbitrators, parties and counsel from several countries, ICSID tribunals do not always hold this second pre-hearing session. A cost-effective alternative is to conduct such subsequent procedural sessions by conference call or video conference.

Consistent with the principle of (reasonable) party autonomy, ICSID tribunals may adopt any procedural sequence and schedule agreed to by the parties, as long as the Convention and the Regulations are not contravened (Arbitration Rule 20). Such agreements are rare in practice. Usually, it is the tribunal which establishes the various steps of the proceedings and their time limits and eventual extensions (Arbitration Rule 26). Under Arbitration Rule 29 and as described below, unless the parties agree otherwise, ICSID arbitration proceedings consist of both a written phase and an oral phase.

Throughout the proceedings, the parties may be represented by counsel or other agents (Arbitration Rule 18). In practice, advocates in ICSID arbitrations tend to be specialized counsel in international law firms, scholars of international law and counsel within the attorney general's office (or equivalent), or ministries of justice and foreign affairs of State parties. The parties' representatives – like the Centre, the Secretariat and the arbitrators – enjoy immunity from legal process and other national restrictions.

Written procedure

As set out in Arbitration Rule 31, the main pleadings in the written phase of an ICSID arbitration usually include a "memorial" (the common name for an advocacy brief in international proceedings) filed by the claimant and a "counter-memorial" filed by the respondent. If the tribunal so requests or if the parties agree, the parties may also file a second round of memorials termed a "reply" for the claimant and a "rejoinder" for the respondent. The tribunal has discretion to order or allow post-hearing memorials.

The tribunal will typically order that the claimant's memorial contain a statement of relevant facts, a statement of law and the claimant's submissions (i.e., pleas) and request for relief. The respondent's counter-memorial, the claimant's reply, and the respondent's rejoinder each must contain a denial or admission of the facts in the prior pleading, any additional relevant facts, a response to the statement of law in the prior pleading, and the party's submissions. In practice, detailed signed witness statements (for fact witnesses) and expert reports (for expert witnesses) are also filed with the pleadings, and form a crucial part of the record.

Convention Article 46 and Arbitration Rule 40 contemplate the filing of counterclaims, "incidental" claims and "additional" claims that arise directly out of the subject matter of the main dispute. The respondent must file any counter-claim no later than in its counter-memorial. The claimant must assert any incidental or additional claims (together called "ancillary claims") no later than in its reply. The tribunal may authorize later filing of ancillary claims by either party for good cause shown. In practice, ICSID tribunals are generally liberal in allowing ancillary claims, which include, for example, claims for interest and costs, provided they are within the scope of the parties' consent to arbitration and otherwise meet the relevant ICSID jurisdictional requirements.

Unlike in other forms of international commercial arbitration, the parties do not transmit their filings directly to the arbitrators. Until the tribunal is constituted, the parties are required to deliver to the Secretariat the original signed version of each filing plus five copies. Thereafter, they must deliver to the Secretariat two copies more than the number of arbitrators on the panel (Arbitration Rule 23). Supporting documentation, witness statements and expert reports are ordinarily filed with the pleading to which they relate and, in any case, must be filed within the time limit for the relevant pleading (Arbitration Rule 24).

Parties may correct errors in the written record, with the permission of the other party or the tribunal, at any time until the award is rendered (Arbitration Rule 25). The secretary to the tribunal, and indeed the ICSID Secretariat staff generally, may take the initiative to point out technical pleading mistakes to the parties' representatives to allow immediate correction and thus avoid confusion and complication.

As in other forms of international commercial arbitration, the written submissions in ICSID cases are generally the most influential part of the record for the arbitrators. ICSID tribunals put a high premium on well-organized, well-researched, clear and measured pleadings, and on reliable and straightforward witness statements and independent expert reports.

Oral procedure

The ICSID oral procedure, like the written procedure, is similar to that followed in ordinary international commercial arbitration. There may be one or more hearings on jurisdiction and merits before the tribunal. These are open only to the parties and their representatives, witnesses and experts, unless the tribunal and the parties agree otherwise (Arbitration Rule 32). Hearings are comparatively short, often no longer than one week even for merits hearings in the most complex cases – hence the premium on excellence and persuasiveness in the written procedure.

In addition to oral argument, the parties may present fact witnesses and experts at the hearing. Arbitration Rule 35 provides that witnesses and experts, who must preface their testimony with declarations of veracity, may be "examined before the tribunal by the parties under the control of its President" and by the tribunal itself. In light of the "control" given to the president in Arbitration, counsel cannot expect to conduct extensive direct examination or overly aggressive cross-examination. The tribunal has discretion to admit written rather than oral testimony and to arrange for oral examination other than before the tribunal itself (Arbitration Rule 36).

Given the importance of written witness statements and expert reports, the main purpose of presenting fact witnesses and experts at the hearing is to allow cross examination by the opposing side and, perhaps most important, questions from the tribunal. Experienced ICSID practitioners know that a hearing is not an occasion to repeat the written submissions, but rather an opportunity to gauge – and respond to – the arbitrators' main concerns. Discernment and responsiveness in advocacy are critical.

Evidence, disclosure and discovery

Arbitration Rule 34 gives the tribunal discretion to decide on both the admissibility and probative value of evidence. An individual tribunal's approach will depend on several factors, not the least of which is the balance of civil and common lawyers on the panel. Strict rules of evidence, such as those developed under national procedural codes, do not apply.

Convention Article 43 provides for voluntary disclosure of evidence, subject to the parties' agreement otherwise. Arbitration Rule 33 requires each party to provide to the tribunal and the other party "precise information regarding the evidence which it intends to produce and that which it intends to request the tribunal to call for, together with an indication of the points to which such evidence will be directed." Arbitration Rule 34 authorizes the tribunal to require the production of documents and the presentation of fact witnesses and experts, and to make site visits.

In sum, in ICSID arbitration any discovery of evidence beyond voluntary disclosure is firmly in the control of the tribunal. Parties to ICSID proceedings cannot expect extensive, US-style document discovery. Depositions are unheard of. To put it bluntly, a claimant investor cannot obtain the evidence necessary to prove its case from the State respondent.

If a party fails to cooperate in the evidentiary process, Arbitration Rule 34(3) directs the ICSID tribunal to take "formal note" of such failure and any reasons given. Although the Arbitration Rules do not contain any further explicit sanction, a party's uncooperative conduct, as in any international commercial arbitration, may lead the tribunal to draw adverse inferences from that lack of cooperation and may affect the allocation of costs. In *AGIP v. Congo*, for example, the Government of Congo's failure to comply with a provisional measure ordering it to produce documentation was reflected in the tribunal's assessment of damages awarded to AGIP.[128]

Objections to jurisdiction

Article 41 of the ICSID Convention affirms that the tribunal "shall be the judge of its own competence," meaning that the tribunal itself is to decide questions regarding its jurisdiction. Given the rapid rise in the number of bilateral investment treaty arbitrations under the Convention, and their unfamiliar jurisdictional foundations, respondent States almost routinely object to ICSID jurisdiction under the relevant treaty. Investors should expect to invest substantial time and resources in the obviously critical jurisdictional phase.

Under Arbitration Rule 41, a party objecting on jurisdictional grounds must do so "as early as possible" in the proceedings, but in any event not later than in its counter-memorial, unless the relevant facts were not known until later. When a party submits a jurisdictional objection, the proceedings on the merits are suspended. The tribunal then establishes a schedule for pleadings on the jurisdictional objection, deciding in particular whether to treat it as a separate preliminary question or to join it to the merits.

When ICSID tribunals deal with jurisdictional objections as preliminary questions, they tend to conduct separate written and oral procedures on jurisdiction. As a practical matter, this may add a year or more to the duration of an ICSID arbitration.

If the tribunal ultimately finds that it has jurisdiction, it typically issues a reasoned decision (rather than an award) and proceeds to calendar further proceedings on the merits. If the tribunal should find that it lacks jurisdiction, the case comes to an end; the tribunal issues a final award dismissing the case for lack of jurisdiction, which is subject to the limited avenues of post-award proceedings available under the Convention (as discussed at the end of this chapter and in Chapter 5). In contrast, decisions finding that the tribunal has jurisdiction are not awards pursuant to the definition of Convention Article 48(3) and are not subject to the post-award

---

[128] *AGIP S.p.A. v. The Government of the People's Republic of Congo*, ICSID Case No. ARB/77/1, Award (30 November 1979), 1 *ICSID Reports* 306, 317-318 (1993).

proceedings available under the Convention. However, the jurisdictional decisions will form an integral part of the final award, once issued, and may be challenged at that stage under the Convention.

Provisional measures

Under Convention Article 47 and Arbitration Rule 39, a party may request at any point during the proceedings that "provisional measures for the preservation of its rights be *recommended* by the Tribunal" (emphasis added). The request for provisional measures must describe the rights to be preserved, the measures requested and the circumstances. Although the tribunal must accord "priority" to requests for provisional measures, it cannot proceed ex parte; it is mandated to give each party the opportunity to comment before recommending provisional measures (Arbitration Rules 39(2) and (4)).

Even with the limitation inherent in the use of the word "recommend" as opposed to the word "order", ICSID tribunals do not readily recommend provisional measures, particularly against State parties. There are, however, instances in which tribunals have recommended provisional measures directing a party to preserve or produce documents,[129] to discontinue parallel proceedings in local courts or not to take steps that would exacerbate the dispute.[130]

A recommendation for provisional measures does not constitute an award and so is not subject to annulment or enforcement proceedings under the Convention. Interestingly, the tribunal in the *Casado and Allende Foundation v. Chile* case expressed the view in dicta that, under general principles of international law, provisional measures under Article 47 should be seen not as mere recommendations in the advisory sense but instead as orders with binding effect on the parties.[131]

As highlighted in Chapter 2, parties arbitrating under the Convention pursuant to an investor-State contract, a bilateral investment treaty or a multilateral investment treaty may not seek provisional measures from an authority other than the tribunal – i.e., a national court – unless this is expressly provided for in the agreement or the relevant treaty (Arbitration Rule 39(5)). Investors anticipating the need for urgent interim measures from local courts in connection with their particular projects must, in the absence of favorable legislation, negotiate for such rights in their investment contracts.

---

[129] *See, e.g., Kaiser Bauxite Company v. Jamaica* (Decision on Jurisdiction and Competence), *supra* note 29; *Liberian Eastern Timber Corporation v. Republic of Liberia*, ICSID Case No. ARB/83/2, Award (31 March 1986) 2 *ICSID Reports* 343 (1994); *AGIP v. Congo* (Award), *supra* note 128.

[130] *See, e.g., Maritime International Nominees Establishment (MINE) v. Republic of Guinea*, ICSID Case ARB/84/4, Award (6 January 1988), 4 *ICSID Reports* 54 (1997); *see also Ceskoslovenska Obchondni Banka, A.S. v. The Slovak Republic* (Decision on Objections to Jurisdiction), *supra* note 67.

[131] *Victor Pey Casado and Presidente Allende Foundation v. Republic of Chile*, ICSID Case No. ARB/98/2, Decision on Provisional Measures (25 September 2001), 16 *ICSID Review – FILJ* 567 (2001).

Default, discontinuance and settlement

ICSID arbitration may proceed in the absence of one party. The very existence of default rules doubtless explains why such instances are rare in practice.

Article 45 of the Convention and Arbitration Rule 42 govern default. If a party fails to appear or to present its case at any stage of the proceedings, the tribunal may, at the request of the other party, render an award on the issues before it. Prior to ruling, however, the tribunal must notify the defaulting party of the other party's request to proceed and, unless satisfied that the defaulting party has no intention to participate, grant a grace period. The defaulting party's failure to present its case is not deemed an admission of the other party's claims. Default proceedings, as in any international commercial arbitration, place a substantial and difficult burden on both the tribunal and the sole participating party. To illustrate, in the *Letco v. Liberia* case, in which Liberia failed to appear or present its case, the tribunal emphasized in the award that it had subjected the claimant's assertions to careful scrutiny and had appointed an accounting firm to examine the claim for damages.[132]

ICSID arbitration proceedings may be discontinued in three ways. First, either party may request a discontinuance, which the tribunal will grant if the other party does not object (Arbitration Rule 44). Second, the proceedings are deemed discontinued if the parties fail to act for six consecutive months or such other time period as may be agreed between them and approved by the tribunal (Arbitration Rule 45). Third, the parties may agree to settle their dispute and request the tribunal to record the terms of their settlement in the form of a final award (Arbitration Rule 43). Such an award on agreed terms allows the parties to benefit from the ICSID enforcement regime (see Chapter 5).

Closure of the proceedings and deliberations

Assuming an ICSID arbitration proceeds through the merits phase, the tribunal declares the proceedings closed once the parties have finished presenting their cases. This may be either at the end of the hearing on the merits or as of the date post-hearing memorials are filed. The tribunal may "exceptionally" reopen the proceedings for new evidence or a "vital need for clarification" on specific points (Arbitration Rule 38). Most important, closure of the proceedings triggers the 120-day period set in Arbitration Rule 46 for the tribunal's rendering of the award.

Pursuant to Arbitration Rule 15, the tribunal must deliberate in private. All arbitrators must keep the deliberations secret. The president chairs the deliberations, just as he or she does initial sessions and the hearings; in the event of incapacity, one of the other members of the tribunal may preside (Arbitration Rules 14 and 17). Any non-unanimous award or decision of the tribunal must be made by the majority, with any abstention counting as a negative vote (Arbitration Rule 16).

---

[132] *LETCO v. Liberia* (Award), *supra* note 129.

Arbitral Proceedings Under the Additional Facility Rules

Arbitration proceedings under the ICSID Additional Facility Rules are conducted in substantially the same manner as those under the ICSID Convention, except for two notable differences (discussed below) concerning the place of the proceedings and provisional measures. The Additional Facility Arbitration Rules contain provisions similar to the Arbitration Rules regarding the conduct of the tribunal's early session(s) (Additional Facility Arbitration Rules 21 to 35); written and oral procedures and evidentiary matters (Additional Facility Arbitration Rules 36 to 44); challenges to the tribunal's competence (Additional Facility Arbitration Rule 45); and default (Additional Facility Arbitration Rule 48), settlement (Additional Facility Arbitration Rule 49) and discontinuance (Additional Facility Arbitration Rules 49 to 51).

Unlike arbitration proceedings under the ICSID Convention, which may take place in any jurisdiction (without effect on the enforceability of the award), proceedings under the Additional Facility Rules must take place in a country that is a party to the New York Convention (Additional Facility Arbitration Rule 19). This rule is intended to facilitate enforcement of ICSID Additional Facility awards by ensuring that, even though such awards do not benefit from the automatic recognition and enforcement regime of the ICSID Convention, they may be readily recognized and enforced under the favorable scheme of the New York Convention (see Chapter 5). As long as this geographical requirement is satisfied, the tribunal may select any place for the arbitration, in consultation with the parties and the Secretariat of the Additional Facility (Additional Facility Arbitration Rule 20).

The Additional Facility procedures for provisional measures also differ slightly from those applicable to ICSID Convention arbitrations. Both the Arbitration Rules and the Additional Facility Arbitration Rules allow parties to request provisional measures from the tribunal and authorize the tribunal to recommend provisional measures at its discretion (Arbitration Rule 39; Additional Facility Arbitration Rule 46). However, while parties arbitrating under the Convention may not request provisional measures from domestic courts unless expressly so agreed (Arbitration Rule 39(5)), the Additional Facility Rules, in terms similar to those found in many international commercial arbitration rules, allow access to local courts without prejudicing the arbitration:

> "The parties may apply to any competent judicial authority for interim or conservatory measures. By doing so they shall not be held to infringe the agreement to arbitrate or to affect the powers of the Tribunal." (Additional Facility Arbitration Rule 46(4))

ICSID Awards

ICSID Convention Awards

Time limits

It is perhaps not surprising that ICSID arbitrations, which necessarily involve issues of State responsibility, proceed slowly. ICSID arbitrations have averaged approximately two to three years from the registration of the initial request to the issuance of the award. Many take longer.

The arbitrators (generally) are not to blame for the extended duration of an ICSID arbitration. It is the written and oral procedures, not the drafting of the award, that typically take the most time. It is not unusual for the parties themselves to request multiple extensions of time and suspension of the proceedings to explore possibilities of settlement. This is, of course, a positive thing, not to be held against the ICSID regime, when assessing its alacrity.

ICSID tribunals have a circumscribed period to draft and issue the award. Under Arbitration Rule 46, the award must be signed within 120 days of the closure of the proceedings, subject to the possibility of a 60-day extension. The Secretary-General, in accordance with Article 49(1) of the ICSID Convention and Arbitration Rule 48, must promptly authenticate the original text of the award and dispatch a certified copy to each party. There is no provision, unlike in the ICC Arbitration Rules, for ICSID to scrutinize or otherwise review a draft award.

The award is deemed rendered on the date the Secretary-General dispatches the certified copies. It is the date of dispatch that triggers the time limits for post-award remedies (see Chapter 5).

The form of awards

The rules concerning the form of ICSID awards do not differ substantially from other international commercial arbitration rules. Under Articles 48(2) and 48(3) of the ICSID Convention, an award must: (a) be in writing; (b) be signed by the members of the tribunal who support it; (c) deal with every question submitted to the tribunal; and (d) state the reasons upon which it is based. These provisions are mandatory, and so may not be deviated from by the parties or by the tribunal.

ICSID Arbitration Rule 47 provides more detail:

"(1) The award shall be in writing and shall contain:
    (a) a precise designation of each party;
    (b) a statement that the Tribunal was established under the Convention, and a description of the method of its constitution;
    (c) the name of each member of the Tribunal, and an identification of the appointing authority of each;
    (d) the names of the agents, counsel and advocates of the parties;

(e) the dates and places of the sittings of the Tribunal;

(f) a summary of the proceeding;

(g) a statement of the facts as found by the Tribunal;

(h) the submissions of the parties;

(i) the decision of the Tribunal on every question submitted to it, together with the reasons upon which the decision is based; and

(j) any decision of the Tribunal regarding the cost of the proceeding.

(2) The award shall be signed by the members of the Tribunal who voted for it; the date of each signature shall be indicated.

(3) Any member of the Tribunal may attach his individual opinion to the award, whether he dissents from the majority or not, or a statement of his dissent."

The requirement that the award contain "the decision of the Tribunal on every question submitted to it" does not mean that the arbitrators must address every argument that may have been advanced by the parties in their pleadings, but only the issues that are decisive. The tribunal's failure to deal explicitly with a decisive issue in the award may constitute a possible ground for annulment, as discussed in Chapter 5.

As noted, Article 48(1) of the ICSID Convention authorizes decisions by a majority vote. Article 48(4) allows arbitrators to attach individual opinions to the award, in the form of either a dissenting or concurring opinion. In ICSID practice, separate opinions are unusual.

Supplementary decision and rectification
Under Article 49 of the ICSID Convention, either party may file with the Secretary-General, within 45 days of the date of the rendering of the final award, a request that the tribunal decide an issue it omitted or "rectify" the award by correcting a "clerical, arithmetical or similar error." Rectification serves merely to provide the parties the opportunity to review the award for obvious, minor mistakes; it is not a mechanism for reconsidering the merits.

Publication
Article 48(5) of the ICSID Convention authorizes the Centre to publish an award or decision only with the consent of both parties. Parties themselves may – and often do – publish awards and decisions unilaterally.

The Secretariat is able to reveal certain information about ICSID cases under Regulations 22 and 23, including the identity of the parties, the date of the request, the membership and constitution of the tribunal, the subject matter of the dispute, and the outcome of the proceedings. The information is published in the biannual ICSID News, in the ICSID Annual Reports, and on the ICSID website.

Additional Facility Awards

Provisions in the Additional Facility Rules dealing with the form of awards are similar to those in the Arbitration Rules. Although not a matter of form, it merits mention that the Additional Facility Rules differ from the Arbitration Rules with respect to applicable law. Additional Facility Arbitration Rule 54 directs the tribunal to apply the substantive law selected by the parties or to decide the dispute ex aequo et bono if the parties have so decided. In contrast, ICSID Convention awards are subject to the choice of law provisions of Article 42, as described above in Chapter 2.

Costs of ICSID Arbitration

In essence, the parties to ICSID arbitrations are liable for three categories of costs: (a) the administrative costs of the Centre; (b) the fees and expenses of the arbitrators; and (c) the attorneys' fees and other expenses incurred by the parties themselves. The tribunal allocates responsibility for these costs as between the parties in the award, which is discussed further below and in Chapter 5.

Advances on Costs

In addition to the non-refundable lodging fee due with the request for arbitration, the Regulations call for the parties to pay an administrative charge of USD3,000 (per the January 2003 Schedule of Fees) following the constitution of the tribunal and then make provisional advances to the Secretariat to cover the costs of the proceedings for three to six month periods at a time (Regulation 14(3)(a)). Without prejudice to the ultimate allocation of costs in the award, the parties must advance the costs of arbitration equally unless the tribunal decides otherwise (Regulation 14(3)(d); Arbitration Rule 28(1)). In annulment proceedings, however, the party seeking annulment must deposit the entire advance on costs (Regulation 14(3)(e)).

Neither the Centre nor the arbitrators serve for free. Under Regulation 14(3)(d), if a party does not pay an advance in full within 30 days of a request for payment, the Secretary-General gives both parties the opportunity to make the payment. If neither party does so within 15 days, the Secretary-General may request the tribunal to suspend the arbitration proceedings. If there is such a suspension for non-payment for more than six months, the Secretary-General may move the tribunal to discontinue the proceedings. In practice, however, the Secretariat consults closely with the parties' representatives on all payment matters throughout the duration of the arbitration.

Level of Costs

The conventional wisdom is that ICSID administrative and arbitrator costs are relatively low compared to those assessed in other international commercial arbitration regimes. On the administrative side, this may be in part due to the World Bank's commitment to subsidize ICSID, undertaken before the adoption of the Convention.[133] As for the arbitrators, the ICSID maximum daily rate (discussed below) is substantially below the rates that the leading arbitrators command in other international arbitrations.

The ICSID cost structure is not based (as in the case, for example, of the ICC) on the amount in dispute, but rather on the administrative services actually provided by the Centre and the time actually devoted by the arbitrators to an individual arbitration (Regulation 14). Unless the parties agree otherwise (which sometimes happens), the arbitrators are compensated according to a maximum daily rate. Pursuant to the January 2003 Schedule of Fees, arbitrators are entitled to USD2,000 per day (pro-rated as appropriate) for hearings, meetings and other work, as well as their reasonable direct expenses, a subsistence allowance and business class travel expenses. In addition to the modest lodging fee and initial administrative fees of USD7,000 and USD3,000, respectively (as of January 2003), the Centre charges for its actual disbursements for interpretation, court reporting and other such services that it arranges in support of an arbitration.

In contrast, the parties' own costs in pursuing an ICSID arbitration are typically high. Given the almost inevitable separate jurisdictional phase (as discussed above), the complexity of investor-State legal and factual issues, the number and length of written pleadings, and the use of fact witnesses and experts in hearings, legal fees mount quickly. The in-house opportunity costs of lawyers and principals (for example, executives, engineers and accountants), who must devote time and other resources to the case, may also be an important factor. The seemingly high costs of the parties must be viewed in perspective, however, as ICSID arbitrations typically involve disputes in major long-term investments where the amount at stake dwarfs the arbitration expenses.

Interest

Whether a successful party is entitled to interest and, if so, how interest is to be calculated are matters to be determined according to the governing substantive law. For the purpose of this Guide, it is sufficient to note that many international arbitration tribunals in the past have maintained that only simple interest is available under international law, while contemporary ICSID tribunals have shown a greater readiness to award compound interest.[134]

---

[133] As discussed in Chapter 1. *See also* Regulations 17 and 18; ICSID *2001 Annual Report* at 23.

[134] *See, e.g., Santa Elena v. Costa Rica* (Award), *supra* note 38; *Emilio Agustín Maffezini v. The Kingdom of Spain*, ICSID Case No. ARB/97/7, Award (13 November 2000), 5 *ICSID Reports* 419 (2002).

Award of Costs

Pursuant to Article 61(2) of the Convention, unless the parties agree otherwise, in the final award the tribunal assesses the parties' arbitration expenses, the fees and expenses of the tribunal itself and the Centre's administrative charges, and allocates those costs between the parties. After the closure of the proceedings, the parties accordingly are required to submit to the tribunal an accounting of their costs, including counsel fees and expenses incurred in producing documentary evidence, fact witnesses and experts.

ICSID tribunal decisions on the allocation of costs between the parties have varied widely, depending on the arbitrators' perception of the reasonableness with which the parties pursued their claims and defenses, the parties' general cooperativeness in achieving cost-effective results, and the novelty of the legal issues presented. Many awards have required the parties to share the costs of the Centre and the arbitrators' fees equally, and to bear their own legal and other expenses.

CHAPTER 5

Recognition, Enforcement and Execution of ICSID Awards

The effectiveness of international commercial arbitration depends to a great extent – some would say entirely – on the degree of finality of the award and the ease with which the award may be enforced by the prevailing party. In this critical respect the rigorous finality provisions and the self-contained enforcement process in the ICSID Convention distinguish ICSID from other international commercial arbitration regimes.

It bears noting that, as with other classes of disputes subject to judicial or arbitral jurisdiction, most of ICSID cases settle. In the cases that do proceed all the way to an award, participants must understand what will happen if the losing party fails to comply with the award voluntarily. In that event, the prevailing party must see the award through phases known as "recognition," "enforcement" and "execution."

"Recognition" is the formal imprimatur that an award is a final and binding decision on issues disputed by the parties. The primary purpose of recognition is to confirm the res judicata effect of an award – that is, to establish that the issues resolved in the award may not be reexamined in other court or arbitration proceedings. Recognition is, by definition, the first legal step in a contested post-award process.

The last step in the post-award process – "execution" – is the prevailing party's actual collection of monetary damages, or actual achievement of other relief granted in the award. Execution generally requires the assistance of local courts, which exercise their authority to cause awards to be satisfied by, for example, issuing judgments and ordering attachment of assets of the award debtor.

The intermediate step of "enforcement" is less precise than the other two. In some legal systems, enforcement refers to the judicial practice of issuing "exequatur," or declaring in an order that an arbitration award is in fact enforceable. In other legal systems, the term loosely refers to an award creditor's legal right to execute its award – i.e., to collect monetary damages or benefit from other remedies granted – and is thus another way of referring to execution. In the context of ICSID arbitration, enforcement is generally indistinguishable from recognition. The two terms are used in a single phrase – recognition and enforcement – that broadly refers to all steps leading up to, but stopping short of, actual execution of an award.

International arbitration awards may not be appealed like court judgments.

Under most national systems, international arbitration awards cannot be reviewed on the merits at all, whether by a court or another arbitral tribunal. The national courts at the place of arbitration nevertheless retain power to set aside awards (at the instance of the losing party before the commencement of enforcement proceedings) or to refuse to enforce awards (in the course of enforcement proceedings commenced by the prevailing party), on grounds that vary somewhat according to national law but in most jurisdictions are extremely limited. Before the 1958 New York Convention came into force,[135] national courts would generally recognize and enforce international arbitration awards (or refuse to do so) according to their domestic laws, including, for example, their particular understanding of comity. Today, awards issued in the territory of the New York Convention's 138 State parties (as of January 2003) benefit from facilitated recognition and enforcement in the territory of any other State party. The New York Convention presumes the validity of international arbitration awards and mandates their enforcement, except on extremely circumscribed procedural and public policy grounds.[136]

One of the greatest strengths of the ICSID Convention is that it is even more favorable to recognition and enforcement than the New York Convention. The ICSID Convention accepts no grounds whatsoever for refusing recognition and enforcement of ICSID tribunal awards. It requires, instead, that the national courts of Contracting States recognize and enforce monetary awards immediately, as if they were final judgments of these States local courts. The courts may not vacate ICSID awards because they are a-national and subject to the ICSID regime rather than to national law. The parties may contest awards only under the limited review mechanism in the ICSID Convention: on restricted grounds, before a three-member ad hoc committee constituted under the Convention, which may only interpret, revise or annul the award. This self-contained delocalized enforcement scheme shelters ICSID arbitration awards from the scrutiny of national courts until an award must be executed, at which time the laws of the country of execution apply.

This chapter addresses each of the steps in the ICSID post-award process – interpretation, revision, annulment and execution. Note that this process applies only to awards rendered under the ICSID Convention, and not to awards issued under the ICSID Additional Facility Rules or the UNCITRAL rules administered by ICSID (like those in NAFTA cases, for example). Awards in the latter categories are governed by the New York Convention, as implemented in Contracting State jurisdictions where they are issued and where their recognition and enforcement ultimately is sought.

---

[135] With the exception of the impact of the Geneva Protocol on Arbitration Clauses of 1923 and the Geneva Convention on the Execution of Foreign Awards of 1927.

[136] For general background on recognition and enforcement of international commercial arbitration awards, see *The Freshfields Guide*, *supra* note 3.

THE FINAL AND BINDING NATURE OF ICSID AWARDS

Article 53(1) of the ICSID Convention, quoted in relevant part, establishes the finality of ICSID awards:

"The award shall be binding on the parties and shall not be subject to any appeal or any other remedy except those provided for in this Convention."

Article 53(1) is straightforward, but two points of qualification are in order. First, an ICSID award binds only the parties to the dispute, not third parties. This point may raise difficult questions in arbitrations between a private investor and "a constituent subdivision or agency of a Contracting State designated to the Centre by that State." It remains unclear, for example, whether in cases where a State's constituent subdivision or agency is designated to the Centre as a party, the State itself is bound when an ICSID tribunal issues an award against the subdivision or agency.[137]

Second, not all ICSID decisions are awards, let alone final awards. Pursuant to Convention Article 48(3), an award is final if it disposes of all questions put to the tribunal. As discussed in Chapter 4, an award is definitely final if the tribunal holds that it lacks jurisdiction or resolves all substantive issues on the merits. An award that affirms jurisdiction, and thus allows the case to proceed to the merits, is not a final award. In *SPP v. Egypt*, when the government of Egypt filed an application to annul the tribunal's decision affirming jurisdiction,[138] the Secretary-General refused to register the application on the ground that it was not an award under the Convention. Orders that recommend provisional measures and procedural decisions are not final awards. Nor is an order discontinuing proceedings a final award, unless it leads to a settlement that is recorded in the form of an award under Convention Article 53(2).

THE ICSID REVIEW REGIME

Parties may seek review under the ICSID Convention only of final awards. Hence, the first step in establishing whether and how a party may challenge a decision issued by an ICSID tribunal is to determine whether the decision is an award and, if so, whether the award is final.

The Convention provides for only three post-award remedies: interpretation, revision and annulment. Article 53(1) precludes parties from challenging awards by appealing to national courts or resorting to "any other remedy except those provided for in this Convention." Furthermore, by operation of Convention Article 26, the

---

[137] A. Broches, *Awards Rendered Pursuant to the ICSID Convention: Binding Force, Finality, Recognition, Enforcement, Execution*, 2 *ICSID Review – FILJ* 287 (1987).

[138] *Southern Pacific Properties (Middle East) Ltd. and Southern Pacific Properties Ltd. (Hong Kong) v. Arab Republic of Egypt*, Decision on Jurisdiction (14 April 1988), 3 *ICSID Reports* 131 (1995).

ICSID review regime is mandatory and exclusive. Parties may not contract out of the regime by agreeing to subject their awards to any other form of review.

Convention Articles 50, 51 and 52 and Arbitration Rules 50 to 55 set out the detailed procedures for filing requests for, respectively, the interpretation, revision and annulment of an award. In accordance with Regulation 16 of the Administrative and Financial Regulations, each of the three procedures requires the advance payment of a non-refundable fee, set in the January 2003 Schedule of Fees at USD7,000. Enforcement of the award may be stayed pending the outcome of these review procedures, under conditions discussed below.

Interpretation of the Award

Article 50 of the ICSID Convention allows either party to apply to the Secretary-General for an "interpretation" of the award's scope or meaning. Interpretation does not entail a review of the merits of the award. Nor does interpretation compromise the finality of the award.

The Convention does not stipulate a deadline by which parties must request interpretation, but it does require that the application specify the points for which interpretation is requested (Arbitration Rule 50(1)(c)(i)). The Secretary-General forwards the request to the tribunal that rendered the award; if the tribunal has dissolved and it cannot be reconstituted, the Secretary-General invites the parties to constitute a new tribunal (Arbitration Rule 51(2) and (3)).

As of January 2003, ICSID had never received a request for interpretation.

Revision of the Award

Either party may also request that an award be "revised," or changed, under Article 51 of the ICSID Convention, but only "on the ground of discovery of some fact of such a nature as decisively to affect the award" (Article 51(1)). Further, the applicant must show that the fact is indeed new—"that when the award was rendered that fact was unknown to the Tribunal and to the applicant, and that the applicant's ignorance of the fact was not due to negligence" (Article 51(1)). The application also must specify the change sought in the award. (See also Arbitration Rule 50(1)(c)(ii).)

A party must file for revision with the Secretary-General within 90 days after discovering the new fact and, in any event, within three years after the award was rendered (Article 51(2); Arbitration Rule 50(3)(a)). If possible, the Secretary-General forwards the application for revision to the original tribunal; otherwise, the Secretary-General arranges for the constitution of a new tribunal (Article 51(3); Arbitration Rule 51(2) and (3)).

As of January 2003, there had been only one request for revision. In that instance, the parties settled the relevant case before the application could be heard.

Annulment of the Award

The most drastic remedy available under the ICSID Convention is the annulment of an award, in whole or in part, under Article 52. Unlike requests for the interpretation or revision of awards under Articles 50 and 51, which may be considered by the original tribunal that issued the award, applications for annulment are put to a new three-member ad hoc committee constituted for that sole purpose.

Annulment proceedings differ from typical judicial appeals in two key respects. First, a successful annulment application leads to the invalidation of the award (or certain of its parts), but never to its amendment. Unlike an appeals court, an ad hoc annulment committee may not substitute its views on a case for that of the original tribunal. The effect of annulment, instead, is to erase the preclusive effect of the award and provide the parties with a second chance to arbitrate the same issues again before an entirely new ICSID tribunal.

Second, an ad hoc committee does not have the jurisdiction to review the merits of the original award in any way. The annulment system is designed to safeguard the integrity, not the outcome, of ICSID arbitration proceedings. Ad hoc committees may annul awards only on the limited grounds described in Article 52(1):

"Either party may request annulment of the award by an application in writing addressed to the Secretary-General on one or more of the following grounds:
(a) that the Tribunal was not properly constituted;
(b) that the Tribunal has manifestly exceeded its powers;
(c) that there was corruption on the part of a member of the Tribunal;
(d) that there has been a serious departure from a fundamental rule of procedure; or
(e) that the award has failed to state the reasons on which it is based."

All of the five ICSID annulment decisions published as of January 2003 have involved the same three grounds: manifest excess of powers, serious departure from a fundamental rule of procedure, and failure to state reasons. (These decisions are described below.) ICSID ad hoc annulment committees have not, to date, invoked the grounds of improper constitution or corruption of tribunals.

Ad hoc committees have found that a tribunal "manifestly exceeded its powers" when it clearly exceeded the competence granted to it by the ICSID Convention, its terms of reference or the remedies available to it under the applicable law. A tribunal's failure to apply the applicable law has also been held to constitute a manifest excess of authority but only, it appears, when the tribunal altogether failed to use, rather than misapplied, the applicable law.[139]

To prevail on a claim that there was "a serious departure from a fundamental rule of procedure," a party must satisfy both prongs of the test, by showing that the rule from which the tribunal departed was fundamental and that the departure was

---

[139] *Klöckner v. Cameroon* (Decision on Annulment), *supra* note 38.

serious.[140] A rule is fundamental if it goes to the heart of the integrity of the arbitration proceedings, as do, for example, the principles of fairness, impartiality, equal treatment, and respect for the right to be heard. A departure is serious, in the view of one ad hoc committee, if it is substantial and material, that is, if it "deprive[s] a party of the benefit or protection which the rule was intended to provide."[141]

An award "has failed to state the reasons on which it is based" if the tribunal is silent as to its reasoning on particular decisions or offers radically contradictory reasonings for particular decisions. Merely insufficient or inadequate reasoning is unlikely to satisfy this requirement; ad hoc committees have been disinclined to annul awards if they are able to reconstruct missing reasoning. Keeping in mind the lack of authority for an ad hoc committee to review the merits of the original award, it is not surprising that faulty reasoning by a tribunal does not constitute a failure to state reasons justifying annulment.

Annulment application procedure

A party must submit its application for annulment to the Secretary-General within 120 days after the award was rendered; in cases of alleged corruption, the request is due within 120 days after the corruption was discovered and, in any event, within three years after the award was rendered (Article 52(2); Arbitration Rule 50(3)(b)). The application must state in detail the Article 52 grounds on which it is based. Upon receiving a request for annulment, the Chairman of the Administrative Council appoints – from the Panel of Arbitrators – the independent three-member ad hoc committee to review the award. The criteria for appointment are strict: in addition to the obvious restriction that the ad hoc committee members may not have sat on the original panel; each must be of another nationality than that of the original arbitrators; and none may be a national of either State affected by the dispute or have been designated to the Panel of Arbitrators by those States (Article 52(3)). Under Convention Article 52(6), if the ad hoc committee annuls the award, either party may resubmit the dispute to a new tribunal constituted afresh under the Convention; there is no "remand" to the original tribunal.

Annulment decisions

As of January 2003, 11 annulment applications had been filed in connection with nine cases (two cases had two sets of annulment proceedings). Two of the 11 applications were dismissed out of hand, for seeking to annul decisions that were not final awards; a third was suspended for non-payment of fees by the applicant; and a

---

[140] *Maritime International Nominees Establishment v. Republic of Guinea*, ICSID Case ARB/84/4, Decision on Annulment (22 December 1989), 4 *ICSID Reports* 79, 87 (1997).
[141] *Id.*

fourth settled before the ad hoc committee reached a decision. As two of the remaining decisions have been kept confidential, there are only five annulment decisions in the public realm.

The first round of ICSID annulment cases, in the 1980s, attracted substantial attention in the legal and investment communities. The ad hoc committees in the first three annulment cases – *Klöckner v. Cameroon, Amco Asia v. Indonesia* and *MINE v. Guinea* – set aside at least parts of all of the three awards under review. In each of the three cases, the parties proceeded to submit the disputes to a second tribunal and, in two of them, then to a second round of annulment proceedings.

Klöckner v. Cameroon arose out of disputes over interlocking contracts for the supply and management of a fertilizer factory in Cameroon. Both the private investor Klöckner and the government of Cameroon raised claims in the arbitration, all of which the original tribunal rejected in 1983.[142] Klöckner applied for annulment, arguing that the tribunal had: (a) manifestly exceeded its power by failing to apply the applicable law and asserting jurisdiction over disputes arising out of a contract with a dispute resolution clause calling for ICC arbitration; (b) seriously departed from fundamental rules of procedure by failing to act impartially, failing to hold a true deliberation and committing other irregularities; and (c) failed to deal with all the questions submitted to it and to state adequately the reasons for deciding the questions it did address. In 1985, the ad hoc committee annulled the award in its entirety, on the basis that the tribunal had manifestly exceeded its powers by failing to apply the applicable law: the ad hoc committee found that the tribunal had postulated, but not actually demonstrated, the application of certain principles of French law.[143] The ad hoc committee also found that the tribunal had failed to explain certain of its rulings: "Despite many readings of the text, it is impossible to discern how and why the Tribunal could reach its decision on this point."[144] A second tribunal rendered a new award, which both parties sought to annul. The second ad hoc committee rejected the parties' applications, for reasons that remain uncertain because the annulment decision (like the second award) was not made public.[145]

In 1984, the tribunal in *Amco v. Indonesia* awarded Amco USD3.2 million in damages for what it found to be the government of Indonesia's unlawful revocation of the investment authorization it had granted Amco for developing and managing a hotel in Indonesia.[146] Indonesia requested annulment of the award on the same three

---

[142] *Klöckner Industrie-Anlagen GmbH and others v. United Republic of Cameroon and Société Camerounaise des Engrais*, ICSID Case No. ARB/81/2, Award (21 October 1983), 2 *ICSID Reports* 9 (1994).

[143] *Klöckner v. Cameroon* (Decision on Annulment), *supra* note 38.

[144] *Id.* at 148.

[145] Both the second award of 26 January 1988 and the second ad hoc committee's Decision of 17 May 1990 are unpublished.

[146] *Amco Asia Corporation and others v. Indonesia*, ICSID Case No. ARB/81/1, Award (20 November 1984), 1 *ICSID Reports* 413 (1993).

grounds invoked by Klöckner: (a) manifest excess of powers; (b) serious departure from fundamental procedural rules; and (c) failure to state reasons. The ad hoc committee annulled the award in 1986 in almost its entirety, ruling that although the tribunal had correctly identified the proper law it had failed actually to apply that law. Having found that the tribunal had thus mistakenly held Indonesia's license revocation to be illegal, the ad hoc committee also annulled the award of damages that hinged on that finding.[147] A new ICSID tribunal issued a second award in Amco's favor in 1990.[148] Both parties again applied for annulment. The second ad hoc committee decided against annulment in 1992, again on grounds that remain uncertain because the annulment decision was not published.

In 1988, in *MINE v. Guinea*, Guinea applied for the partial annulment of the award granted by the original tribunal to MINE for damages in the amount of approximately USD12 million.[149] Guinea claimed that the tribunal had: (a) failed to apply any law at all; (b) seriously departed from a fundamental rule of procedure by adopting a theory of damages that had not been advanced or discussed by the parties; and (c) failed both to state reasons for certain of its findings and to answer other questions put to it. The *MINE v. Guinea* ad hoc committee let stand the original tribunal's rulings on Guinea's liability, but annulled the tribunal's ruling on damages for failure to state reasons. Among other things, the ad hoc committee found that the tribunal had failed to address two issues raised by Guinea that, if correct, would have substantially reduced the award of both damages and interest.[150] The parties began a second ICSID arbitration, which they settled mid-course.

The first ad hoc committees in *Klöckner* and *Amco* were severely criticized. Commentators argued that the committees had overstepped their mandates by examining the merits of the awards they reviewed and thereby effectively turning into an appeals process what the ICSID Convention's drafters had intended to be only a safety net against egregiously irregular awards.[151] Because the first two annulments seemed to presage a cycle of appellate-type proceedings, it was widely feared that the annulment process in practice would undercut the much-touted finality of ICSID awards and undermine investor confidence in ICSID arbitration. However, as early as the late 1980s, many commentators believed that the ICSID system had reestablished some of its balance, as a result of the more measured holding of the ad hoc committee in *MINE* in 1989 and the decisions of the second ad hoc committees in *Klöckner II* in 1990 and *Amco II* in 1992 not to annul the second round of awards in those cases.[152]

---

[147] *Amco Asia Corporation and others v. Indonesia*, ICSID Case No. ARB/81/1, Decision on the Application for Annulment, (16 May 1986), 1 *ICSID Reports* 509 (1993).

[148] *Amco v. Indonesia* (Award in Resubmitted Case), ICSID *supra* note 39.

[149] *MINE v. Guinea* (Award), *supra* note 130.

[150] *MINE v. Guinea (*Decision on Annulment*)*, *supra* note 140.

[151] *See* Schreuer, *supra* note 4, at 893, 901.

[152] *Id.* at 900-901.

After a quiet decade, the winter of 2000-2001 witnessed the filing of three annulment applications within weeks of one another. The annulment proceedings in *Philippe Gruslin v. Malaysia* were quickly discontinued because the applicant failed to pay the requisite ICSID fees. Those in *Wena Hotels Ltd. v. Arab Republic of Egypt* and *Compañia de Aguas del Aconquija S.A. and Vivendi Universal v. Argentine Republic* were completed and the decisions published. As the jurisdiction of the original tribunals in the underlying cases in *Wena* and *Vivendi* was based on bilateral investment treaties, rather than on the ICSID arbitration agreements at the heart of the *Klöckner-Amco-MINE* trilogy of decisions, these two annulment decisions addressed a host of new issues.

In *Wena*, the government of Egypt sought the annulment of an award holding it responsible for the expropriation of Wena, a United Kingdom hotel management company. Egypt argued that the original tribunal had: (a) manifestly exceeded its authority by failing to apply the applicable law; (b) seriously departed from fundamental rules of procedure by, among other things, depriving Egypt of its right to be heard and inappropriately shifting the parties' burdens of proof; and (c) failed both to state reasons for certain of its findings and to address all questions put to it. The ad hoc committee rejected all grounds for annulment, including Egypt's claim that the tribunal had misconstrued Convention Article 42, the choice of law article in the Convention (see Chapter 4), when it applied the relevant UK-Egypt bilateral investment treaty and other international law without regard for Egyptian law. In particular, the ad hoc committee held that the tribunal had not manifestly exceeded its authority when it applied the substantive provisions of the BIT and supplemented the treaty with other international law, even though the parties had not expressly selected international law as the governing law.[153] Although that holding appeared to hinge only on an interpretation of Article 42, the *Wena* annulment decision revealed certain of the new challenges posed by BIT-based ICSID arbitrations (see Chapter 3).

As noted in Chapter 3, the dispute in *Vivendi* arose out of a concession contract for the operation of the water and sewage system of the Tucumán province in Argentina. After the original tribunal dismissed the French investor's claim in its entirety,[154] the investor sought partial annulment of the award on grounds that the tribunal had: (a) manifestly exceeded its powers in failing to exercise jurisdiction over treaty claims it mistakenly construed as contractual claims; (b) seriously departed from a fundamental rule of procedure in not giving the investor the opportunity to present its case on a jurisdictional matter; and (c) failed to state the reasons upon which the award was based. The *Vivendi* ad hoc committee partially annulled the award, deciding, among other things, that the tribunal had exceeded its powers by finding that it had jurisdiction of the investor's treaty breach claims against the province of Tucumán but then refusing to consider, as its mandate

---

[153] *Wena Hotels v. Egypt* (Decision on Annulment), *supra* note 71.
[154] *Vivendi v. Argentina* (Award), *supra* note 71.

required, the merits of those treaty claims because they overlapped with contract claims requiring (in the tribunal's view) consideration by local administrative tribunals.[155]

Waiving the right to seek annulment

Parties that wish to avoid the uncertainty created by the prospect of ICSID annulment proceedings may consider waiving the right to annulment in the arbitration agreement. While the validity of such waivers apparently has not been tested, some commentators contend that Convention Article 52 is not subject to modification by the parties and that such waivers could be challenged before an ad hoc committee.[156] In any event, investors and host States alike should be mindful that, given the Convention's exclusion of any recourse to external review, a waiver of their right to annulment (if effective) would foreclose the only remedy available to them to challenge a truly rogue award.

Stay of Enforcement Pending Review Proceedings

Pending resolution of an application for interpretation, revision or annulment, the enforcement of an award may be stayed. Article 53(1) of the Convention provides, in relevant part:

> "Each party shall abide by and comply with the terms of the award except to the extent that enforcement shall have been stayed pursuant to the relevant provisions of this Convention."

The effect of a stay, simply put, is to suspend the losing party's obligation "to abide by and comply with" the award. On the one hand, because this phrase has been construed to encompass both recognition and enforcement of the award, a stay effectively freezes all binding aspects of the award, including its res judicata effect.[157] On the other hand, a stay does not affect the intrinsic legal validity of the award, at least not until the award has been interpreted, revised or annulled.

It is generally for the relevant tribunal or ad hoc committee to decide, in its discretion, whether to grant a stay (Convention Articles 50(2), 51(4) and 52(5)). A stay is automatic in only one specific situation: when, in revision or annulment proceedings, the moving party requests the stay at the time it files its application (Convention Articles 51(4) and 52(5)). In this instance, the Secretary-General may not refuse the request for the initial stay and must notify the parties of the stay. This stay terminates automatically when the tribunal or ad hoc committee is constituted, unless the tribunal or ad hoc committee extends it, at a party's request, within

---

[155] *Vivendi v. Argentina* (Decision on Annulment), *supra* note 101.

[156] Schreuer, *supra* note 4, at 908-910.

[157] Broches, *supra* note 137, at 317.

30 days (Arbitration Rule 54(2)). The practice is for tribunals and ad hoc committees to consider a further stay only on a request from a party and to hear both sides before entering a stay.

The guiding principles for ordering a stay of an award, as they have evolved in ICSID practice, are similar to those that apply to requests for provisional measures. In determining whether to grant a stay, the ad hoc committee in *Amco v. Indonesia* found it particularly relevant to consider whether: (a) enforcement of the award, if upheld, would be prompt; (b) the party requesting the stay was engaged in dilatory tactics; (c) the party requesting the stay offered security; and (d) proceeding with enforcement would likely cause irreparable injury to the award debtor because, for example, it would have difficulty recovering monies paid under the award if the award were later annulled.[158]

Requests for a stay of enforcement are most commonly submitted in annulment proceedings involving monetary awards. For example, the first ad hoc committee in *Amco v. Indonesia* ordered that enforcement of the monetary award issued against Indonesia be stayed on the condition that Indonesia provide an irrevocable and unconditional bank guarantee for payment in accordance with the final decision of the ad hoc committee.[159] In *MINE v. Guinea*, Guinea applied for, and obtained, a stay of enforcement of the monetary award on the ground that Guinea would suffer undue hardship if MINE seized its assets, but the ad hoc committee refused to require a bank guarantee from Guinea in return for prolonging the stay of enforcement because it would inappropriately alter the existing balance between the parties.[160]

RECOGNITION AND ENFORCEMENT

Article 54(1) is the heart of the ICSID Convention's automatic recognition and enforcement mechanism:

> "Each Contracting State shall recognize an award rendered pursuant to this Convention as binding and enforce the pecuniary obligations imposed by that award within its territories as if it were a final judgment of a court in that State. A Contracting State with a federal constitution may enforce such an award in or through its federal courts and may provide that such courts shall treat the award as if it were a final judgment of the courts of a constituent state."

Article 54(1) distinguishes pecuniary (i.e., monetary) awards from non-pecuniary awards, which might encompass performance obligations concerning employment

---

[158] *Amco v. Indonesia* (Decision on the Application for Annulment), *supra* note 147.

[159] *Id.* at 513.

[160] *Maritime International Nominees Establishment v. Republic of Guinea*, ICSID Case ARB/84/4, Interim Order No. 1 on Guinea's Application for Stay of Enforcement of the Award (12 August 1988), 4 *ICSID Reports* 111, 113-116 (1997).

and management matters, restitution of seized property, or application of taxation or currency transfer restrictions. The recognition and enforcement of ICSID monetary awards is simultaneous and automatic: the Convention prohibits the competent authorities of Contracting States from subjecting ICSID monetary awards to review under their national law or any other law. Article 54(1) also mandates automatic recognition – but not enforcement – of non-monetary awards, presumably leaving such awards to be enforced under the New York Convention, if it applies, or by other means.

Given this difference in treatment of monetary and non-monetary awards under the ICSID regime, parties should consider attempting to frame all their claims as monetary claims or, at very least, asking for monetary forms of relief as alternatives to specific performance claims. For example, an investor could seek specific performance of a State's obligation to reinstate a license and also, as an alternative, liquidated damages for non-performance of that obligation under the governing law.

Under Convention Article 54(2), a party seeking recognition and enforcement of an ICSID award in the territory of a Contracting State must provide a certified copy of the award to the competent court or other authority designated by the State. It is also Article 54(2) that requires each Contracting State to notify the Secretary-General of the designation of such competent court or other authority. Some States, for example the United Kingdom, have taken the opportunity to include with these notifications detailed instructions for parties applying for the recognition, enforcement and execution of an ICSID award in their territory (i.e., requirements as to time limits, currencies, evidence that the award is not subject to annulment). Other Contracting States have provided little, if any, guidance. In all cases, as requirements vary from one Contracting State to another, a party with an ICSID award in its favor must seek the advice of local counsel before initiating recognition and enforcement proceedings.

Execution

Recognition and Enforcement Versus Execution

Under the Convention, the recognition and enforcement of ICSID awards, on the one hand, and their execution, on the other, are distinct procedures. Typically, a prevailing party seeking to collect under an award will petition a national court to recognize and enforce the award and then, in a separate procedure, seek an execution order against the losing party's assets in that jurisdiction.

These two steps – recognition and enforcement, and execution – are subject to different laws. While the ICSID Convention specifically insulates awards from review under national laws at the recognition and enforcement stage, it offers no such guarantees at the time awards are to be executed against specific assets. The Convention, however supportive of foreign investment and investors, does not obligate a Contracting State to execute an ICSID award in circumstances where an equivalent final judgment of its own courts could not be executed. In such circumstances, national law on sovereign immunity from execution prevails.

Convention Article 54(3) stipulates that the execution of ICSID awards "shall be governed by the laws concerning the execution of judgments in force in the State in whose territories such execution is sought." Article 55 reiterates and emphasizes this:

> "Nothing in Article 54 shall be construed as derogating from the law in force in any Contracting State relating to immunity of that State or of any State from execution."

In other words, national courts in Contracting States must recognize and enforce awards according to the Convention, i.e. immediately, but they may execute them according to their own national law.

Although in theory this distinction raises the spectre of complicated execution proceedings, parties generally comply voluntarily with ICSID awards, as they do with awards delivered under the auspices of other respected arbitration institutions. In actual practice, payment is often the result of a post-award settlement. Of the 20 some ICSID cases that resulted in damage awards through 2002, only three led to execution proceedings (albeit convoluted ones, as described below).

The ICSID system is largely self-enforcing because Contracting States presumably recognize that blocking the execution of awards against them would alienate the very investors they are trying to attract by ratifying the ICSID Convention. Although investment disputes do not proceed in a political vacuum, it would certainly be inconsistent for a State to sign bilateral investment treaties and enact pro-investment legislation and then flagrantly evade the obligations they create. Award-debtor States may also fear political fallout within the World Bank community: their recalcitrance could alienate other Contracting States, which have undertaken to enforce ICSID awards on the understanding that all State parties to the Convention would do the same.

Sovereign Immunity from Execution

As the combined effect of Convention Articles 54(3) and 55 is to subject the execution of ICSID awards to national laws on sovereign immunity, prospective investors should examine these laws with great care. Sovereign immunity laws vary greatly from one State to another. Some shield States with absolute immunity from execution, for example, whereas others allow execution against sovereign assets used for commercial purposes or against assets related to the obligation to be enforced. In addition, national laws extend sovereign immunity to a greater or lesser degree to the State's constituent subdivisions and agencies. Most important, under the law of the vast majority of countries, a waiver of sovereign immunity from suit – evidenced, as relevant here, by ratification of the ICSID Convention – does not imply a waiver of sovereign immunity from execution.

As noted, as of January 2003, foreign investors with favorable ICSID awards have been required to pursue execution proceedings in only three cases. All were procedurally complicated and raised issues regarding the immunity of sovereign assets used for commercial purposes. In *Benvenuti and Bonfant v. Congo*, Benvenuti applied to the Tribunal de Grande Instance of Paris for an order enforcing its ICSID award. The court granted the enforcement order, but added that it could not be executed against assets of the Congo located in France without the court's prior authorization because those assets might be protected by sovereign immunity.[161] Benvenuti appealed the decision to the Paris Court of Appeal, which struck out the qualifying language in the order on the grounds that it contradicted the ICSID Convention's simplified enforcement procedure and that the court had exceeded its authority by making a finding on the execution of the award when it had been asked only to enforce it.[162]

Execution efforts in *SOABI v. Senegal* led to similar results.[163] The Tribunal de Grande Instance of Paris granted SOABI an order for the enforcement of its ICSID award against Senegal. The Paris Court of Appeal reversed the order and blocked execution of the award, because it was not satisfied that SOABI would enforce the award only against assets specifically earmarked by Senegal for economic and commercial activities.[164] The Court of Cassation then reversed the Court of Appeal, on the ground that the lower court's enforcement order in itself did not amount to an act of execution entitling Senegal to claim sovereign immunity.[165]

In *LETCO v. Liberia*, LETCO obtained an award of damages in the amount of approximately USD9 million (after rectification) for breach of forestry concessions.[166] The US District Court for the Southern District of New York, a federal court of first instance, granted an order for the recognition and enforcement of LETCO's award against Liberia.[167] Shortly thereafter, a writ of execution was issued in LETCO's favor attaching various registration fees and taxes owed to the government of Liberia. Liberia appealed the execution order, arguing that those fees and taxes were sovereign assets immune from execution under the US Foreign Sovereign Immunities Act (*FSIA*). The court agreed and quashed the execution

---

[161] *Benvenuti & Bonfant Srl. v. The Government People's Republic of the Congo, ICSID* Case No. ARB 77/2, Decision of Tribunal de Grande Instance, Paris (13 January 1981), 1 *ICSID Reports* 368 (1993).

[162] *Benvenuti & Bonfant Srl. v. The Government People's Republic of the Congo,* ICSID Case No. ARB 77/2, Decision of Cour d'Appel, Paris (26 June 1981), 1 *ICSID Reports* 368 (1993).

[163] *Société Ouest Africaine de Bétons Industriels (SOABI) v. State of Senegal,* ICSID Case No. ARB/82/1, Award (25 February 1988), 2 *ICSID Reports* 164 (1994).

[164] *Société Ouest Africaine de Bétons Industriels (SOABI) v. State of Senegal,* ICSID Case No. ARB/82/1, Decision of Cour d'Appel, Paris (5 December 1989), 2 *ICSID Reports* 337 (1994).

[165] *Société Ouest Africaine de Bétons Industriels (SOABI) v. State of Senegal,* ICSID Case No. ARB/82/1, Decision of Cour de Cassation (11 June 1991), 2 *ICSID Reports* 341 (1994).

[166] *LETCO v. Liberia* (Decision on Rectification), *supra* note 23.

[167] *Liberian Eastern Timber Corporation v. Republic of Liberia,* ICSID Case No. ARB/83/2, Decision of United States District Court, Southern District of New York (5 September 1986), 2 *ICSID Reports* 384 (1994).

order, but it also gave LETCO leave to seek execution against commercial assets of the government of Liberia, under the commercial exception to general immunity in the FSIA.[168] LETCO then obtained execution orders attaching bank accounts of the Embassy of Liberia in Washington, DC. The US District Court for the District of Columbia (again, a federal court of first instance) quashed those orders, finding that the accounts were immune from attachment under the FSIA even though they contained funds used for both public purposes and commercial activities. The court ruled that the use of certain embassy funds for commercial activities incidental to embassy operations did not deprive the entire bank accounts of the mantle of sovereign immunity.[169]

Given the possible complications illustrated by the *Benvenuti*, *SOABI* and *LETCO* execution efforts, investors should assess possible execution fora carefully before finalizing investments and certainly before they initiate collection proceedings on ICSID awards. An investor with a monetary award in hand should attempt to locate the losing State's assets and then obtain comparative law advice to identify jurisdictions that allow attachment of at least certain categories of sovereign assets.

An alternative at the investment stage, of course, is for the investor to request the relevant State expressly to waive any and all sovereign immunity from execution in the relevant investment contract. The practical (and political) reality, however, is that States and State entities, although willing to waive their immunity from suit in ICSID contracts, rarely are able to take the next step and waive the immunity of State assets from attachment by foreign investors. Further, even when the relevant State or State entity is prepared to provide a waiver of execution immunity, the investor must also make sure to obtain advice about the validity of such a waiver under the sovereign immunity laws of expected enforcement jurisdictions.

Recourse for Failure to Recognize, Enforce or Execute ICSID Awards

Investors have limited recourse against States that choose to refuse to recognize, enforce and execute ICSID awards in spite of their Convention obligations. An investor cannot bring proceedings against the delinquent State in its own name, but must rely on its home State to institute proceedings on its behalf, perhaps even before the International Court of Justice. Although Article 27 of the ICSID Convention expressly bars a Contracting State from espousing its nationals' claims directly against another State (an otherwise accepted expression of diplomatic

---

[168] *Liberian Eastern Timber Corporation v. Republic of Liberia*, ICSID Case No. ARB/83/2, Decision of United States District Court, Southern District of New York (12 December 1986), 2 *ICSID Reports* 384 (1994) 73 (S.D.N.Y. 1986)., 650 *F.Supp.* (The Decision was affirmed on appeal on 19 May 1987 with no published opinion.).

[169] *Liberian Eastern Timber Corporation v. Republic of Liberia*, ICSID Case No. ARB/83/2, Decision of United States District Court, District of Columbia (16 April 1987), 2 *ICSID Reports* 390 (1994), 659 *F.Supp.* 606 (D.D.C. 1987).

protection under international law), Article 64 allows an investor's home State to do so for the specific purpose of enforcing against the host State a Convention obligation it has failed to honor. This default procedure obviously requires the good offices of the investor's home government, which, depending on the political circumstances, may be reluctant to proceed against a fellow Contracting State. As of January 2003, no Contracting State had yet invoked its rights under Article 64.

ANNEX 1

CONVENTION ON THE SETTLEMENT OF INVESTMENT DISPUTES BETWEEN STATES AND NATIONALS OF OTHER STATES

PREAMBLE

The Contracting States

Considering the need for international cooperation for economic development, and the role of private international investment therein;

Bearing in mind the possibility that from time to time disputes may arise in connection with such investment between Contracting States and nationals of other Contracting States;

Recognizing that while such disputes would usually be subject to national legal processes, international methods of settlement may be appropriate in certain cases;

Attaching particular importance to the availability of facilities for international conciliation or arbitration to which Contracting States and nationals of other Contracting States may submit such disputes if they so desire;

Desiring to establish such facilities under the auspices of the International Bank for Reconstruction and Development;

Recognizing that mutual consent by the parties to submit such disputes to conciliation or to arbitration through such facilities constitutes a binding agreement which requires in particular that due consideration be given to any recommendation of conciliators, and that any arbitral award be complied with; and

Declaring that no Contracting State shall by the mere fact of its ratification, acceptance or approval of this Convention and without its consent be deemed to be under any obligation to submit any particular dispute to conciliation or arbitration,

Have agreed as follows:

Lucy Reed, Jan Paulsson and Nigel Blackaby, Guide to ICSID Arbitration, 111–218
© 2004 *Kluwer Law International. Printed in The Netherlands*

CHAPTER I
International Centre for Settlement of Investment Disputes

Section 1
Establishment and Organization

Article 1

(1) There is hereby established the International Centre for Settlement of Investment Disputes (hereinafter called the Centre).

(2) The purpose of the Centre shall be to provide facilities for conciliation and arbitration of investment disputes between Contracting States and nationals of other Contracting States in accordance with the provisions of this Convention.

Article 2

The seat of the Centre shall be at the principal office of the International Bank for Reconstruction and Development (hereinafter called the Bank). The seat may be moved to another place by decision of the Administrative Council adopted by a majority of two-thirds of its members.

Article 3

The Centre shall have an Administrative Council and a Secretariat and shall maintain a Panel of Conciliators and a Panel of Arbitrators.

Section 2
The Administrative Council

Article 4

(1) The Administrative Council shall be composed of one representative of each Contracting State. An alternate may act as representative in case of his principal's absence from a meeting or inability to act.

(2) In the absence of a contrary designation, each governor and alternate governor of the Bank appointed by a Contracting State shall be *ex officio* its representative and its alternate respectively.

Article 5

The President of the Bank shall be *ex officio* Chairman of the Administrative Council (hereinafter called the Chairman) but shall have no vote. During his absence or inability to act and during any vacancy in the office of President of the Bank, the person for the time being acting as President shall act as Chairman of the Administrative Council.

Article 6

(1) Without prejudice to the powers and functions vested in it by other provisions of this Convention, the Administrative Council shall:

(a) adopt the administrative and financial regulations of the Centre;
(b) adopt the rules of procedure for the institution of conciliation and arbitration proceedings;
(c) adopt the rules of procedure for conciliation and arbitration proceedings (hereinafter called the Conciliation Rules and the Arbitration Rules);
(d) approve arrangements with the Bank for the use of the Bank's administrative facilities and services;
(e) determine the conditions of service of the Secretary-General and of any Deputy Secretary-General;
(f) adopt the annual budget of revenues and expenditures of the Centre;
(g) approve the annual report on the operation of the Centre.
The decisions referred to in sub-paragraphs (a), (b), (c) and (f) above shall be adopted by a majority of two-thirds of the members of the Administrative Council.

(2) The Administrative Council may appoint such committees as it considers necessary.
(3) The Administrative Council shall also exercise such other powers and perform such other functions as it shall determine to be necessary for the implementation of the provisions of this Convention.

Article 7

(1) The Administrative Council shall hold an annual meeting and such other meetings as may be determined by the Council, or convened by the Chairman, or convened by the Secretary-General at the request of not less than five members of the Council.
(2) Each member of the Administrative Council shall have one vote and, except as otherwise herein provided, all matters before the Council shall be decided by a majority of the votes cast.
(3) A quorum for any meeting of the Administrative Council shall be a majority of its members.
(4) The Administrative Council may establish, by a majority of two-thirds of its members, a procedure whereby the Chairman may seek a vote of the Council without convening a meeting of the Council. The vote shall be considered valid only if the majority of the members of the Council cast their votes within the time limit fixed by the said procedure.

Article 8

Members of the Administrative Council and the Chairman shall serve without remuneration from the Centre.

Section 3
The Secretariat

Article 9

The Secretariat shall consist of a Secretary-General, one or more Deputy Secretaries-General and staff.

Article 10

(1) The Secretary-General and any Deputy Secretary-General shall be elected by the

Administrative Council by a majority of two-thirds of its members upon the nomination of the Chairman for a term of service not exceeding six years and shall be eligible for re-election. After consulting the members of the Administrative Council, the Chairman shall propose one or more candidates for each such office.

(2) The offices of Secretary-General and Deputy Secretary-General shall be incompatible with the exercise of any political function. Neither the Secretary-General nor any Deputy Secretary-General may hold any other employment or engage in any other occupation except with the approval of the Administrative Council.

(3) During the Secretary-General's absence or inability to act, and during any vacancy of the office of Secretary-General, the Deputy Secretary-General shall act as Secretary-General. If there shall be more than one Deputy Secretary-General, the Administrative Council shall determine in advance the order in which they shall act as Secretary-General.

Article 11

The Secretary-General shall be the legal representative and the principal officer of the Centre and shall be responsible for its administration, including the appointment of staff, in accordance with the provisions of this Convention and the rules adopted by the Administrative Council. He shall perform the function of registrar and shall have the power to authenticate arbitral awards rendered pursuant to this Convention, and to certify copies thereof.

Section 4
The Panels

Article 12

The Panel of Conciliators and the Panel of Arbitrators shall each consist of qualified persons, designated as hereinafter provided, who are willing to serve thereon.

Article 13

(1) Each Contracting State may designate to each Panel four persons who may but need not be its nationals.

(2) The Chairman may designate ten persons to each Panel. The persons so designated to a Panel shall each have a different nationality.

Article 14

(1) Persons designated to serve on the Panels shall be persons of high moral character and recognized competence in the fields of law, commerce, industry or finance, who may be relied upon to exercise independent judgment. Competence in the field of law shall be of particular importance in the case of persons on the Panel of Arbitrators.

(2) The Chairman, in designating persons to serve on the Panels, shall in addition pay due regard to the importance of assuring representation on the Panels of the principal legal systems of the world and of the main forms of economic activity.

Article 15

(1) Panel members shall serve for renewable periods of six years.

(2) In case of death or resignation of a member of a Panel, the authority which designated the member shall have the right to designate another person to serve for the remainder of that member's term.

(3) Panel members shall continue in office until their successors have been designated.

Article 16

(1) A person may serve on both Panels.

(2) If a person shall have been designated to serve on the same Panel by more than one Contracting State, or by one or more Contracting States and the Chairman, he shall be deemed to have been designated by the authority which first designated him or, if one such authority is the State of which he is a national, by that State.

(3) All designations shall be notified to the Secretary-General and shall take effect from the date on which the notification is received.

Section 5
Financing the Centre

Article 17

If the expenditure of the Centre cannot be met out of charges for the use of its facilities, or out of other receipts, the excess shall be borne by Contracting States which are members of the Bank in proportion to their respective subscriptions to the capital stock of the Bank, and by Contracting States which are not members of the Bank in accordance with rules adopted by the Administrative Council.

Section 6
Status, Immunities and Privileges

Article 18

The Centre shall have full international legal personality. The legal capacity of the Centre shall include the capacity:

    (a) to contract;
    (b) to acquire and dispose of movable and immovable property;
    (c) to institute legal proceedings.

Article 19

To enable the Centre to fulfil its functions, it shall enjoy in the territories of each Contracting State the immunities and privileges set forth in this Section.

Article 20

The Centre, its property and assets shall enjoy immunity from all legal process, except when the Centre waives this immunity.

Article 21

The Chairman, the members of the Administrative Council, persons acting as conciliators or arbitrators or members of a Committee appointed pursuant to paragraph (3) of Article 52, and the officers and employees of the Secretariat

   (a) shall enjoy immunity from legal process with respect to acts performed by them in the exercise of their functions, except when the Centre waives this immunity;
   (b) not being local nationals, shall enjoy the same immunities from immigration restrictions, alien registration requirements and national service obligations, the same facilities as regards exchange restrictions and the same treatment in respect of travelling facilities as are accorded by Contracting States to the representatives, officials and employees of comparable rank of other Contracting States.

Article 22

The provisions of Article 21 shall apply to persons appearing in proceedings under this Convention as parties, agents, counsel, advocates, witnesses or experts; provided, however, that sub-paragraph (b) thereof shall apply only in connection with their travel to and from, and their stay at, the place where the proceedings are held.

Article 23

(1) The archives of the Centre shall be inviolable, wherever they may be.
(2) With regard to its official communications, the Centre shall be accorded by each Contracting State treatment not less favourable than that accorded to other international organizations.

Article 24

(1) The Centre, its assets, property and income, and its operations and transactions authorized by this Convention shall be exempt from all taxation and customs duties. The Centre shall also be exempt from liability for the collection or payment of any taxes or customs duties.
(2) Except in the case of local nationals, no tax shall be levied on or in respect of expense allowances paid by the Centre to the Chairman or members of the Administrative Council, or on or in respect of salaries, expense allowances or other emoluments paid by the Centre to officials or employees of the Secretariat.
(3) No tax shall be levied on or in respect of fees or expense allowances received by persons acting as conciliators, or arbitrators, or members of a Committee appointed pursuant to paragraph (3) of Article 52, in proceedings under this Convention, if the sole jurisdictional basis for such tax is the location of the Centre or the place where such proceedings are conducted or the place where such fees or allowances are paid.

CHAPTER II
Jurisdiction of the Centre

Article 25

(1) The jurisdiction of the Centre shall extend to any legal dispute arising directly out of an investment, between a Contracting State (or any constituent subdivision or agency of a Contracting State designated to the Centre by that State) and a national of another Contracting State, which the parties to the dispute consent in writing to submit to the Centre. When the parties have given their consent, no party may withdraw its consent unilaterally.
(2) "National of another Contracting State" means:

    (a) any natural person who had the nationality of a Contracting State other than the State party to the dispute on the date on which the parties consented to submit such dispute to conciliation or arbitration as well as on the date on which the request was registered pursuant to paragraph (3) of Article 28 or paragraph (3) of Article 36, but does not include any person who on either date also had the nationality of the Contracting State party to the dispute; and

    (b) any juridical person which had the nationality of a Contracting State other than the State party to the dispute on the date on which the parties consented to submit such dispute to conciliation or arbitration and any juridical person which had the nationality of the Contracting State party to the dispute on that date and which, because of foreign control, the parties have agreed should be treated as a national of another Contracting State for the purposes of this Convention.

(3) Consent by a constituent subdivision or agency of a Contracting State shall require the approval of that State unless that State notifies the Centre that no such approval is required.
(4) Any Contracting State may, at the time of ratification, acceptance or approval of this Convention or at any time thereafter, notify the Centre of the class or classes of disputes which it would or would not consider submitting to the jurisdiction of the Centre. The Secretary-General shall forthwith transmit such notification to all Contracting States. Such notification shall not constitute the consent required by paragraph (1).

Article 26

Consent of the parties to arbitration under this Convention shall, unless otherwise stated, be deemed consent to such arbitration to the exclusion of any other remedy. A Contracting State may require the exhaustion of local administrative or judicial remedies as a condition of its consent to arbitration under this Convention.

Article 27

(1) No Contracting State shall give diplomatic protection, or bring an international claim, in respect of a dispute which one of its nationals and another Contracting State shall have consented to submit or shall have submitted to arbitration under this Convention, unless such other Contracting State shall have failed to abide by and comply with the award rendered in such dispute.
(2) Diplomatic protection, for the purposes of paragraph (1), shall not include informal diplomatic exchanges for the sole purpose of facilitating a settlement of the dispute.

CHAPTER III
Conciliation

Section 1
Request for Conciliation

Article 28

(1) Any Contracting State or any national of a Contracting State wishing to institute conciliation proceedings shall address a request to that effect in writing to the Secretary-General who shall send a copy of the request to the other party.

(2) The request shall contain information concerning the issues in dispute, the identity of the parties and their consent to conciliation in accordance with the rules of procedure for the institution of conciliation and arbitration proceedings.

(3) The Secretary-General shall register the request unless he finds, on the basis of the information contained in the request, that the dispute is manifestly outside the jurisdiction of the Centre. He shall forthwith notify the parties of registration or refusal to register.

Section 2
Constitution of the Conciliation Commission

Article 29

(1) The Conciliation Commission (hereinafter called the Commission) shall be constituted as soon as possible after registration of a request pursuant to Article 28.

(2) (a) The Commission shall consist of a sole conciliator or any uneven number of conciliators appointed as the parties shall agree.

(b) Where the parties do not agree upon the number of conciliators and the method of their appointment, the Commission shall consist of three conciliators, one conciliator appointed by each party and the third, who shall be the president of the Commission, appointed by agreement of the parties.

Article 30

If the Commission shall not have been constituted within 90 days after notice of registration of the request has been dispatched by the Secretary-General in accordance with paragraph (3) of Article 28, or such other period as the parties may agree, the Chairman shall, at the request of either party and after consulting both parties as far as possible, appoint the conciliator or conciliators not yet appointed.

Article 31

(1) Conciliators may be appointed from outside the Panel of Conciliators, except in the case of appointments by the Chairman pursuant to Article 30.

(2) Conciliators appointed from outside the Panel of Conciliators shall possess the qualities stated in paragraph (1) of Article 14.

Section 3
Conciliation Proceedings

Article 32

(1) The Commission shall be the judge of its own competence.

(2) Any objection by a party to the dispute that that dispute is not within the jurisdiction of the Centre, or for other reasons is not within the competence of the Commission, shall be considered by the Commission which shall determine whether to deal with it as a preliminary question or to join it to the merits of the dispute.

Article 33

Any conciliation proceeding shall be conducted in accordance with the provisions of this Section and, except as the parties otherwise agree, in accordance with the Conciliation Rules in effect on the date on which the parties consented to conciliation. If any question of procedure arises which is not covered by this Section or the Conciliation Rules or any rules agreed by the parties, the Commission shall decide the question.

Article 34

(1) It shall be the duty of the Commission to clarify the issues in dispute between the parties and to endeavour to bring about agreement between them upon mutually acceptable terms. To that end, the Commission may at any stage of the proceedings and from time to time recommend terms of settlement to the parties. The parties shall cooperate in good faith with the Commission in order to enable the Commission to carry out its functions, and shall give their most serious consideration to its recommendations.

(2) If the parties reach agreement, the Commission shall draw up a report noting the issues in dispute and recording that the parties have reached agreement. If, at any stage of the proceedings, it appears to the Commission that there is no likelihood of agreement between the parties, it shall close the proceedings and shall draw up a report noting the submission of the dispute and recording the failure of the parties to reach agreement. If one party fails to appear or participate in the proceedings, the Commission shall close the proceedings and shall draw up a report noting that party's failure to appear or participate.

Article 35

Except as the parties to the dispute shall otherwise agree, neither party to a conciliation proceeding shall be entitled in any other proceeding, whether before arbitrators or in a court of law or otherwise, to invoke or rely on any views expressed or statements or admissions or offers of settlement made by the other party in the conciliation proceedings, or the report or any recommendations made by the Commission.

CHAPTER IV
Arbitration

Section I
Request for Arbitration

Article 36

(1) Any Contracting State or any national of a Contracting State wishing to institute arbitration proceedings shall address a request to that effect in writing to the Secretary-General who shall send a copy of the request to the other party.

(2) The request shall contain information concerning the issues in dispute, the identity of the parties and their consent to arbitration in accordance with the rules of procedure for the institution of conciliation and arbitration proceedings.

(3) The Secretary-General shall register the request unless he finds, on the basis of the information contained in the request, that the dispute is manifestly outside the jurisdiction of the Centre. He shall forthwith notify the parties of registration or refusal to register.

Section 2
Constitution of the Tribunal

Article 37

(1) The Arbitral Tribunal (hereinafter called the Tribunal) shall be constituted as soon as possible after registration of a request pursuant to Article 36.

(2) (a) The Tribunal shall consist of a sole arbitrator or any uneven number of arbitrators appointed as the parties shall agree.

(b) Where the parties do not agree upon the number of arbitrators and the method of their appointment, the Tribunal shall consist of three arbitrators, one arbitrator appointed by each party and the third, who shall be the president of the Tribunal, appointed by agreement of the parties.

Article 38

If the Tribunal shall not have been constituted within 90 days after notice of registration of the request has been dispatched by the Secretary-General in accordance with paragraph (3) of Article 36, or such other period as the parties may agree, the Chairman shall, at the request of either party and after consulting both parties as far as possible, appoint the arbitrator or arbitrators not yet appointed. Arbitrators appointed by the Chairman pursuant to this Article shall not be nationals of the Contracting State party to the dispute or of the Contracting State whose national is a party to the dispute.

Article 39

The majority of the arbitrators shall be nationals of States other than the Contracting State party to the dispute and the Contracting State whose national is a party to the dispute; provided, however, that the foregoing provisions of this Article shall not apply if the sole arbitrator or each individual member of the Tribunal has been appointed by agreement of the parties.

Article 40

(1) Arbitrators may be appointed from outside the Panel of Arbitrators, except in the case of appointments by the Chairman pursuant to Article 38.
(2) Arbitrators appointed from outside the Panel of Arbitrators shall possess the qualities stated in paragraph (1) of Article 14.

Section 3
Powers and Functions of the Tribunal

Article 41

(1) The Tribunal shall be the judge of its own competence.
(2) Any objection by a party to the dispute that that dispute is not within the jurisdiction of the Centre, or for other reasons is not within the competence of the Tribunal, shall be considered by the Tribunal which shall determine whether to deal with it as a preliminary question or to join it to the merits of the dispute.

Article 42

(1) The Tribunal shall decide a dispute in accordance with such rules of law as may be agreed by the parties. In the absence of such agreement, the Tribunal shall apply the law of the Contracting State party to the dispute (including its rules on the conflict of laws) and such rules of international law as may be applicable.
(2) The Tribunal may not bring in a finding of *non liquet* on the ground of silence or obscurity of the law.
(3) The provisions of paragraphs (1) and (2) shall not prejudice the power of the Tribunal to decide a dispute *ex aequo et bono* if the parties so agree.

Article 43

Except as the parties otherwise agree, the Tribunal may, if it deems it necessary at any stage of the proceedings,

(a) call upon the parties to produce documents or other evidence, and
(b) visit the scene connected with the dispute, and conduct such inquiries there as it may deem appropriate.

Article 44

Any arbitration proceeding shall be conducted in accordance with the provisions of this Section and, except as the parties otherwise agree, in accordance with the Arbitration Rules in effect on the date on which the parties consented to arbitration. If any question of procedure arises which is not covered by this Section or the Arbitration Rules or any rules agreed by the parties, the Tribunal shall decide the question.

Article 45

(1) Failure of a party to appear or to present his case shall not be deemed an admission of the other party's assertions.

(2) If a party fails to appear or to present his case at any stage of the proceedings the other party may request the Tribunal to deal with the questions submitted to it and to render an award. Before rendering an award, the Tribunal shall notify, and grant a period of grace to, the party failing to appear or to present its case, unless it is satisfied that that party does not intend to do so.

Article 46

Except as the parties otherwise agree, the Tribunal shall, if requested by a party, determine any incidental or additional claims or counterclaims arising directly out of the subject-matter of the dispute provided that they are within the scope of the consent of the parties and are otherwise within the jurisdiction of the Centre.

Article 47

Except as the parties otherwise agree, the Tribunal may, if it considers that the circumstances so require, recommend any provisional measures which should be taken to preserve the respective rights of either party.

Section 4
The Award

Article 48

(1) The Tribunal shall decide questions by a majority of the votes of all its members.

(2) The award of the Tribunal shall be in writing and shall be signed by the members of the Tribunal who voted for it.

(3) The award shall deal with every question submitted to the Tribunal, and shall state the reasons upon which it is based.

(4) Any member of the Tribunal may attach his individual opinion to the award, whether he dissents from the majority or not, or a statement of his dissent.

(5) The Centre shall not publish the award without the consent of the parties.

Article 49

(1) The Secretary-General shall promptly dispatch certified copies of the award to the parties. The award shall be deemed to have been rendered on the date on which the certified copies were dispatched.

(2) The Tribunal upon the request of a party made within 45 days after the date on which the award was rendered may after notice to the other party decide any question which it had omitted to decide in the award, and shall rectify any clerical, arithmetical or similar error in the award. Its decision shall become part of the award and shall be notified to the parties in the same manner as the award. The periods of time provided for under paragraph (2) of Article 51 and paragraph (2) of Article 52 shall run from the date on which the decision was rendered.

Section 5
Interpretation, Revision and Annulment of the Award

Article 50

(1) If any dispute shall arise between the parties as to the meaning or scope of an award, either party may request interpretation of the award by an application in writing addressed to the Secretary-General.

(2) The request shall, if possible, be submitted to the Tribunal which rendered the award. If this shall not be possible, a new Tribunal shall be constituted in accordance with Section 2 of this Chapter. The Tribunal may, if it considers that the circumstances so require, stay enforcement of the award pending its decision.

Article 51

(1) Either party may request revision of the award by an application in writing addressed to the Secretary-General on the ground of discovery of some fact of such a nature as decisively to affect the award, provided that when the award was rendered that fact was unknown to the Tribunal and to the applicant and that the applicant's ignorance of that fact was not due to negligence.

(2) The application shall be made within 90 days after the discovery of such fact and in any event within three years after the date on which the award was rendered.

(3) The request shall, if possible, be submitted to the Tribunal which rendered the award. If this shall not be possible, a new Tribunal shall be constituted in accordance with Section 2 of this Chapter.

(4) The Tribunal may, if it considers that the circumstances so require, stay enforcement of the award pending its decision. If the applicant requests a stay of enforcement of the award in his application, enforcement shall be stayed provisionally until the Tribunal rules on such request.

Article 52

(1) Either party may request annulment of the award by an application in writing addressed to the Secretary-General on one or more of the following grounds:

    (a) that the Tribunal was not properly constituted;
    (b) that the Tribunal has manifestly exceeded its powers;
    (c) that there was corruption on the part of a member of the Tribunal;
    (d) that there has been a serious departure from a fundamental rule of procedure; or
    (e) that the award has failed to state the reasons on which it is based.

(2) The application shall be made within 120 days after the date on which the award was rendered except that when annulment is requested on the ground of corruption such application shall be made within 120 days after discovery of the corruption and in any event within three years after the date on which the award was rendered.

(3) On receipt of the request the Chairman shall forthwith appoint from the Panel of Arbitrators an ad hoc Committee of three persons. None of the members of the Committee shall have been a member of the Tribunal which rendered the award, shall be of the same nationality as any such member, shall be a national of the State party to the dispute or of the

State whose national is a party to the dispute, shall have been designated to the Panel of Arbitrators by either of those States, or shall have acted as a conciliator in the same dispute. The Committee shall have the authority to annul the award or any part thereof on any of the grounds set forth in paragraph (1).

(4) The provisions of Articles 41-45, 48, 49, 53 and 54, and of Chapters VI and VII shall apply mutatis mutandis to proceedings before the Committee.

(5) The Committee may, if it considers that the circumstances so require, stay enforcement of the award pending its decision. If the applicant requests a stay of enforcement of the award in his application, enforcement shall be stayed provisionally until the Committee rules on such request.

(6) If the award is annulled the dispute shall, at the request of either party, be submitted to a new Tribunal constituted in accordance with Section 2 of this Chapter.

Section 6
Recognition and Enforcement of the Award

Article 53

(1) The award shall be binding on the parties and shall not be subject to any appeal or to any other remedy except those provided for in this Convention. Each party shall abide by and comply with the terms of the award except to the extent that enforcement shall have been stayed pursuant to the relevant provisions of this Convention.

(2) For the purposes of this Section, "award" shall include any decision interpreting, revising or annulling such award pursuant to Articles 50, 51 or 52.

Article 54

(1) Each Contracting State shall recognize an award rendered pursuant to this Convention as binding and enforce the pecuniary obligations imposed by that award within its territories as if it were a final judgment of a court in that State. A Contracting State with a federal constitution may enforce such an award in or through its federal courts and may provide that such courts shall treat the award as if it were a final judgment of the courts of a constituent state.

(2) A party seeking recognition or enforcement in the territories of a Contracting State shall furnish to a competent court or other authority which such State shall have designated for this purpose a copy of the award certified by the Secretary-General. Each Contracting State shall notify the Secretary-General of the designation of the competent court or other authority for this purpose and of any subsequent change in such designation.

(3) Execution of the award shall be governed by the laws concerning the execution of judgments in force in the State in whose territories such execution is sought.

Article 55

Nothing in Article 54 shall be construed as derogating from the law in force in any Contracting State relating to immunity of that State or of any foreign State from execution.

CHAPTER V
Replacement and Disqualification of Conciliators and Arbitrators

Article 56

(1) After a Commission or a Tribunal has been constituted and proceedings have begun, its composition shall remain unchanged; provided, however, that if a conciliator or an arbitrator should die, become incapacitated, or resign, the resulting vacancy shall be filled in accordance with the provisions of Section 2 of Chapter III or Section 2 of Chapter IV.

(2) A member of a Commission or Tribunal shall continue to serve in that capacity notwithstanding that he shall have ceased to be a member of the Panel.

(3) If a conciliator or arbitrator appointed by a party shall have resigned without the consent of the Commission or Tribunal of which he was a member, the Chairman shall appoint a person from the appropriate Panel to fill the resulting vacancy.

Article 57

A party may propose to a Commission or Tribunal the disqualification of any of its members on account of any fact indicating a manifest lack of the qualities required by paragraph (1) of Article 14. A party to arbitration proceedings may, in addition, propose the disqualification of an arbitrator on the ground that he was ineligible for appointment to the Tribunal under Section 2 of Chapter IV.

Article 58

The decision on any proposal to disqualify a conciliator or arbitrator shall be taken by the other members of the Commission or Tribunal as the case may be, provided that where those members are equally divided, or in the case of a proposal to disqualify a sole conciliator or arbitrator, or a majority of the conciliators or arbitrators, the Chairman shall take that decision. If it is decided that the proposal is well-founded the conciliator or arbitrator to whom the decision relates shall be replaced in accordance with the provisions of Section 2 of Chapter III or Section 2 of Chapter IV.

CHAPTER VI
Cost of Proceedings

Article 59

The charges payable by the parties for the use of the facilities of the Centre shall be determined by the Secretary-General in accordance with the regulations adopted by the Administrative Council.

Article 60

(1) Each Commission and each Tribunal shall determine the fees and expenses of its members within limits established from time to time by the Administrative Council and after consultation with the Secretary-General.

(2) Nothing in paragraph (1) of this Article shall preclude the parties from agreeing in advance with the Commission or Tribunal concerned upon the fees and expenses of its members.

Article 61

(1) In the case of conciliation proceedings the fees and expenses of members of the Commission as well as the charges for the use of the facilities of the Centre, shall be borne equally by the parties. Each party shall bear any other expenses it incurs in connection with the proceedings.

(2) In the case of arbitration proceedings the Tribunal shall, except as the parties otherwise agree, assess the expenses incurred by the parties in connection with the proceedings, and shall decide how and by whom those expenses, the fees and expenses of the members of the Tribunal and the charges for the use of the facilities of the Centre shall be paid. Such decision shall form part of the award.

CHAPTER VII
Place of Proceedings

Article 62

Conciliation and arbitration proceedings shall be held at the seat of the Centre except as hereinafter provided.

Article 63

Conciliation and arbitration proceedings may be held, if the parties so agree,

(a) at the seat of the Permanent Court of Arbitration or of any other appropriate institution, whether private or public, with which the Centre may make arrangements for that purpose; or

(b) at any other place approved by the Commission or Tribunal after consultation with the Secretary-General.

CHAPTER VIII
Disputes Between Contracting States

Article 64

Any dispute arising between Contracting States concerning the interpretation or application of this Convention which is not settled by negotiation shall be referred to the International Court of Justice by the application of any party to such dispute, unless the States concerned agree to another method of settlement.

CHAPTER IX
Amendment

Article 65

Any Contracting State may propose amendment of this Convention. The text of a proposed amendment shall be communicated to the Secretary-General not less than 90 days prior to the meeting of the Administrative Council at which such amendment is to be considered and shall forthwith be transmitted by him to all the members of the Administrative Council.

Article 66

(1) If the Administrative Council shall so decide by a majority of two-thirds of its members, the proposed amendment shall be circulated to all Contracting States for ratification, acceptance or approval. Each amendment shall enter into force 30 days after dispatch by the depositary of this Convention of a notification to Contracting States that all Contracting States have ratified, accepted or approved the amendment.

(2) No amendment shall affect the rights and obligations under this Convention of any Contracting State or of any of its constituent subdivisions or agencies, or of any national of such State arising out of consent to the jurisdiction of the Centre given before the date of entry into force of the amendment.

CHAPTER X
Final Provisions

Article 67

This Convention shall be open for signature on behalf of States members of the Bank. It shall also be open for signature on behalf of any other State which is a party to the Statute of the International Court of Justice and which the Administrative Council, by a vote of two-thirds of its members, shall have invited to sign the Convention.

Article 68

(1) This Convention shall be subject to ratification, acceptance or approval by the signatory States in accordance with their respective constitutional procedures.

(2) This Convention shall enter into force 30 days after the date of deposit of the twentieth instrument of ratification, acceptance or approval. It shall enter into force for each State which subsequently deposits its instrument of ratification, acceptance or approval 30 days after the date of such deposit.

Article 69

Each Contracting State shall take such legislative or other measures as may be necessary for making the provisions of this Convention effective in its territories.

Article 70

This Convention shall apply to all territories for whose international relations a Contracting State is responsible, except those which are excluded by such State by written notice to the depositary of this Convention either at the time of ratification, acceptance or approval or subsequently.

Article 71

Any Contracting State may denounce this Convention by written notice to the depositary of this Convention. The denunciation shall take effect six months after receipt of such notice.

Article 72

Notice by a Contracting State pursuant to Articles 70 or 71 shall not affect the rights or obligations under this Convention of that State or of any of its constituent subdivisions or agencies or of any national of that State arising out of consent to the jurisdiction of the Centre given by one of them before such notice was received by the depositary.

Article 73

Instruments of ratification, acceptance or approval of this Convention and of amendments thereto shall be deposited with the Bank which shall act as the depositary of this Convention. The depositary shall transmit certified copies of this Convention to States members of the Bank and to any other State invited to sign the Convention.

Article 74

The depositary shall register this Convention with the Secretariat of the United Nations in accordance with Article 102 of the Charter of the United Nations and the Regulations thereunder adopted by the General Assembly.

Article 75

The depositary shall notify all signatory States of the following:

  (a) signatures in accordance with Article 67;
  (b) deposits of instruments of ratification, acceptance and approval in accordance with Article 73;
  (c) the date on which this Convention enters into force in accordance with Article 68;
  (d) exclusions from territorial application pursuant to Article 70;
  (e) the date on which any amendment of this Convention enters into force in accordance with Article 66; and
  (f) denunciations in accordance with Article 71.

DONE at Washington, in the English, French and Spanish languages, all three texts being equally authentic, in a single copy which shall remain deposited in the archives of the International Bank for Reconstruction and Development, which has indicated by its signature below its agreement to fulfil the functions with which it is charged under this Convention.

ANNEX 2

LIST OF ICSID CONTRACTING STATES
(as of November 3, 2003)

State	Signature	Deposit of Ratification	Entry into Force of Convention
Afghanistan	Sep 30, 1966	June 25, 1968	July 25, 1968
Albania	Oct 15, 1991	Oct 15, 1991	Nov 14, 1991
Algeria	Apr 17, 1995	Feb 21, 1996	Mar 22, 1996
Argentina	May 21, 1991	Oct 19, 1994	Nov 18, 1994
Armenia	Sep 16, 1992	Sep 16, 1992	Oct 16, 1992
Australia	Mar 24, 1975	May 2, 1991	June 1, 1991
Austria	May 17, 1966	May 25, 1971	June 24, 1971
Azerbaijan	Sep 18, 1992	Sep 18, 1992	Oct 18, 1992
Bahamas	Oct 19, 1995	Oct 19, 1995	Nov 18, 1995
Bahrain	Sep 22, 1995	Feb 14, 1996	Mar 15, 1996
Bangladesh	Nov 20, 1979	Mar 27, 1980	Apr 26, 1980
Barbados	May 13, 1981	Nov 1, 1983	Dec 1, 1983
Belarus	July 10, 1992	July 10, 1992	Aug 9, 1992
Belgium	Dec 15, 1965	Aug 27, 1970	Sep 26, 1970
Belize	Dec 19, 1986		
Benin	Sep 10, 1965	Sep 6, 1966	Oct 14, 1966
Bolivia	May 3, 1991	June 23, 1995	July 23, 1995
Bosnia and Herzegovina	Apr 25, 1997	May 14, 1997	June 13, 1997
Botswana	Jan 15, 1970	Jan 15, 1970	Feb 14, 1970
Brunei Darussalam	Sep 16, 2002	Sep 16, 2002	Oct 16, 2002
Bulgaria	Mar 21, 2000	Apr 13, 2001	May 13, 2001
Burkina Faso	Sep 16, 1965	Aug 29, 1966	Oct 14, 1966
Burundi	Feb 17, 1967	Nov 5, 1969	Dec 5, 1969
Cambodia	Nov 5, 1993		
Cameroon	Sep 23, 1965	Jan 3, 1967	Feb 2, 1967
Central African Republic	Aug 26, 1965	Feb 23, 1966	Oct 14, 1966
Chad	May 12, 1966	Aug 29, 1966	Oct 14, 1966
Chile	Jan 25, 1991	Sep 24, 1991	Oct 24, 1991
China	Feb 9, 1990	Jan 7, 1993	Feb 6, 1993
Colombia	May 18, 1993	July 15, 1997	Aug 14, 1997
Comoros	Sep 26, 1978	Nov 7, 1978	Dec 7, 1978
Congo	Dec 27, 1965	June 23, 1966	Oct 14, 1966
Congo, Democratic Rep of	Oct 29, 1968	Apr 29, 1970	May 29, 1970
Costa Rica	Sep 29, 1981	Apr 27, 1993	May 27, 1993

Table (continued)

State	Signature	Deposit of Ratification	Entry into Force of Convention
Côte d'Ivoire	June 30, 1965	Feb 16, 1966	Oct 14, 1966
Croatia	June 16, 1997	Sep 22, 1998	Oct 22, 1998
Cyprus	Mar 9, 1966	Nov 25, 1966	Dec 25, 1966
Czech Republic	Mar 23, 1993	Mar 23, 1993	Apr 22, 1993
Dominican Republic	Mar 20, 2000		
Denmark	Oct 11, 1965	Apr 24, 1968	May 24, 1968
Ecuador	Jan 15, 1986	Jan 15, 1986	Feb 14, 1986
Egypt, Arab Rep of	Feb 11, 1972	May 3, 1972	June 2, 1972
El Salvador	June 9, 1982	Mar 6, 1984	Apr 5, 1984
Estonia	June 23, 1992	June 23, 1992	Jul 23, 1992
Ethiopia	Sep 21, 1965		
Fiji	July 1, 1977	Aug 11, 1977	Sep 10, 1977
Finland	July 14, 1967	Jan 9, 1969	Feb 8, 1969
France	Dec 22, 1965	Aug 21, 1967	Sep 20, 1967
Gabon	Sep 21, 1965	Apr 4, 1966	Oct 14, 1966
Gambia, The	Oct 1, 1974	Dec 27, 1974	Jan 26, 1975
Georgia	Aug 7, 1992	Aug 7, 1992	Sep 6, 1992
Germany	Jan 27, 1966	Apr 18, 1969	May 18, 1969
Ghana	Nov 26, 1965	July 13, 1966	Oct 14, 1966
Greece	Mar 16, 1966	Apr 21, 1969	May 21, 1969
Grenada	May 24, 1991	May 24, 1991	June 23, 1991
Guatemala	Nov 9, 1995	Jan 21, 2003	Feb 20, 2003
Guinea	Aug 27,1968	Nov 4, 1968	Dec 4, 1968
Guinea-Bissau	Sep 4, 1991		
Guyana	July 3, 1969	July 11, 1969	Aug 10, 1969
Haiti	Jan 30, 1985		
Honduras	May 28, 1986	Feb 14, 1989	Mar 16, 1989
Hungary	Oct 1, 1986	Feb 4, 1987	Mar 6, 1987
Iceland	July 25, 1966	July 25, 1966	Oct 14, 1966
Indonesia	Feb 16, 1968	Sep 28, 1968	Oct 28, 1968
Ireland	Aug 30, 1966	Apr 7, 1981	May 7, 1981
Israel	June 16, 1980	June 22, 1983	July 22, 1983
Italy	Nov 18, 1965	Mar 29, 1971	Apr 28, 1971
Jamaica	June 23, 1965	Sep 9, 1966	Oct 14, 1966
Japan	Sep 23, 1965	Aug 17, 1967	Sep 16, 1967
Jordan	July 14, 1972	Oct 30, 1972	Nov 29, 1972
Kazakhstan	July 23, 1992	Sep 21, 2000	Oct 21, 2000
Kenya	May 24, 1966	Jan 3, 1967	Feb 2, 1967
Kyrgyz, Rep of	June 9, 1995		
Korea, Rep of	Apr 18, 1966	Feb 21, 1967	Mar 23, 1967
Kuwait	Feb 9, 1978	Feb 2, 1979	Mar 4, 1979

Table (continued)

State	Signature	Deposit of Ratification	Entry into Force of Convention
Latvia	Aug 8, 1997	Aug 8, 1997	Sep 7, 1997
Lebanon	Mar 26, 2003	Mar 26, 2003	Apr 25, 2003
Lesotho	Sep 19, 1968	July 8, 1969	Aug 7, 1969
Liberia	Sep 3, 1965	June 16, 1970	July 16, 1970
Lithuania	July 6, 1992	July 6, 1992	Aug 5, 1992
Luxembourg	Sep 28, 1965	July 30, 1970	Aug 29, 1970
Macedonia, former Yugoslav Rep of	Sep 16, 1998	Oct 27, 1998	Nov 26, 1998
Madagascar	June 1, 1966	Sep 6, 1966	Oct 14, 1966
Malawi	June 9, 1966	Aug 23, 1966	Oct 14, 1966
Malaysia	Oct 22, 1965	Aug 8, 1966	Oct 14, 1966
Mali	Apr 9, 1976	Jan 3, 1978	Feb 2, 1978
Malta	Apr 24, 2002	Nov 3, 2003	Nov 3, 2003
Mauritania	July 30, 1965	Jan 11, 1966	Oct 14, 1966
Mauritius	June 2, 1969	June 2, 1969	July 2, 1969
Micronesia	June 24, 1993	June 24, 1993	July 24, 1993
Moldova	Aug 12,1992		
Mongolia	June 14, 1991	June 14, 1991	July 14, 1991
Morocco	Oct 11, 1965	May 11, 1967	June 10, 1967
Mozambique	Apr 4, 1995	June 7, 1995	July 7, 1995
Namibia	Oct 26, 1998		
Nepal	Sep 28, 1965	Jan 7, 1969	Feb 6, 1969
Netherlands	May 25, 1966	Sep 14, 1966	Oct 14, 1966
New Zealand	Sep 2, 1970	Apr 2, 1980	May 2, 1980
Nicaragua	Feb 4, 1994	Mar 20, 1995	Apr 19, 1995
Niger	Aug 23, 1965	Nov 14, 1966	Dec 14, 1966
Nigeria	July 13, 1965	Aug 23, 1965	Oct 14, 1966
Norway	June 24, 1966	Aug 16, 1967	Sep 15, 1967
Oman	May 5, 1995	July 24, 1995	Aug 23, 1995
Pakistan	July 6, 1965	Sep 15, 1966	Oct 15, 1966
Panama	Nov 22, 1995	Apr 8, 1996	May 8, 1996
Papua New Guinea	Oct 20, 1978	Oct 20, 1978	Nov 19, 1978
Paraguay	July 27, 1981	Jan 7, 1983	Feb 6, 1983
Peru	Sep 4, 1991	Aug 9, 1993	Sep 8, 1993
Philippines	Sep 26, 1978	Nov 17, 1978	Dec 17, 1978
Portugal	Aug 4, 1983	July 2, 1984	Aug 1, 1984
Romania	Sep 6, 1974	Sep 12, 1975	Oct 12, 1975
Russian Federation	June 16, 1992		
Rwanda	Apr 21, 1978	Oct 15, 1979	Nov 14, 1979
Saint Vincent and the Grenadines	Aug 7, 2001	Dec 16, 2002	Jan 15, 2003
Samoa	Feb 3, 1978	Apr 25, 1978	May 25, 1978
Sao Tome and Principe	Oct 1, 1999		

Table (continued)

State	Signature	Deposit of Ratification	Entry into Force of Convention
Saudi Arabia	Sep 28, 1979	May 8, 1980	June 7, 1980
Senegal	Sep 26, 1966	Apr 21, 1967	May 21, 1967
Serbia and Montenegro	July 31, 2002		
Seychelles	Feb 16, 1978	Mar 20, 1978	Apr 19, 1978
Sierra Leone	Sep 27, 1965	Aug 2, 1966	Oct 14, 1966
Singapore	Feb 2, 1968	Oct 14, 1968	Nov 13, 1968
Slovak Republic	Sep 27, 1993	May 27, 1994	June 26, 1994
Slovenia	Mar 7, 1994	Mar 7, 1994	Apr 6, 1994
Solomon Islands	Nov 12, 1979	Sep 8, 1981	Oct 8, 1981
Somalia	Sep 27, 1965	Feb 29, 1968	Mar 30, 1968
Spain	Mar 21, 1994	Aug 18, 1994	Sept 17, 1994
Sri Lanka	Aug 30, 1967	Oct 12, 1967	Nov 11, 1967
St Kitts & Nevis	Oct 14, 1994	Aug 4, 1995	Sep 3, 1995
St Lucia	June 4, 1984	June 4, 1984	July 4, 1984
Sudan	Mar 15, 1967	Apr 9, 1973	May 9, 1973
Swaziland	Nov 3, 1970	June 14, 1971	July 14, 1971
Sweden	Sep 25, 1965	Dec 29, 1966	Jan 28, 1967
Switzerland	Sep 22, 1967	May 15, 1968	June 14, 1968
Tanzania	Jan 10, 1992	May 18, 1992	June 17, 1992
Thailand	Dec 6, 1985		
Timor-Leste	July 23, 2002	July 23, 2002	Aug 22, 2002
Togo	Jan 24, 1966	Aug 11,967	Sep 10, 1967
Tonga	May 1, 1989	Mar 21, 1990	Apr 20, 1990
Trinidad and Tobago	Oct 5, 1966	Jan 3, 1967	Feb 2, 1967
Tunisia	May 5, 1965	June 22, 1966	Oct 14, 1966
Turkey	June 24, 1987	Mar 3, 1989	Apr 2, 1989
Turkmenistan	Sep 26, 1992	Sep 26, 1992	Oct 26, 1992
Uganda	June 7, 1966	June 7, 1966	Oct 14, 1966
Ukraine	Apr 3, 1998	June 7, 2000	July 7, 2000
United Arab Emirates	Dec 23, 1981	Dec 23, 1981	Jan 22, 1982
United Kingdom of Great Britain and Northern Ireland	May 26, 1965	Dec 19, 1966	Jan 18, 1967
United States of America	Aug 27, 1965	June 10, 1966	Oct 14, 1966
Uruguay	May 28, 1992	Aug 9, 2000	Sep 8, 2000
Uzbekistan	Mar 17, 1994	July 26, 1995	Aug 25, 1995
Venezuela	Aug 18, 1993	May 2, 1995	June 1, 1995
Yemen, Republic of	Oct 28, 1997		
Zambia	June 17, 1970	June 17, 1970	July 17, 1970
Zimbabwe	Mar 25, 1991	May 20, 1994	June 19, 1994

ANNEX 3

RULES OF PROCEDURE FOR THE INSTITUTION OF
CONCILIATION AND ARBITRATION PROCEEDINGS
(effective 1 January 2003)

(INSTITUTION RULES)

Rule 1
The Request

(1) Any Contracting State or any national of a Contracting State wishing to institute conciliation or arbitration proceedings under the Convention shall address a request to that effect in writing to the Secretary-General at the seat of the Centre. The request shall indicate whether it relates to a conciliation or an arbitration proceeding. It shall be drawn up in an official language of the Centre, shall be dated, and shall be signed by the requesting party or its duly authorized representative.

(2) The request may be made jointly by the parties to the dispute.

Rule 2
Contents of the Request

(1) The request shall:

- (a) designate precisely each party to the dispute and state the address of each;
- (b) state, if one of the parties is a constituent subdivision or agency of a Contracting State, that it has been designated to the Centre by that State pursuant to Article 25(1) of the Convention;
- (c) indicate the date of consent and the instruments in which it is recorded, including, if one party is a constituent subdivision or agency of a Contracting State, similar data on the approval of such consent by that State unless it had notified the Centre that no such approval is required;
- (d) indicate with respect to the party that is a national of a Contracting State:
  - (i) its nationality on the date of consent; and
  - (ii) if the party is a natural person:
    - (A) his nationality on the date of the request; and
    - (B) that he did not have the nationality of the Contracting State party to the dispute either on the date of consent or on the date of the request; or
  - (iii) if the party is a juridical person which on the date of consent had the nationality of the Contracting State party to the dispute, the agreement of the parties that it should be treated as a national of another Contracting State for the purposes of the Convention;
- (e) contain information concerning the issues in dispute indicating that there is, between the parties, a legal dispute arising directly out of an investment; and

(f) state, if the requesting party is a juridical person, that it has taken all necessary internal actions to authorize the request.

(2) The information required by subparagraphs (1)(c), (1)(d)(iii), and (1)(f) shall be supported by documentation.

(3) "Date of consent" means the date on which the parties to the dispute consented in writing to submit it to the Centre; if both parties did not act on the same day, it means the date on which the second party acted.

Rule 3
Optional Information in the Request

The request may in addition set forth any provisions agreed by the parties regarding the number of conciliators or arbitrators and the method of their appointment, as well as any other provisions agreed concerning the settlement of the dispute.

Rule 4
Copies of the Request

(1) The request shall be accompanied by five additional signed copies. The Secretary-General may require such further copies as he may deem necessary.

(2) Any documentation submitted with the request shall conform to the requirements of Administrative and Financial Regulation 30.

Rule 5
Acknowledgement of the Request

(1) On receiving a request the Secretary-General shall:

    (a) send an acknowledgement to the requesting party;
    (b) take no other action with respect to the request until he has received payment of the prescribed fee.

(2) As soon as he has received the fee for lodging the request, the Secretary-General shall transmit a copy of the request and of the accompanying documentation to the other party.

Rule 6
Registration of the Request

(1) The Secretary-General shall, subject to Rule 5(1)(b), as soon as possible, either:

    (a) register the request in the Conciliation or the Arbitration Register and on the same day notify the parties of the registration; or
    (b) if he finds, on the basis of the information contained in the request, that the dispute is manifestly outside the jurisdiction of the Centre, notify the parties of his refusal to register the request and of the reasons therefor.

(2) A proceeding under the Convention shall be deemed to have been instituted on the date of the registration of the request.

Rule 7
Notice of Registration

The notice of registration of a request shall:

(a) record that the request is registered and indicate the date of the registration and of the dispatch of that notice;

(b) notify each party that all communications and notices in connection with the proceeding will be sent to the address stated in the request, unless another address is indicated to the Centre;

(c) unless such information has already been provided, invite the parties to communicate to the Secretary-General any provisions agreed by them regarding the number and the method of appointment of the conciliators or arbitrators;

(d) invite the parties to proceed, as soon as possible, to constitute a Conciliation Commission in accordance with Articles 29 to 31 of the Convention, or an Arbitral Tribunal in accordance with Articles 37 to 40;

(e) remind the parties that the registration of the request is without prejudice to the powers and functions of the Conciliation Commission or Arbitral Tribunal in regard to jurisdiction, competence and the merits; and

(f) be accompanied by a list of the members of the Panel of Conciliators or of Arbitrators of the Centre.

Rule 8
Withdrawal of the Request

The requesting party may, by written notice to the Secretary-General, withdraw the request before it has been registered. The Secretary-General shall promptly notify the other party, unless, pursuant to Rule 5(1)(b), the request had not been transmitted to it.

Rule 9
Final Provisions

(1) The texts of these Rules in each official language of the Centre shall be equally authentic.

(2) These Rules may be cited as the "Institution Rules" of the Centre.

RULES OF PROCEDURE
FOR ARBITRATION PROCEEDINGS
(effective 1 January 2003)

(ARBITRATION RULES)

CHAPTER I
Establishment of the Tribunal

Rule 1
General Obligations

(1) Upon notification of the registration of the request for arbitration, the parties shall, with all possible dispatch, proceed to constitute a Tribunal, with due regard to Section 2 of Chapter IV of the Convention.

(2) Unless such information is provided in the request, the parties shall communicate to the Secretary-General as soon as possible any provisions agreed by them regarding the number of arbitrators and the method of their appointment.

(3) The majority of the arbitrators shall be nationals of States other than the State party to the dispute and of the State whose national is a party to the dispute, unless the sole arbitrator or each individual member of the Tribunal is appointed by agreement of the parties. Where the Tribunal is to consist of three members, a national of either of these States may not be appointed as an arbitrator by a party without the agreement of the other party to the dispute. Where the Tribunal is to consist of five or more members, nationals of either or these States may not be appointed as arbitrators by a party if appointment by the other party of the same number of arbitrators of either of these nationalities would result in a majority of arbitrators of these nationalities.

(4) No person who had previously acted as a conciliator or arbitrator in any proceeding for the settlement of the dispute may be appointed as a member of the Tribunal.

Rule 2
Method of Constituting the Tribunal
in the Absence of Previous Agreement

(1) If the parties, at the time of the registration of the request for arbitration, have not agreed upon the number of arbitrators and the method of their appointment, they shall, unless they agree otherwise, follow the following procedure:

    (a) the requesting party shall, within 10 days after the registration of the request, propose to the other party the appointment of a sole arbitrator or of a specified uneven number of arbitrators and specify the method proposed for their appointment;

    (b) within 20 days after receipt of the proposals made by the requesting party, the other party shall:

(i) accept such proposals; or

(ii) make other proposals regarding the number of arbitrators and the method of their appointment;

(c) within 20 days after receipt of the reply containing any such other proposals, the requesting party shall notify the other party whether it accepts or rejects such proposals.

(2) The communications provided for in paragraph (1) shall be made or promptly confirmed in writing and shall either be transmitted through the Secretary-General or directly between the parties with a copy to the Secretary-General. The parties shall promptly notify the Secretary-General of the contents of any agreement reached.

(3) At any time 60 days after the registration of the request, if no agreement on another procedure is reached, either party may inform the Secretary-General that it chooses the formula provided for in Article 37(2)(b) of the Convention. The Secretary-General shall thereupon promptly inform the other party that the Tribunal is to be constituted in accordance with that Article.

Rule 3
Appointment of Arbitrators to a Tribunal Constituted in Accordance with Convention Article 37(2)(b)

(1) If the Tribunal is to be constituted in accordance with Article 37(2)(b) of the Convention:

(a) either party shall in a communication to the other party:
  (i) name two persons, identifying one of them, who shall not have the same nationality as nor be a national of either party, as the arbitrator appointed by it, and the other as the arbitrator proposed to be the President of the Tribunal; and
  (ii) invite the other party to concur in the appointment of the arbitrator proposed to be the President of the Tribunal and to appoint another arbitrator;

(b) promptly upon receipt of this communication the other party shall, in its reply:
  (i) name a person as the arbitrator appointed by it, who shall not have the same nationality as nor be a national of either party; and
  (ii) concur in the appointment of the arbitrator proposed to be the President of the Tribunal or name another person as the arbitrator proposed to be President;

(c) promptly upon receipt of the reply containing such a proposal, the initiating party shall notify the other party whether it concurs in the appointment of the arbitrator proposed by that party to be the President of the Tribunal.

(2) The communications provided for in this Rule shall be made or promptly confirmed in writing and shall either be transmitted through the Secretary-General or directly between the parties with a copy to the Secretary-General.

Rule 4
Appointment of Arbitrators by the Chairman of the Administrative Council

(1) If the Tribunal is not constituted within 90 days after the dispatch by the Secretary-General of the notice of registration, or such other period as the parties may agree, either party may, through the Secretary-General, address to the Chairman of the Administrative Council a

request in writing to appoint the arbitrator or arbitrators not yet appointed and to designate an arbitrator to be the President of the Tribunal.

(2) The provision of paragraph (1) shall apply *mutatis mutandis* in the event that the parties have agreed that the arbitrators shall elect the President of the Tribunal and they fail to do so.

(3) The Secretary-General shall forthwith send a copy of the request to the other party.

(4) The Chairman shall use his best efforts to comply with that request within 30 days after its receipt. Before he proceeds to make an appointment or designation, with due regard to Articles 38 and 40 (1) of the Convention, he shall consult with both parties as far as possible.

(5) The Secretary-General shall promptly notify the parties of any appointment or designation made by the Chairman.

Rule 5
Acceptance of Appointments

(1) The party or parties concerned shall notify the Secretary-General of the appointment of each arbitrator and indicate the method of his appointment.

(2) As soon as the Secretary-General has been informed by a party or the Chairman of the Administrative Council of the appointment of an arbitrator, he shall seek an acceptance from the appointee.

(3) If an arbitrator fails to accept his appointment within 15 days, the Secretary-General shall promptly notify the parties, and if appropriate the Chairman, and invite them to proceed to the appointment of another arbitrator in accordance with the method followed for the previous appointment.

Rule 6
Constitution of the Tribunal

(1) The Tribunal shall be deemed to be constituted and the proceeding to have begun on the date the Secretary-General notifies the parties that all the arbitrators have accepted their appointment.

(2) Before or at the first session of the Tribunal, each arbitrator shall sign a declaration in the following form:

> "To the best of my knowledge there is no reason why I should not serve on the Arbitral Tribunal constituted by the International Centre for Settlement of Investment Disputes with respect to a dispute between ... and ...
>
> "I shall keep confidential all information coming to my knowledge as a result of my participation in this proceeding, as well as the contents of any award made by the Tribunal.
>
> "I shall judge fairly as between the parties, according to the applicable law, and shall not accept any instruction or compensation with regard to the proceeding from any source except as provided in the Convention on the Settlement of Investment Disputes between States and Nationals of Other States and in the Regulations and Rules made pursuant thereto.
>
> "A statement of my past and present professional, business and other relationships (if any) with the parties is attached hereto."

Any arbitrator failing to sign a declaration by the end of the first session of the Tribunal shall be deemed to have resigned.

Rule 7
Replacement of Arbitrators

At any time before the Tribunal is constituted, each party may replace any arbitrator appointed by it and the parties may by common consent agree to replace any arbitrator. The procedure of such replacement shall be in accordance with Rules 1, 5 and 6.

Rule 8
Incapacity or Resignation of Arbitrators

(1) If an arbitrator becomes incapacitated or unable to perform the duties of his office, the procedure in respect of the disqualification of arbitrators set forth in Rule 9 shall apply.

(2) An arbitrator may resign by submitting his resignation to the other members of the Tribunal and the Secretary-General. If the arbitrator was appointed by one of the parties, the Tribunal shall promptly consider the reasons for his resignation and decide whether it consents thereto. The Tribunal shall promptly notify the Secretary-General of its decision.

Rule 9
Disqualification of Arbitrators

(1) A party proposing the disqualification of an arbitrator pursuant to Article 57 of the Convention shall promptly, and in any event before the proceeding is declared closed, file its proposal with the Secretary-General, stating its reasons therefor.

(2) The Secretary-General shall forthwith:

(a) transmit the proposal to the members of the Tribunal and, if it relates to a sole arbitrator or to a majority of the members of the Tribunal, to the Chairman of the Administrative Council; and

(b) notify the other party of the proposal.

(3) The arbitrator to whom the proposal relates may, without delay, furnish explanations to the Tribunal or the Chairman, as the case may be.

(4) Unless the proposal relates to a majority of the members of the Tribunal, the other members shall promptly consider and vote on the proposal in the absence of the arbitrator concerned. If those members are equally divided, they shall, through the Secretary-General, promptly notify the Chairman of the proposal, of any explanation furnished by the arbitrator concerned and of their failure to reach a decision.

(5) Whenever the Chairman has to decide on a proposal to disqualify an arbitrator, he shall use his best efforts to take that decision within 30 days after he has received the proposal.

(6) The proceeding shall be suspended until a decision has been taken on the proposal.

Rule 10
Procedure during a Vacancy on the Tribunal

(1) The Secretary-General shall forthwith notify the parties and, if necessary, the Chairman of the Administrative Council of the disqualification, death, incapacity or resignation of an arbitrator and of the consent, if any, of the Tribunal to a resignation.

(2) Upon the notification by the Secretary-General of a vacancy on the Tribunal, the proceeding shall be or remain suspended until the vacancy has been filled.

Rule 11
Filling Vacancies on the Tribunal

(1) Except as provided in paragraph (2), a vacancy resulting from the disqualification, death, incapacity or resignation of an arbitrator shall be promptly filled by the same method by which his appointment had been made.

(2) In addition to filling vacancies relating to arbitrators appointed by him, the Chairman of the Administrative Council shall appoint a person from the Panel of Arbitrators:

(a) to fill a vacancy caused by the resignation, without the consent of the Tribunal, of an arbitrator appointed by a party; or

(b) at the request of either party, to fill any other vacancy, if no new appointment is made and accepted within 45 days of the notification of the vacancy by the Secretary-General.

(3) The procedure for filling a vacancy shall be in accordance with Rules 1, 4(4), 4(5), 5 and, *mutatis mutandis*, 6(2).

Rule 12
Resumption of Proceeding after Filling a Vacancy

As soon as a vacancy on the Tribunal has been filled, the proceeding shall continue from the point it had reached at the time the vacancy occurred. The newly appointed arbitrator may, however, require that the oral procedure be recommenced, if this had already been started.

CHAPTER II
Working of the Tribunal

Rule 13
Sessions of the Tribunal

(1) The Tribunal shall hold its first session within 60 days after its constitution or such other period as the parties may agree. The dates of that session shall be fixed by the President of the Tribunal after consultation with its members and the Secretary-General. If upon its constitution the Tribunal has no President because the parties have agreed that the President shall be elected by its members, the Secretary-General shall fix the dates of that session. In both cases, the parties shall be consulted as far as possible.

(2) The dates of subsequent sessions shall be determined by the Tribunal, after consultation with the Secretary-General and with the parties as far as possible.

(3) The Tribunal shall meet at the seat of the Centre or at such other place as may have been agreed by the parties in accordance with Article 63 of the Convention. If the parties agree that the proceeding shall be held at a place other than the Centre or an institution with which the Centre has made the necessary arrangements, they shall consult with the Secretary-General and request the approval of the Tribunal. Failing such approval, the Tribunal shall meet at the seat of the Centre.

(4) The Secretary-General shall notify the members of the Tribunal and the parties of the dates and place of the sessions of the Tribunal in good time.

Rule 14
Sittings of the Tribunal

(1) The President of the Tribunal shall conduct its hearings and preside at its deliberations.
(2) Except as the parties otherwise agree, the presence of a majority of the members of the Tribunal shall be required at its sittings.
(3) The President of the Tribunal shall fix the date and hour of its sittings.

Rule 15
Deliberations of the Tribunal

(1) The deliberations of the Tribunal shall take place in private and remain secret.
(2) Only members of the Tribunal shall take part in its deliberations. No other person shall be admitted unless the Tribunal decides otherwise.

Rule 16
Decisions of the Tribunal

(1) Decisions of the Tribunal shall be taken by a majority of the votes of all its members. Abstention shall count as a negative vote.
(2) Except as otherwise provided by these Rules or decided by the Tribunal, it may take any decision by correspondence among its members, provided that all of them are consulted. Decisions so taken shall be certified by the President of the Tribunal.

Rule 17
Incapacity of the President

If at any time the President of the Tribunal should be unable to act, his functions shall be performed by one of the other members of the Tribunal, acting in the order in which the Secretary-General had received the notice of their acceptance of their appointment to the Tribunal.

Rule 18
Representation of the Parties

(1) Each party may be represented or assisted by agents, counsel or advocates whose names and authority shall be notified by that party to the Secretary-General, who shall promptly inform the Tribunal and the other party.
(2) For the purposes of these Rules, the expression "party" includes, where the context so admits, an agent, counsel or advocate authorized to represent that party.

CHAPTER III
General Procedural Provisions

Rule 19
Procedural Orders

The Tribunal shall make the orders required for the conduct of the proceeding.

Rule 20
Preliminary Procedural Consultation

(1) As early as possible after the constitution of a Tribunal, its President shall endeavor to ascertain the views of the parties regarding questions of procedure. For this purpose he may request the parties to meet him. He shall, in particular, seek their views on the following matters:

    (a) the number of members of the Tribunal required to constitute a quorum at its sittings;
    (b) the language or languages to be used in the proceeding;
    (c) the number and sequence of the pleadings and the time limits within which they are to be filed;
    (d) the number of copies desired by each party of instruments filed by the other;
    (e) dispensing with the written or the oral procedure;
    (f) the manner in which the cost of the proceeding is to be apportioned; and
    (g) the manner in which the record of the hearings shall be kept.

(2) In the conduct of the proceeding the Tribunal shall apply any agreement between the parties on procedural matters, except as otherwise provided in the Convention or the Administrative and Financial Regulations.

Rule 21
Pre Hearing Conference

(1) At the request of the Secretary-General or at the discretion of the President of the Tribunal, a pre hearing conference between the Tribunal and the parties may be held to arrange for an exchange of information and the stipulation of uncontested facts in order to expedite the proceeding.
(2) At the request of the parties, a pre hearing conference between the Tribunal and the parties, duly represented by their authorized representatives, may be held to consider the issues in dispute with a view to reaching an amicable settlement.

Rule 22
Procedural Languages

(1) The parties may agree on the use of one or two languages to be used in the proceeding, provided, that, if they agree on any language that is not an official language of the Centre, the Tribunal, after consultation with the Secretary-General, gives its approval. If the parties do not agree on any such procedural language, each of them may select one of the official languages (i.e. English, French and Spanish) for this purpose.

(2) If two procedural languages are selected by the parties, any instruments may be filed in either language. Either language may be used at the hearings, subject, if the Tribunal so requires, to translation and interpretation. The orders and the award of the Tribunal shall be rendered and the record kept in both procedural languages, both versions being equally authentic.

Rule 23
Copies of Instruments

Except as otherwise provided by the Tribunal after consultation with the parties and the Secretary-General, every request, pleading, application, written observation, supporting documentation, if any, or other instrument shall be filed in the form of a signed original accompanied by the following number of additional copies:

(a) before the number of members of the Tribunal has been determined: five;
(b) after the number of members of the Tribunal has been determined: two more than the number of its members.

Rule 24
Supporting Documentation

Supporting documentation shall ordinarily be filed together with the instrument to which it relates, and in any case within the time limit fixed for the filing of such instrument.

Rule 25
Correction of Errors

An accidental error in any instrument or supporting document may, with the consent of the other party or by leave of the Tribunal, be corrected at any time before the award is rendered.

Rule 26
Time Limits

(1) Where required, time limits shall be fixed by the Tribunal by assigning dates for the completion of the various steps in the proceeding. The Tribunal may delegate this power to its President.
(2) The Tribunal may extend any time limit that it has fixed. If the Tribunal is not in session, this power shall be exercised by its President.
(3) Any step taken after expiration of the applicable time limit shall be disregarded unless the Tribunal, in special circumstances and after giving the other party an opportunity of stating its views, decides otherwise.

Rule 27
Waiver

A party which knows or should have known that a provision of the Administrative and Financial Regulations, of these Rules, of any other rules or agreement applicable to the proceeding, or of an order of the Tribunal has not been complied with and which fails to state promptly its objections thereto, shall be deemed – subject to Article 45 of the Convention – to have waived its right to object.

Rule 28
Cost of Proceeding

(1) Without prejudice to the final decision on the payment of the cost of the proceeding, the Tribunal may, unless otherwise agreed by the parties, decide:

  (a) at any stage of the proceeding, the portion which each party shall pay, pursuant to Administrative and Financial Regulation 14, of the fees and expenses of the Tribunal and the charges for the use of the facilities of the Centre;

  (b) with respect to any part of the proceeding, that the related costs (as determined by the Secretary-General) shall be borne entirely or in a particular share by one of the parties.

(2) Promptly after the closure of the proceeding, each party shall submit to the Tribunal a statement of costs reasonably incurred or borne by it in the proceeding and the Secretary-General shall submit to the Tribunal an account of all amounts paid by each party to the Centre and of all costs incurred by the Centre for the proceeding. The Tribunal may, before the award has been rendered, request the parties and the Secretary-General to provide additional information concerning the cost of the proceeding.

CHAPTER IV
Written and Oral Procedures

Rule 29
Normal Procedures

Except if the parties otherwise agree, the proceeding shall comprise two distinct phases: a written procedure followed by an oral one.

Rule 30
Transmission of the Request

As soon as the Tribunal is constituted, the Secretary-General shall transmit to each member a copy of the request by which the proceeding was initiated, of the supporting documentation, of the notice of registration and of any communication received from either party in response thereto.

Rule 31
The Written Procedure

(1) In addition to the request for arbitration, the written procedure shall consist of the following pleadings, filed within time limits set by the Tribunal:

(a) a memorial by the requesting party;
(b) a counter-memorial by the other party; and, if the parties so agree or the Tribunal deems it necessary:
(c) a reply by the requesting party; and
(d) a rejoinder by the other party.

(2) If the request was made jointly, each party shall, within the same time limit determined by the Tribunal, file its memorial and, if the parties so agree or the Tribunal deems it necessary, its reply; however, the parties may instead agree that one of them shall, for the purposes of paragraph (1), be considered as the requesting party.
(3) A memorial shall contain: a statement of the relevant facts; a statement of law; and the submissions. A counter-memorial, reply or rejoinder shall contain an admission or denial of the facts stated in the last previous pleading; any additional facts, if necessary; observations concerning the statement of law in the last previous pleading; a statement of law in answer thereto; and the submissions.

Rule 32
The Oral Procedure

(1) The oral procedure shall consist of the hearing by the Tribunal of the parties, their agents, counsel and advocates, and of witnesses and experts.
(2) The Tribunal shall decide, with the consent of the parties, which other persons besides the parties, their agents, counsel and advocates, witnesses and experts during their testimony, and officers of the Tribunal may attend the hearings.
(3) The members of the Tribunal may, during the hearings, put questions to the parties, their agents, counsel and advocates, and ask them for explanations.

Rule 33
Marshalling of Evidence

Without prejudice to the rules concerning the production of documents, each party shall, within time limits fixed by the Tribunal, communicate to the Secretary-General, for transmission to the Tribunal and the other party, precise information regarding the evidence which it intends to produce and that which it intends to request the Tribunal to call for, together with an indication of the points to which such evidence will be directed.

Rule 34
Evidence: General Principles

(1) The Tribunal shall be the judge of the admissibility of any evidence adduced and of its probative value.
(2) The Tribunal may, if it deems it necessary at any stage of the proceeding:

(a) call upon the parties to produce documents, witnesses and experts; and
(b) visit any place connected with the dispute or conduct inquiries there.

(3) The parties shall cooperate with the Tribunal in the production of the evidence and in the other measures provided for in paragraph (2). The Tribunal shall take formal note of the

failure of a party to comply with its obligations under this paragraph and of any reasons given for such failure.

(4) Expenses incurred in producing evidence and in taking other measures in accordance with paragraph (2) shall be deemed to constitute part of the expenses incurred by the parties within the meaning of Article 61(2) of the Convention.

Rule 35
Examination of Witnesses and Experts

(1) Witnesses and experts shall be examined before the Tribunal by the parties under the control of its President. Questions may also be put to them by any member of the Tribunal.

(2) Each witness shall make the following declaration before giving his evidence:

> "I solemnly declare upon my honour and conscience that I shall speak the truth, the whole truth and nothing but the truth."

(3) Each expert shall make the following declaration before making his statement:

> "I solemnly declare upon my honour and conscience that my statement will be in accordance with my sincere belief."

Rule 36
Witnesses and Experts: Special Rules

Notwithstanding Rule 35 the Tribunal may:

> (a) admit evidence given by a witness or expert in a written deposition; and
> (b) with the consent of both parties, arrange for the examination of a witness or expert otherwise than before the Tribunal itself. The Tribunal shall define the subject of the examination, the time limit, the procedure to be followed and other particulars. The parties may participate in the examination.

Rule 37
Visits and Inquiries

If the Tribunal considers it necessary to visit any place connected with the dispute or to conduct an inquiry there, it shall make an order to this effect. The order shall define the scope of the visit or the subject of the inquiry, the time limit, the procedure to be followed and other particulars. The parties may participate in any visit or inquiry.

Rule 38
Closure of the Proceeding

(1) When the presentation of the case by the parties is completed, the proceeding shall be declared closed.

(2) Exceptionally, the Tribunal may, before the award has been rendered, reopen the proceeding on the ground that new evidence is forthcoming of such a nature as to constitute a decisive factor, or that there is a vital need for clarification on certain specific points.

CHAPTER V
Particular Procedures

Rule 39
Provisional Measures

(1) At any time during the proceeding a party may request that provisional measures for the preservation of its rights be recommended by the Tribunal. The request shall specify the rights to be preserved, the measures the recommendation of which is requested, and the circumstances that require such measures.

(2) The Tribunal shall give priority to the consideration of a request made pursuant to paragraph (1).

(3) The Tribunal may also recommend provisional measures on its own initiative or recommend measures other than those specified in a request. It may at any time modify or revoke its recommendations.

(4) The Tribunal shall only recommend provisional measures, or modify or revoke its recommendations, after giving each party an opportunity of presenting its observations.

(5) Nothing in this Rule shall prevent the parties, provided that they have so stipulated in the agreement recording their consent, from requesting any judicial or other authority to order provisional measures, prior to the institution of the proceeding, or during the proceeding, for the preservation of their respective rights and interests.

Rule 40
Ancillary Claims

(1) Except as the parties otherwise agree, a party may present an incidental or additional claim or counter-claim arising directly out of the subject-matter of the dispute, provided that such ancillary claim is within the scope of the consent of the parties and is otherwise within the jurisdiction of the Centre.

(2) An incidental or additional claim shall be presented not later than in the reply and a counter-claim no later than in the counter-memorial, unless the Tribunal, upon justification by the party presenting the ancillary claim and upon considering any objection of the other party, authorizes the presentation of the claim at a later stage in the proceeding.

(3) The Tribunal shall fix a time limit within which the party against which an ancillary claim is presented may file its observations thereon.

Rule 41
Objections to Jurisdiction

(1) Any objection that the dispute or any ancillary claim is not within the jurisdiction of the Centre or, for other reasons, is not within the competence of the Tribunal shall be made as early as possible. A party shall file the objection with the Secretary-General no later than the expiration of the time limit fixed for the filing of the counter-memorial, or, if the objection relates to an ancillary claim, for the filing of the rejoinder – unless the facts on which the objection is based are unknown to the party at that time.

(2) The Tribunal may on its own initiative consider, at any stage of the proceeding, whether

the dispute or any ancillary claim before it is within the jurisdiction of the Centre and within its own competence.

(3) Upon the formal raising of an objection relating to the dispute, the proceeding on the merits shall be suspended. The President of the Tribunal, after consultation with its other members, shall fix a time limit within which the parties may file observations on the objection.

(4) The Tribunal shall decide whether or not the further procedures relating to the objection shall be oral. It may deal with the objection as a preliminary question or join it to the merits of the dispute. If the Tribunal overrules the objection or joins it to the merits, it shall once more fix time limits for the further procedures.

(5) If the Tribunal decides that the dispute is not within the jurisdiction of the Centre or not within its own competence, it shall render an award to that effect.

Rule 42
Default

(1) If a party (in this Rule called the "defaulting party") fails to appear or to present its case at any stage of the proceeding, the other party may, at any time prior to the discontinuance of the proceeding, request the Tribunal to deal with the questions submitted to it and to render an award.

(2) The Tribunal shall promptly notify the defaulting party of such a request. Unless it is satisfied that that party does not intend to appear or to present its case in the proceeding, it shall, at the same time, grant a period of grace and to this end:

   (a) if that party had failed to file a pleading or any other instrument within the time limit fixed therefor, fix a new time limit for its filing; or
   (b) if that party had failed to appear or present its case at a hearing, fix a new date for the hearing.

The period of grace shall not, without the consent of the other party, exceed 60 days.

(3) After the expiration of the period of grace or when, in accordance with paragraph (2), no such period is granted, the Tribunal shall resume the consideration of the dispute. Failure of the defaulting party to appear or to present its case shall not be deemed an admission of the assertions made by the other party.

(4) The Tribunal shall examine the jurisdiction of the Centre and its own competence in the dispute and, if it is satisfied, decide whether the submissions made are well-founded in fact and in law. To this end, it may, at any stage of the proceeding, call on the party appearing to file observations, produce evidence or submit oral explanations.

Rule 43
Settlement and Discontinuance

(1) If, before the award is rendered, the parties agree on a settlement of the dispute or otherwise to discontinue the proceeding, the Tribunal, or the Secretary-General if the Tribunal has not yet been constituted, shall, at their written request, in an order take note of the discontinuance of the proceeding.

(2) If the parties file with the Secretary-General the full and signed text of their settlement and in writing request the Tribunal to embody such settlement in an award, the Tribunal may record the settlement in the form of its award.

Rule 44
Discontinuance at Request of a Party

If a party requests the discontinuance of the proceeding, the Tribunal, or the Secretary-General if the Tribunal has not yet been constituted, shall in an order fix a time limit within which the other party may state whether it opposes the discontinuance. If no objection is made in writing within the time limit, the other party shall be deemed to have acquiesced in the discontinuance and the Tribunal, or if appropriate the Secretary-General, shall in an order take note of the discontinuance of the proceeding. If objection is made, the proceeding shall continue.

Rule 45
Discontinuance for Failure of Parties to Act

If the parties fail to take any steps in the proceeding during six consecutive months or such period as they may agree with the approval of the Tribunal, or of the Secretary-General if the Tribunal has not yet been constituted, they shall be deemed to have discontinued the proceeding and the Tribunal, or if appropriate the Secretary-General, shall, after notice to the parties, in an order take note of the discontinuance.

CHAPTER VI
The Award

Rule 46
Preparation of the Award

The award (including any individual or dissenting opinion) shall be drawn up and signed within 120 days after closure of the proceeding. The Tribunal may, however, extend this period by a further 30 days if it would otherwise be unable to draw up the award.

Rule 47
The Award

(1) The award shall be in writing and shall contain:

    (a) a precise designation of each party;
    (b) a statement that the Tribunal was established under the Convention, and a description of the method of its constitution;
    (c) the name of each member of the Tribunal, and an identification of the appointing authority of each;
    (d) the names of the agents, counsel and advocates of the parties;
    (e) the dates and place of the sittings of the Tribunal;
    (f) a summary of the proceeding;
    (g) a statement of the facts as found by the Tribunal;
    (h) the submissions of the parties;
    (i) the decision of the Tribunal on every question submitted to it, together with the reasons upon which the decision is based; and

(j) any decision of the Tribunal regarding the cost of the proceeding.

(2) The award shall be signed by the members of the Tribunal who voted for it; the date of each signature shall be indicated.

(3) Any member of the Tribunal may attach his individual opinion to the award, whether he dissents from the majority or not, or a statement of his dissent.

Rule 48
Rendering of the Award

(1) Upon signature by the last arbitrator to sign, the Secretary-General shall promptly:

(a) authenticate the original text of the award and deposit it in the archives of the Centre, together with any individual opinions and statements of dissent; and

(b) dispatch a certified copy of the award (including individual opinions and statements of dissent) to each party, indicating the date of dispatch on the original text and on all copies.

(2) The award shall be deemed to have been rendered on the date on which the certified copies were dispatched.

(3) The Secretary-General shall, upon request, make available to a party additional certified copies of the award.

(4) The Centre shall not publish the award without the consent of the parties. The Centre may, however, include in its publications excerpts of the legal rules applied by the Tribunal.

Rule 49
Supplementary Decisions and Rectification

(1) Within 45 days after the date on which the award was rendered, either party may request, pursuant to Article 49(2) of the Convention, a supplementary decision on, or the rectification of, the award. Such a request shall be addressed in writing to the Secretary-General. The request shall:

(a) identify the award to which it relates;

(b) indicate the date of the request;

(c) state in detail:

(i) any question which, in the opinion of the requesting party, the Tribunal omitted to decide in the award; and

(ii) any error in the award which the requesting party seeks to have rectified; and

(d) be accompanied by a fee for lodging the request.

(2) Upon receipt of the request and of the lodging fee, the Secretary-General shall forthwith:

(a) register the request;

(b) notify the parties of the registration;

(c) transmit to the other party a copy of the request and of any accompanying documentation; and

(d) transmit to each member of the Tribunal a copy of the notice of registration, together with a copy of the request and of any accompanying documentation.

(3) The President of the Tribunal shall consult the members on whether it is necessary for the Tribunal to meet in order to consider the request. The Tribunal shall fix a time limit for the parties to file their observations on the request and shall determine the procedure for its consideration.

(4) Rules 46-48 shall apply, *mutatis mutandis*, to any decision of the Tribunal pursuant to this Rule.

(5) If a request is received by the Secretary-General more than 45 days after the award was rendered, he shall refuse to register the request and so inform forthwith the requesting party.

CHAPTER VII
Interpretation, Revision and Annulment of the Award

Rule 50
The Application

(1) An application for the interpretation, revision or annulment of an award shall be addressed in writing to the Secretary-General and shall:

(a) identify the award to which it relates;

(b) indicate the date of the application;

(c) state in detail:

   (i) in an application for interpretation, the precise points in dispute;

   (ii) in an application for revision, pursuant to Article 51(1) of the Convention, the change sought in the award, the discovery of some fact of such a nature as decisively to affect the award, and evidence that when the award was rendered that fact was unknown to the Tribunal and to the applicant, and that the applicant's ignorance of that fact was not due to negligence;

   (iii) in an application for annulment, pursuant to Article 52(1) of the Convention, the grounds on which it is based. These grounds are limited to the following:

   • that the Tribunal was not properly constituted;

   • that the Tribunal has manifestly exceeded its powers;

   • that there was corruption on the part of a member of the Tribunal;

   • that there has been a serious departure from a fundamental rule of procedure;

   • that the award has failed to state the reasons on which it is based;

(d) be accompanied by the payment of a fee for lodging the application.

(2) Without prejudice to the provisions of paragraph (3), upon receiving an application and the lodging fee, the Secretary-General shall forthwith:

(a) register the application;

(b) notify the parties of the registration; and

(c) transmit to the other party a copy of the application and of any accompanying documentation.

(3) The Secretary-General shall refuse to register an application for:

(a) revision, if, in accordance with Article 51(2) of the Convention, it is not made within 90 days after the discovery of the new fact and in any event within three years after the date on which the award was rendered (or any subsequent decision or correction);

(b) annulment, if, in accordance with Article 52(2) of the Convention, it is not made:

  (i) within 120 days after the date on which the award was rendered (or any subsequent decision or correction) if the application is based on any of the following grounds:

  - the Tribunal was not properly constituted;
  - the Tribunal has manifestly exceeded its powers;
  - there has been a serious departure from a fundamental rule of procedure;
  - the award has failed to state the reasons on which it is based;

  (ii) in the case of corruption on the part of a member of the Tribunal, within 120 days after discovery thereof, and in any event within three years after the date on which the award was rendered (or any subsequent decision or correction).

(4) If the Secretary-General refuses to register an application for revision, or annulment, he shall forthwith notify the requesting party of his refusal.

Rule 51
Interpretation or Revision: Further Procedures

(1) Upon registration of an application for the interpretation or revision of an award, the Secretary-General shall forthwith:

(a) transmit to each member of the original Tribunal a copy of the notice of registration, together with a copy of the application and of any accompanying documentation; and

(b) request each member of the Tribunal to inform him within a specified time limit whether that member is willing to take part in the consideration of the application.

(2) If all members of the Tribunal express their willingness to take part in the consideration of the application, the Secretary-General shall so notify the members of the Tribunal and the parties. Upon dispatch of these notices the Tribunal shall be deemed to be reconstituted.

(3) If the Tribunal cannot be reconstituted in accordance with paragraph (2), the Secretary-General shall so notify the parties and invite them to proceed, as soon as possible, to constitute a new Tribunal, including the same number of arbitrators, and appointed by the same method, as the original one.

Rule 52
Annulment: Further Procedures

(1) Upon registration of an application for the annulment of an award, the Secretary-General shall forthwith request the Chairman of the Administrative Council to appoint an ad hoc Committee in accordance with Article 52(3) of the Convention.

(2) The Committee shall be deemed to be constituted on the date the Secretary-General notifies the parties that all members have accepted their appointment. Before or at the first session of the Committee, each member shall sign a declaration conforming to that set forth in Rule 6(2).

Rule 53
Rules of Procedure

The provisions of these Rules shall apply *mutatis mutandis* to any procedure relating to the interpretation, revision or annulment of an award and to the decision of the Tribunal or Committee.

Rule 54
Stay of Enforcement of the Award

(1) The party applying for the interpretation, revision or annulment of an award may in its application, and either party may at any time before the final disposition of the application, request a stay in the enforcement of part or all of the award to which the application relates. The Tribunal or Committee shall give priority to the consideration of such a request.

(2) If an application for the revision or annulment of an award contains a request for a stay of its enforcement, the Secretary-General shall, together with the notice of registration, inform both parties of the provisional stay of the award. As soon as the Tribunal or Committee is constituted it shall, if either party requests, rule within 30 days on whether such stay should be continued; unless it decides to continue the stay, it shall automatically be terminated.

(3) If a stay of enforcement has been granted pursuant to paragraph (1) or continued pursuant to paragraph (2), the Tribunal or Committee may at any time modify or terminate the stay at the request of either party. All stays shall automatically terminate on the date on which a final decision is rendered on the application, except that a Committee granting the partial annulment of an award may order the temporary stay of enforcement of the unannulled portion in order to give either party an opportunity to request any new Tribunal constituted pursuant to Article 52(6) of the Convention to grant a stay pursuant to Rule 55(3).

(4) A request pursuant to paragraph (1), (2) (second sentence) or (3) shall specify the circumstances that require the stay or its modification or termination. A request shall only be granted after the Tribunal or Committee has given each party an opportunity of presenting its observations.

(5) The Secretary-General shall promptly notify both parties of the stay of enforcement of any award and of the modification or termination of such a stay, which shall become effective on the date on which he dispatches such notification.

Rule 55
Resubmission of Dispute after an Annulment

(1) If a Committee annuls part or all of an award, either party may request the resubmission of the dispute to a new Tribunal. Such a request shall be addressed in writing to the Secretary-General and shall:

  (a) identify the award to which it relates;
  (b) indicate the date of the request;
  (c) explain in detail what aspect of the dispute is to be submitted to the Tribunal; and
  (d) be accompanied by a fee for lodging the request.

(2) Upon receipt of the request and of the lodging fee, the Secretary-General shall forthwith:

  (a) register it in the Arbitration Register;

(b) notify both parties of the registration;
(c) transmit to the other party a copy of the request and of any accompanying documentation; and
(d) invite the parties to proceed, as soon as possible, to constitute a new Tribunal, including the same number of arbitrators, and appointed by the same method, as the original one.

(3) If the original award had only been annulled in part, the new Tribunal shall not reconsider any portion of the award not so annulled. It may, however, in accordance with the procedures set forth in Rule 54, stay or continue to stay the enforcement of the unannulled portion of the award until the date its own award is rendered.

(4) Except as otherwise provided in paragraphs (1)-(3), these Rules shall apply to a proceeding on a resubmitted dispute in the same manner as if such dispute had been submitted pursuant to the Institution Rules.

CHAPTER VIII
General Provisions

Rule 56
Final Provisions

(1) The texts of these Rules in each official language of the Centre shall be equally authentic.
(2) These Rules may be cited as the "Arbitration Rules" of the Centre.

ANNEX 5

MODEL ICSID CLAUSES

INTRODUCTION

The International Centre for Settlement of Investment Disputes (ICSID or the Centre) is a public international organization established by a multilateral treaty, the 1965 Convention on the Settlement of Investment Disputes between States and Nationals of Other States (the Convention).[1] As of April 15, 1998, 129 countries had signed and ratified the Convention to become Contracting States.[2]

The purpose of ICSID, as set forth in Article 1(2) of the Convention, is to provide facilities for the conciliation and arbitration of investment disputes between Contracting States and nationals of other Contracting States. The jurisdiction of the Centre, or in other terms the scope of the Convention, is elaborated upon in Article 25(1) of the Convention. It defines ICSID's jurisdiction as extending to "any legal dispute arising directly out of an investment, between a Contracting State (or any constituent subdivision or agency of a Contracting State designated to the Centre by that State) and a national of another Contracting State, which the parties to the dispute consent in writing to submit to the Centre."

The consent of the parties has been described as the "cornerstone" of the jurisdiction of the Centre as thus defined.[3] The present brochure suggests clauses to record such consent. Also proposed in this brochure are clauses for use in conjunction with the Rules Governing the Additional Facility for the Administration of Proceedings by the Secretariat of ICSID (the Additional Facility Rules)[4] which are available for certain types of proceedings between States and foreign nationals falling outside the scope of the Convention. A concluding section of the brochure contains an example of an ad hoc arbitration clause designating the Secretary-General of the Centre as appointing authority of arbitrators.

The only formal requirement that the Convention establishes with respect to the consent of the parties is that such consent be in writing. In many cases, as in the ones envisaged in this brochure, the consent of both parties will be set forth in a single instrument. However, the parties' consents may also be recorded in separate instruments.[5] Nor is any special form of

---

[1] The Convention, 575 U.N.T.S. 159, is reprinted, together with the Report of the World Bank Executive Directors on the Convention, in Doc. ICSID/2. Pursuant to Article 6(1) of the Convention, the Administrative Council of the Centre has adopted Administrative and Financial Regulations, Rules of Procedure for the Institution of Conciliation and Arbitration Proceedings (Institution Rules), Rules of Procedure for Conciliation Proceedings (Conciliation Rules) and Rules of Procedure for Arbitration Proceedings (Arbitration Rules). References in this brochure to such Regulations and Rules are to those adopted with effect from September 26, 1984 and reprinted in ICSID Basic Documents, Doc. ICSID/15 (Jan. 1985).

[2] *See* Doc. ICSID/3, List of Contracting States and Other Signatories of the Convention.

[3] Report of the World Bank Executive Directors on the Convention, *supra* note 1, at para. 23.

[4] The Additional Facility Rules are reprinted in Doc. ICSID/11 (June 1979).

[5] For example, the consent of the State party may be set forth in its investment legislation or in a bilateral investment treaty concluded by it. *See* Report of the World Bank Executive Directors on the Convention, *supra* note 1, at para. 24.

words required. The following clauses thus are intended merely as models. Actual clauses will vary in substance and terminology according to the circumstances of each case.

In general, the Contracting State party is in the proposed clauses called the "Host State" and the national of another Contracting State "the Investor." Square brackets: [ ] are used to indicate optional material or, if separated by a virgule: [ ]/[ ], to indicate alternative formulations. Underscored material indicates a blank to be filled in accordance with the underscored directions. For simplicity, the clauses generally refer only to arbitration; however, in several of them (in particular, Clauses 9, 16, 17 and 19) the words: "arbitration," "arbitrators," "Arbitral Tribunal" or "Arbitration Rules" can be replaced by corresponding references to "conciliation," "conciliators," "Conciliation Commission" or "Conciliation Rules," or by a reference to both conciliation and arbitration.

I. BASIC SUBMISSION CLAUSES

A. Consent in Respect of Future Disputes

Under the Convention, consent may be given in advance, with respect to a defined class of future disputes. Clauses relating to future disputes are a common feature of investment agreements between Contracting States and investors who are nationals of other Contracting States.

Clause 1

The [Government]/[name of constituent subdivision or agency] of name of Contracting State (hereinafter the "Host State") and name of investor (hereinafter the "Investor") hereby consent to submit to the International Centre for Settlement of Investment Disputes (hereinafter the "Centre") any[6] dispute arising out of or relating to this agreement for settlement by [conciliation]/[arbitration]/ [conciliation followed, if the dispute remains unresolved within time limit of the communication of the report of the Conciliation Commission to the parties, by arbitration] pursuant to the Convention on the Settlement of Investment Disputes between States and Nationals of Other States (hereinafter the "Convention").

B. Consent in Respect of Existing Disputes

Consent may also be given in respect of a particular, existing dispute.

Clause 2

The [Government]/[name of constituent subdivision or agency] of name of Contracting State (hereinafter the "Host State") and name of investor (hereinafter the "Investor") hereby consent to submit to the International Centre for Settlement of Investment Disputes (hereinafter the "Centre") for settlement by [conciliation]/[arbitration]/[conciliation followed, if the dispute remains unresolved within time limit of the communication of the report of the Conciliation Commission to the parties, by arbitration] pursuant to the

---

[6] If a restrictive clause such as clause 4 is added, the word "any" may have to be qualified.

Convention on the Settlement of Investment Disputes between States and Nationals of Other States, the following dispute arising out of the investment described below: . . .

II. SPECIAL CLAUSES RELATING TO THE SUBJECT-MATTER OF THE DISPUTE

A. Stipulation that Transaction Constitutes an Investment

While the Convention requires that the dispute arise "directly out of an investment," it deliberately does not define the latter term. The Report of the World Bank Executive Directors on the Convention explains that such definition was not attempted "given the essential requirement of consent by the parties."[7] Parties thus have much, though not unlimited, discretion to determine whether their transaction constitutes an investment.[8] The fact that the parties consent to submit a dispute to the Centre of course implies that they consider it to arise out of an investment. If the parties wish to strengthen the presumption, they may include an explicit statement to this effect in the consent agreement.

Clause 3

It is hereby stipulated that the transaction to which this agreement relates is an investment.

B. Limitation of Subject-Matter of Disputes Submitted to the Centre

The Convention does not require that the parties to an investment arrangement must agree to submit to the Centre all the disputes that might arise out of the transaction. They may decide to submit only particular types of questions, or to submit all with certain exceptions, as illustrated by the following clause.

Clause 4

The consent to the jurisdiction of the Centre recorded in <u>citation of basic clause above</u> shall [only]/[not] extend to disputes related to the following matters: . . .

III. SPECIAL CLAUSES RELATING TO THE PARTIES

A. Constituent Subdivision or Governmental Agency

When the party representing the Contracting State is not the government itself but only a "constituent subdivision" or a governmental "agency," then two special requirements must be fulfilled pursuant to Article 25(1) and (3) of the Convention:

(a) the subdivision or agency must be designated by the Contracting State to the Centre; and
(b) the consent given by the subdivision or agency must be either:

---

[7] Report of the World Bank Executive Directors on the Convention, *supra* note 1, at para. 27.
[8] For brief descriptions of the different kinds of transaction involved in actual cases submitted to the Centre, see ICSID Cases, Doc. ICSID/16/Rev. 5 (Nov. 30, 1996).

(i)   approved by the State; or

(ii) one as to which the State has notified the Centre that no such approval is required.

While the clause suggested below does not[9] directly fulfill these requirements, it constitutes a convenient reminder of the steps that should be undertaken – preferably before the effective date of the consent clause.

Clause 5

The <u>name of constituent subdivision or agency</u> is [a constituent subdivision]/[an agency] of the Host State, which has been designated to the Centre by the Government of that State in accordance with Article 25(l) of the Convention. In accordance with Article 25(3) of the Convention, the Host State [hereby gives its approval to this consent agreement][10] /[has given its approval to this consent agreement in <u>citation of instrument in which approval is expressed</u>]/[has notified the Centre that no approval of [this type of consent agreement]/[of consent agreements by the <u>name of constituent subdivision or agency</u> is required]].

B. Stipulation of Nationality of Investor

If the investor is a natural person, the Convention requires that the investor be a national of a Contracting State other than the host State both on the date of consent and on the date of the registration of the request for conciliation or arbitration, and the investor may not on either of these two dates also have the nationality of the host State. If the investor is a juridical person then, except as noted in Section III(C) below, it must merely have the nationality of a Contracting State other than the host State on the date of consent. While the Convention does not require that nationality be specified in the consent agreement and a stipulation of nationality cannot correct an actual disability (again except as stated in Section III(C)), it may be useful to specify, by means of a clause such as the one below, the nationality of the investor.

Clause 6

It is hereby stipulated by the parties that the Investor is a national of <u>name of another Contracting State</u>.

C. Agreement that a Juridical Person is Under Foreign Control

If the investor is a juridical person that on the date of consent has the nationality of the host State, then Article 25(2)(b) of the Convention still permits the Centre to assume jurisdiction if the parties have agreed that "because of foreign control" the juridical person "should be treated as a national of another Contracting State for the purposes of [the] Convention." When this is the case, the parties may record their agreement as to the nationality of the investor in a clause such as the one set forth below.

---

9   With the exception of the alternative presented in the text accompanying *infra* note 10.

10 This alternative can only be used if the government is also a party to the agreement.

Clause 7

It is hereby agreed that, although the Investor is a national of the Host State, it is controlled by nationals of <u>name(s) of other Contracting State(s)</u> and shall be treated as a national of [that]/[those] State[s] for the purposes of the Convention.

D. Preservation of Rights of Investor after Compensation

A number of States have developed schemes for insuring their nationals, generally through governmental agencies, against losses that may be suffered in relation to foreign investments. There are also at present two intergovernmental agencies – the Multilateral Investment Guarantee Agency and the Inter-Arab Investment Guarantee Corporation – that administer similar investment insurance schemes. If such a governmental or intergovernmental agency indemnifies an investor, the agency will normally become subrogated to the investor's rights. The agency may nevertheless be unable to avail itself of such agreement providing for the resolution of disputes under the Convention as may originally have been concluded between the investor and the host State. This is so because ICSID's facilities are not available for proceedings between governmental entities or between governments and intergovernmental organizations. It may therefore be necessary that in any dispute the proceeding be conducted by the investor. The following clause may be used to cover this situation.

Clause 8

It is hereby agreed that the right of the Investor to refer a dispute to the Centre pursuant to this agreement shall not be affected by the fact that the Investor has received full or partial compensation from any third party with respect to any loss or injury that is the subject of the dispute [; provided that the Host State may require evidence that such third party agrees to the exercise of that right by the Investor].

IV. METHOD OF CONSTITUTING THE TRIBUNAL

Article 37(2)(a) of the Convention provides that an Arbitral Tribunal "shall consist of a sole arbitrator or any uneven number of arbitrators"; under Article 39 of the Convention, the majority of the arbitrators must be nationals of States other than the host and the home State of the investor, unless each individual arbitrator is appointed by agreement of the parties; and according to Article 40(2) of the Convention arbitrators appointed from outside the Panel of Arbitrators of the Centre must possess the qualities required for those serving on that Panel."[11]

Except for the above requirements, the parties are free to constitute their Tribunal in any

---

[11] In addition to the Panel of Arbitrators, the Centre maintains a Panel of Conciliators. Each Panel consists of up to four persons designated by each Contracting State and up to ten persons designated by the Chairman of the Administrative Council of ICSID. The designees, who all serve for renewable periods of six years, are listed in Doc. ICSID/10. The qualities that they must possess are set forth in Article 14(1) of the Convention which provides that "[p]ersons designated to serve on the Panels shall be persons of high moral character and recognized competence in the fields of law, commerce, industry or finance, who may be relied upon to exercise independent judgment. Competence in the field of law shall be of particular importance in the case of persons on the Panel of Arbitrators."

way they wish. If they have not reached an agreement thereon by the time the request for arbitration has been registered, Arbitration Rule 2 provides a procedure for agreeing on how to constitute a Tribunal; however, if the parties are unable to reach an agreement, then either may, at the expiration of the 60-day period provided for in Arbitration Rule 2(3), invoke the automatic formula provided for in Article 37(2)(b) of the Convention.[12] If the parties can agree in advance on the method of constituting their Tribunal, it would seem best to record this in the consent agreement by means of a clause such as the following.

Clause 9

Any Arbitral Tribunal constituted pursuant to this agreement shall consist of [a sole arbitrator]/[uneven total number arbitrators, number appointed by each party, and an arbitrator, who shall be President of the Tribunal, appointed by [agreement of the parties]/ [title of neutral official]/[agreement of the parties or, failing such agreement, by title of neutral official]].

V. APPLICABLE LAW

A. *Specification of System of Law*

Article 42(1) of the Convention provides that a Tribunal shall decide a dispute in accordance with such rules of law as may be agreed by the parties. The parties are free to agree on rules of law defined as they choose. They may refer to a national law, international law, a combination of national and international law, or a law frozen in time or subject to certain modifications.[13]

Clause 10

Any Arbitral Tribunal constituted pursuant to this agreement shall apply specification of system of law [as in force on the date on which this agreement is signed]/[subject to the following modifications: . . .].

B. *Ex Aequo et Bono Power*

Article 42(3) of the Convention provides that a Tribunal may decide a dispute *ex aequo et bono*

---

[12] Under the formula in Article 37(2)(b) of the Convention the Tribunal will consist of three arbitrators, one appointed by each party and a third, presiding, arbitrator appointed by agreement of the parties. Should the Tribunal remain to be constituted at the expiration of the 90-day period provided for in Article 38 of the Convention and Arbitration Rule 4, or such other period as the parties may agree, then either party may request the Chairman of the Administrative Council of ICSID to appoint the arbitrator or arbitrators not yet appointed. Under Arbitration Rule 4, the Chairman must comply with such requests within 30 days. If, as possible under clause 9 above, a neutral official other than the Chairman may be called upon to appoint arbitrators, it is advisable to obtain the official's consent in advance (*compare infra* sec. XII).

[13] If the parties do not reach agreement on the matter, then Article 42(1) of the Convention specifies that the Tribunal shall apply "the law of the Contracting State party to the dispute (including its rules on the conflict of laws) and such rules of international law as may be applicable."

if the parties so agree. If the parties wish to give the Tribunal the authority so to decide, they may use a clause such as follows.

Clause 11

Any Arbitral Tribunal constituted pursuant to this agreement shall have the power to decide a dispute *ex aequo et bono*.

VI. CLAUSES RELATING TO OTHER REMEDIES

A. Agreement that Other Remedies are Not Excluded

The first sentence of Article 26 of the Convention provides that the consent of the parties to arbitration "shall, unless otherwise stated, be deemed consent to such arbitration to the exclusion of any other remedy." Since this provision permits the parties to "state otherwise," they may do so by means of a clause along the following lines.

Clause 12

The consent to the jurisdiction of the Centre recorded in citation of basic clause above shall not preclude either party hereto from resorting to the following alternative remedy: identification of other type of proceeding. While such other proceeding is pending, no arbitration proceeding pursuant to the Convention shall be instituted.

B. Requirement to Exhaust Local Remedies

The second sentence of Article 26 of the Convention permits a Contracting State to "require the exhaustion of local administrative or judicial remedies as a condition of its consent to arbitration under this Convention." If a State so requires, a clause along the following lines might be included in the consent agreement.

Clause 13

Before either party hereto institutes an arbitration proceeding under the Convention with respect to a particular dispute, that party must have taken all steps necessary to exhaust the [following] [administrative] [and] [judicial] remedies available under the laws of the Host State with respect to that dispute [list of required remedies], unless the other party hereto waives that requirement in writing.

C. Provisional Measures

Article 47 of the Convention provides that, except as the parties otherwise agree, a Tribunal may, if it considers the circumstances so require, recommend any provisional measures which should be taken to preserve the respective rights of either party. Under Arbitration Rule 39(5) the parties may, if they have so provided in their consent agreement, also request a court or other authority to order provisional measures. If the parties wish thus to provide for the possibility of seeking court-ordered provisional measures, they may use a clause such as the following for the purpose.

Clause 14

Without prejudice to the power of the Arbitral Tribunal to recommend provisional measures, either party hereto may request any judicial or other authority to order any provisional or conservatory measure, including attachment, prior to the institution of the arbitration proceeding, or during the proceeding, for the preservation of its rights and interests.

VII. WAIVER OF IMMUNITY FROM EXECUTION OF THE AWARD

Under Article 54 of the Convention, all Contracting States, whether or not parties to the dispute, must recognize awards rendered pursuant to the Convention as binding and enforce the pecuniary obligations imposed thereby. Article 55 of the Convention nevertheless makes it clear that a State does not by becoming a party to the Convention waive such immunity from execution of an award as the State might enjoy under national laws. Such a waiver may, however, be effected by an express stipulation of which the following is an example.

Clause 15

The Host State hereby waives any right of sovereign immunity as to it and its property in respect of the enforcement and execution of any award rendered by an Arbitral Tribunal constituted pursuant to this agreement.

VIII. RULES OF PROCEDURE

A. Use of Current Version of Rules of Procedure

Article 44 of the Convention provides that arbitration proceedings shall in general and "except as the parties otherwise agree" be conducted in accordance with the Arbitration Rules of the Centre in effect on the date on which the parties consented to arbitration under the Convention. The parties may however wish to provide that the Arbitration Rules should always apply in their most up-to-date form. This can be accomplished by a clause along the lines of the following.

Clause 16

Any arbitration proceeding pursuant to this agreement shall be conducted in accordance with the Arbitration Rules of the Centre in effect on the date on which the proceeding is instituted.

B. Substitution of Particular Procedural Rules

Instead of using the Arbitration Rules of the Centre, the parties may prefer to substitute their own dispositions for some of the ICSID ones.[14]

---

[14] In doing so, the parties should take care that their rules do not contravene any of the binding provisions (i.e., those that do not permit the parties to agree on alternatives) of the Convention, of the Administrative and Financial Regulations, or of the Institution Rules of the Centre.

Clause 17

Any arbitration proceeding pursuant to this agreement shall be conducted in accordance with the Arbitration Rules of the Centre except that the following provisions shall be substituted for the Rules indicated below: ...

IX. DIVISION OF COSTS

Article 61(2) of the Convention provides that, except as the parties otherwise agree, the Arbitral Tribunal shall assess the expenses incurred by the parties in connection with an arbitration proceeding and shall decide how and by whom those expenses, as well as the fees and expenses of the members of the Tribunal and the charges of the Centre, shall be paid.[15] If the parties wish to make an advance agreement on this point, they may do so by means of a clause along the following lines.

Clause 18

In any arbitration proceeding conducted pursuant to this agreement, the fees and expenses of the members of the Arbitral Tribunal as well as the charges for the use of the facilities of the Centre shall be [borne equally by the parties hereto]/[divided between the parties hereto as follows: ...].

X. PLACE OF PROCEEDINGS

Under Articles 62 and 63 of the Convention, proceedings may be held at:

(a) the seat of the Centre (in Washington, D.C.);
(b) the seat of any institution with which the Centre has made the necessary arrangements (Article 63(a) of the Convention singles out the Permanent Court of Arbitration at The Hague as an example of such an institution);[16] or
(c) any other place agreed by the parties (in which case Article 63(b) of the Convention requires that the venue also be approved by the Tribunal after consultation with the Secretary-General).

If the parties wish to address this matter in advance, they may do so by means of a clause such as the one below, bearing in mind the fact that the designation of a place of proceedings will if it falls under Article 63(b) of the Convention be subject to the approval of the Tribunal after consultation with the Secretary-General.

Clause 19

The parties hereto hereby agree that any arbitration proceeding conducted pursuant to this agreement shall be held at/in name of institution or place.

---

[15] Article 61(1) of the Convention provides that in the case of conciliation proceedings the fees and expenses of the members of the Conciliation Commission, as well as the charges for the use of the facilities of the Centre, shall be borne equally by the parties.
[16] Other such institutions include the Asian-African Legal Consultative Committee's Regional Centres for Commercial Arbitration at Cairo and Kuala Lumpur.

XI. CLAUSES REFERRING TO THE ADDITIONAL FACILITY RULES

The Additional Facility Rules were approved by the Administrative Council of ICSID in 1978. Under these Rules, the Secretariat of the Centre is authorized to administer the following types of proceedings between States (or subdivisions or agencies of States) and nationals of other States which fall outside the scope of the Convention:

(a) conciliation and arbitration proceedings for the settlement of investment disputes between parties one of which is not a Contracting State or a national of a Contracting State;
(b) conciliation and arbitration proceedings between parties at least one of which is a Contracting State or a national of a Contracting State for the settlement of disputes that do not directly arise out of an investment; and
(c) fact-finding proceedings.

A. Additional Facility Conciliation/Arbitration

According to Article 4 of the Additional Facility Rules, any agreement providing for conciliation or arbitration proceedings under the Additional Facility in respect of existing or future disputes requires the approval of the Secretary-General of the Centre. The parties may apply for such approval at any time prior to the institution of proceedings, but it is advisable that such agreements be submitted for approval before they are concluded.

In practice, agreements providing for Additional Facility conciliation or arbitration are most commonly concluded in respect of investment disputes which cannot be brought under the Convention because either the host or the home State of the investor is not a Contracting State. For such cases, Article 4 of the Additional Facility Rules requires that the Secretary-General give his approval of the agreement for recourse to Additional Facility conciliation or arbitration only if the parties also consent to have recourse to conciliation or arbitration under the Convention (in lieu of the Additional Facility) if, by the time that proceedings are instituted, both the host and the home States are Contracting States.[17] The latter type of consent may conveniently be coupled with the reference to the Additional Facility in a single clause. An arbitration clause of this type might read as follows.

Clause 20

The Government of <u>name of host State</u> (hereinafter the "Host State") and <u>name of investor</u> (hereinafter the "Investor"), a national of <u>name of home State</u> (hereinafter the "Home State"), hereby consent to submit to the International Centre for Settlement of Investment Disputes (hereinafter the "Centre") any dispute arising out of or relating to this agreement for settlement by arbitration pursuant to:

(a) the Convention on the Settlement of Investment Disputes between States and Nationals of Other States (hereinafter the "Convention") if the Host State and the Home State have both become parties to the Convention at the time when any proceeding hereunder is instituted, or
(b) the Arbitration (Additional Facility) Rules of the Centre if the jurisdictional

---

[17] For cases not involving an investment, Article 4 of the Additional Facility Rules requires that the Secretary-General give his approval only if he is satisfied that the underlying transaction has features that distinguish it from an "ordinary commercial transaction."

requirements *ratione personae* of Article 25 of the Convention remain unfulfilled at the time specified in (a) above.

B. Additional Facility Fact-Finding

Additional Facility fact-finding is intended as a mechanism for preventing, rather than settling, disputes. Under Article 16 of the Fact-Finding (Additional Facility) Rules, the proceeding ends with a report that is "limited to findings of fact." The report has no binding character and must not even contain recommendations. Fact-finding can, however, provide parties with impartial assessments of facts which, if accepted by them, may prevent differences of view on specific factual issues from escalating into legal disputes. Also in contrast to the position with regard to conciliation and arbitration under the Additional Facility, any State and national of any other State (irrespective of whether these be Contracting States) may have recourse to Additional Facility fact-finding and the parties' agreement in this respect is not subject to approval by the Secretary-General of the Centre. Such an agreement might read as follows.

Clause 21

The parties hereto hereby agree to submit to the International Centre for Settlement of Investment Disputes (hereinafter "the Centre") for an inquiry under the Additional Facility (Fact-Finding) Rules of the Centre [the following questions of fact: ...]/[any questions of fact related to the following matters: ...].

XII. DESIGNATION OF THE SECRETARY-GENERAL OF ICSID AS APPOINTING AUTHORITY OF AD HOC ARBITRATORS

From time to time, parties to existing or potential disputes seek the assistance of the Secretary-General of the Centre in arranging for ad hoc (i.e., noninstitutional) arbitration by having him appoint some or all of the arbitrators in certain defined contingencies. This may in particular be done in the context of agreements providing for arbitration in accordance with the Arbitration Rules of the United Nations Commission on International Trade Law (UNCITRAL)[18], which are specially designed for ad hoc proceedings. Although the Secretary-General has often undertaken to act as appointing authority of ad hoc arbitrators, he is not obliged to do so. It is thus advisable for parties wishing to entrust such a task to the Secretary-General to obtain his consent in advance, preferably before the agreement incorporating the assignment is concluded.

The following is an example of a clause referring to the Secretary-General of ICSID as appointing authority of ad hoc arbitrators. This is a clause providing for arbitration under the UNCITRAL Arbitration Rules. It is based on the model text published with those Rules, to which the designation of the Secretary-General is added here.

---

[18] U.N. Doc. A/31/17 (1976).

Clause 22

Any dispute, controversy or claim arising out of or relating to this contract, or the breach, termination or invalidity thereof, shall be settled by arbitration in accordance with the UNCITRAL Arbitration Rules as at present in force. The appointing authority shall be the Secretary-General of the International Centre for Settlement of Investment Disputes. [The number of arbitrators shall be [one]/[three]. The place of arbitration shall be <u>name of town or country</u>. The languages to be used in the arbitral proceedings shall be <u>name of language(s)</u>.]

ANNEX 6

MODEL UK BILATERAL INVESTMENT TREATY

[DRAFT] AGREEMENT [   ]

BETWEEN THE GOVERNMENT OF THE UNITED KINGDOM OF GREAT BRITAIN AND NORTHERN IRELAND

AND

THE GOVERNMENT OF

FOR THE PROMOTION AND PROTECTION OF INVESTMENTS

The Government of the United Kingdom of Great Britain and Northern Ireland and the Government of   ;

Desiring to create favourable conditions for greater investment by nationals and companies of one State in the territory of the other State;

Recognising that the encouragement and reciprocal protection under international agreement of such investments will be conducive to the stimulation of individual business initiative and will increase prosperity in both States;

Have agreed as follows:

ARTICLE 1

Definitions

For the purposes of this Agreement:

(a) "investment" means every kind of asset and in particular, though not exclusively, includes:
   (i) movable and immovable property and any other property rights such as mortgages, liens or pledges;
   (ii) shares in and stock and debentures of a company and any other form of participation in a company;
   (iii) claims to money or to any performance under contract having a financial value;
   (iv) intellectual property rights, goodwill, technical processes and know-how;
   (v) business concessions conferred by law or under contract, including concessions to search for, cultivate, extract or exploit natural resources.

   A change in the form in which assets are invested does not affect their character as investments and the term "investment" includes all investments, whether made before or after the date of entry into force of this Agreement;

(b) "returns" means the amounts yielded by an investment and in particular, though not exclusively, includes profit, interest, capital gains, dividends, royalties and fees;

167

(c) "nationals" means:
    (i) in respect of the United Kingdom: physical persons deriving their status as United Kingdom nationals from the law in force in the United Kingdom;
    (ii) in respect of _____ : _____ ;
(d) "companies" means:
    (i) in respect of the United Kingdom: corporations, firms and associations incorporated or constituted under the law in force in any part of the United Kingdom or in any territory to which this Agreement is extended in accordance with the provisions of Article 12;
    (ii) in respect of _____ : _____ ;
(e) "territory" means:
    (i) in respect of the United Kingdom: Great Britain and Northern Ireland, including the territorial sea and maritime area situated beyond the territorial sea of the United Kingdom which has been or might in the future be designated under the national law of the United Kingdom in accordance with international law as an area within which the United Kingdom may exercise rights with regard to the sea-bed and subsoil and the natural resources and any territory to which this Agreement is extended in accordance with the provisions of Article 12;
    (ii) in respect of _____ : _____ .

ARTICLE 2

Promotion and Protection of Investment

(1) Each Contracting Party shall encourage and create favourable conditions for nationals or companies of the other Contracting Party to invest capital in its territory, and, subject to its right to exercise powers conferred by its laws, shall admit such capital.

(2) Investments of nationals or companies of each Contracting Party shall at all times be accorded fair and equitable treatment and shall enjoy full protection and security in the territory of the other Contracting Party. Neither Contracting Party shall in any way impair by unreasonable or discriminatory measures the management, maintenance, use, enjoyment or disposal of investments in its territory of nationals or companies of the other Contracting Party. Each Contracting Party shall observe any obligation it may have entered into with regard to investments of nationals or companies of the other Contracting Party.

ARTICLE 3

National Treatment and Most-favoured-nation Provisions

(1) Neither Contracting Party shall in its territory subject investments or returns of nationals or companies of the other Contracting Party to treatment less favourable than that which it accords to investments or returns of its own nationals or companies or to investments or returns of nationals or companies of any third State.

(2) Neither Contracting Party shall in its territory subject nationals or companies of the other Contracting Party, as regards their management, maintenance, use, enjoyment or disposal of their investments, to treatment less favourable that that which it accords to its own nationals or companies or to nationals or companies of any third State.

(3) For the avoidance of doubt it is confirmed that the treatment provided for in paragraphs (1) and (2) above shall apply to the provisions of Articles 1 to 11 of this Agreement.

ARTICLE 4

Compensation for Losses

(1) Nationals or companies of one Contracting Party whose investments in the territory of the other Contracting Party suffer losses owing to war or other armed conflict, revolution, a state of national emergency, revolt, insurrection or riot in the territory of the latter Contracting Party shall be accorded by the latter Contracting Party treatment, as regards restitution, indemnification, compensation or other settlement, no less favourable that that which the latter Contracting Party accords to its own nationals or companies or to nationals or companies of any third State. Resulting payments shall be freely transferable.

(2) Without prejudice to paragraph (1) of this Article, nationals or companies of one Contracting Party who in any of the situations referred to in that paragraph suffer losses in the territory of the other Contracting Party resulting from:

    (a) requisitioning of their property by its forces or authorities, or

    (b) destruction of their property by its forces or authorities, which was not caused in combat action or was not required by the necessity of the situation,

shall be accorded restitution or adequate compensation. Resulting payments shall be freely transferable.

ARTICLE 5

Expropriation

(1) Investments of nationals or companies of either Contracting Party shall not be nationalised, expropriated or subjected to measures having effect equivalent to nationalisation or expropriation (hereinafter referred to as "expropriation") in the territory of the other Contracting Party except for a public purpose related to the internal needs of that Party on a non-discriminatory basis and against prompt, adequate and effective compensation. Such compensation shall amount to the genuine value of the investment expropriated immediately before the expropriation or before the impending expropriation became public knowledge, whichever is the earlier, shall include interest at a normal commercial rate until the date of payment, shall be made without delay, be effectively realizable and be freely transferable. The national or company affected shall have a right, under the law of the Contracting Party making the expropriation, to prompt review, by a judicial or other independent authority of that Party, of his or its case and of the valuation of his or its investment in accordance with the principles set out in this paragraph.

(2) Where a Contracting Party expropriates the assets of a company which is incorporated or constituted under the law in force in any part of its own territory, and in which nationals or companies of the other Contracting Party own shares, it shall ensure that the provisions of paragraph (1) of this Article are applied to the extent necessary to guarantee prompt, adequate and effective compensation in respect of their investment to such nationals or companies of the other Contracting Party who are owners of those shares.

ARTICLE 6

Repatriation of Investment and Returns

Each Contracting Party shall in respect of investments guarantee to nationals or companies of the other Contracting Party the unrestricted transfer of their investments and returns. Transfers shall be effected without delay in the convertible currency in which the capital was originally invested or in any other convertible currency agreed by the investor and the Contracting Party concerned. Unless otherwise agreed by the investor transfers shall be made at the rate of exchange applicable on the date of transfer pursuant to the exchange regulations in force.

ARTICLE 7

Exceptions

The provisions of this Agreement relative to the grant of treatment not less favourable that that accorded to the nationals or companies of either Contracting Party or of any third State shall not be construed so as to oblige one Contracting Party to extend to the nationals or companies of the other the benefit of any treatment, preference or privilege resulting from:

(a) any existing or future customs union or similar international agreement to which either of the Contracting Parties is or may become a party; or

(b) any international agreement or arrangement relating wholly or mainly to taxation or any domestic legislation relating wholly or mainly to taxation.

[Preferred]

ARTICLE 8

Reference to International Centre for Settlement of Investment Disputes

(1) Each Contracting Party hereby consents to submit to the International Centre for the Settlement of Investment Disputes (hereinafter referred to as "the Centre") for settlement by conciliation or arbitration under the Convention on the Settlement of Investment Disputes between States and Nationals of Other States opened for signature at Washington DC on 18 March 1965 any legal dispute arising between that Contracting Party and a national or company of the other Contracting Party concerning an investment of the latter in the territory of the former.

(2) A company which is incorporated or constituted under the law in force in the territory of one Contracting Party and in which before such a dispute arises the majority of shares are owned by nationals or companies of the other Contracting Party shall in accordance with Article 25 (2) (b) of the Convention be treated for the purposes of the Convention as a company of the other Contracting Party.

(3) If any such dispute should arise and agreement cannot be reached within three months between the parties to this dispute through pursuit of local remedies or otherwise, then, if the national or company affected also consents in writing to submit the dispute to the Centre for settlement by conciliation or arbitration under the Convention, either party may institute proceedings by addressing a request to that effect to the Secretary-General of the Centre as provided in Articles 28 and 36 of the Convention. In the event of disagreement as to whether conciliation or arbitration is the more appropriate procedure the national or company affected shall have the right to choose. The Contracting Party which is a party to the dispute shall not raise as an objection at any stage of the proceedings or enforcement of an award the fact that the national or company which is the other party to the dispute has received in pursuance of an insurance contract an indemnity in respect of some or all of his or its losses.

(4) Neither Contracting Party shall pursue through the diplomatic channel any dispute referred to the Centre unless:

(a) the Secretary-General of the Centre, or a conciliation commission or an arbitral tribunal constituted by it, decides that the dispute is not within the jurisdiction of the Centre; or

(b) the other Contracting Party shall fail to abide by or to comply with any award rendered by an arbitral tribunal.

[Alternative]

ARTICLE 8

Settlement of Disputes between an Investor and a Host State

(1) Disputes between a national or company of one Contracting Party and the other Contracting Party concerning an obligation of the latter under this Agreement in relation to an investment of the former which have not been amicably settled shall, after a period of three months from written notification of a claim, be submitted to international arbitration if the national or company concerned so wishes.

(2) Where the dispute is referred to international arbitration, the national or company and the Contracting Party concerned in the dispute may agree to refer the dispute either to:

(a) the International Centre for the Settlement of Investment Disputes (having regard to the provisions, where applicable, of the Convention on the Settlement of Investment Disputes between States and Nationals of other States, opened for signature at Washington DC on 18 March 1965 and the Additional Facility for the Administration of Conciliation, Arbitration and Fact-Finding Proceedings); or

(b) the Court of Arbitration of the International Chamber of Commerce; or

(c) an international arbitrator or ad hoc arbitration tribunal to be appointed by a special agreement or established under the Arbitration Rules of the United Nations Commission on International Trade Law.

If after a period of three months from written notification of the claim there is no agreement to one of the above alternative procedures, the dispute shall at the request in writing of the national or company concerned be submitted to arbitration under the Arbitration Rules of the United Nations Commission on International Trade Law as then in force. The parties to the dispute may agree in writing to modify these Rules.

ARTICLE 9

Disputes between the Contracting Parties

(1) Disputes between the Contracting Parties concerning the interpretation or application of this Agreement should, if possible, be settled through the diplomatic channel.

(2) If a dispute between the Contracting Parties cannot thus be settled, it shall upon the request of either Contracting Party be submitted to an arbitral tribunal.

(3) Such an arbitral tribunal shall be constituted for each individual case in the following way. Within two months of the receipt of the request for arbitration, each Contracting Party shall appoint one member of the tribunal. Those two members shall then select a national of a third State who on approval by the two Contracting Parties shall be appointed Chairman of the tribunal. The Chairman shall be appointed within two months from the date of appointment of the other two members.

(4) If within the periods specified in paragraph (3) of this Article the necessary appointments

have not been made, either Contracting Party may, in the absence of any other agreement, invite the President of the International Court of Justice to make any necessary appointments. If the President is a national of either Contracting Party or if he is otherwise prevented from discharging the said function, the Vice-President shall be invited to make the necessary appointments. If the Vice-President is a national of either Contracting Party or if he too is prevented from discharging the said function, the Member of the International Court of Justice next in seniority who is not a national of either Contracting Party shall be invited to make the necessary appointments.

(5) The arbitral tribunal shall reach its decision by a majority of votes. Such decision shall be binding on both Contracting Parties. Each Contracting Party shall bear the cost of its own member of the tribunal and of its representation in the arbitral proceedings; the cost of the Chairman and the remaining costs shall be borne in equal parts by the Contracting Parties. The tribunal may, however, in its decision direct that a higher proportion of costs shall be borne by one of the two Contracting Parties, and this award shall be binding on both Contracting Parties. The tribunal shall determine its own procedure.

ARTICLE 10

Subrogation

(1) If one Contracting Party or its designated Agency ("the first Contracting Party") makes a payment under an indemnity given in respect of an investment in the territory of the other Contracting Party ("the second Contracting Party"), the second Contracting Party shall recognise:

(a) the assignment to the first Contracting Party by law or by legal transaction
   of all the rights and claims of the party indemnified; and
(b) that the first Contracting Party is entitled to exercise such rights and enforce such
   claims by virtue of subrogation, to the same extent as the party
   indemnified.

(2) The first Contracting Party shall be entitled in all circumstances to the same treatment in respect of:

(a) the rights and claims acquired by it by virtue of the assignment, and
(b) any payments received in pursuance of those rights and claims,

as the party indemnified was entitled to receive by virtue of this Agreement in respect of the investment concerned and its related returns.

(3) Any payments received in non-convertible currency by the first Contracting Party in pursuance of the rights and claims acquired shall be freely available to the first Contracting Party for the purpose of meeting any expenditure incurred in the territory of the second Contracting Party.

ARTICLE 11

Application of other Rules

If the provisions of law of either Contracting Party or obligations under international law existing at present or established hereafter between the Contracting Parties in addition to the present Agreement contain rules, whether general or specific, entitling investments by nationals or companies of the other Contracting Party to a treatment more favourable than is provided for by the present Agreement, such rules shall to the extent that they are more favourable prevail over the present Agreement.

ARTICLE 12

Territorial Extension

At the time of [signature] [entry into force] [ratification] of this Agreement, or at any time thereafter, the provisions of this Agreement may be extended to such territories for whose international relations the Government of the United Kingdom are responsible as may be agreed between the Contracting Parties in an Exchange of Notes.

ARTICLE 13

Entry into Force

[This Agreement shall enter into force on the day of signature.]

or

[Each Contracting Party shall notify the other in writing of the completion of the constitutional formalities required in its territory for the entry into force of this Agreement. This Agreement shall enter into force on the date of the latter of the two notifications.]

or

[The Agreement shall be ratified and shall enter into force on the exchange of Instruments of Ratification.]

ARTICLE 14

Duration and Termination

This Agreement shall remain in force for a period of ten years. Thereafter it shall continue in force until the expiration of twelve months from the date on which either Contracting Party shall have given written notice of termination to the other. Provided that in respect of investments made whilst the Agreement is in force, its provisions shall continue in effect with respect to such investments for a period of twenty years after the date of termination and without prejudice to the application thereafter of the rules of general international law.

In witness whereof the undersigned, duly authorised thereto by their respective Governments, have signed this Agreement.

Done in duplicate at .... this ....
day of .... 200_ [in the English and ....
languages, both texts being equally authoritative].

For the Government of

For the Government of the United Kingdom of
Great Britain and Northern Ireland:

106th Congress
2d Session

SENATE Treaty Doc.

106-25

INVESTMENT TREATY WITH BAHRAIN

MESSAGE

FROM

THE PRESIDENT OF THE UNITED STATES

TRANSMITTING

THE TREATY BETWEEN THE GOVERNMENT OF THE UNITED STATES OF AMERICA AND THE GOVERNMENT OF THE STATE OF BAHRAIN CONCERNING THE ENCOURAGEMENT AND RECIPROCAL PROTECTION OF INVESTMENT WITH ANNEX AND PROTOCOL, SIGNED, AT WASHINGTON ON SEPTEMBER 29, 1999

MAY 23, 2000.–Treaty was read the first time and, together with the accompanying papers, referred to the Committee on Foreign Relations and ordered to be printed for the use of the Senate

U.S. GOVERNMENT PRINTING OFFICE

79-118 WASHINGTON : 2000

LETTER OF TRANSMITTAL

* * * * * *

The White House, *May 23, 2000.*

To the Senate of the United States:

With a view to receiving the advice and consent of the Senate to ratification, I transmit herewith the Treaty Between the Government of the United States of America and the Government of the State of Bahrain Concerning the Encouragement and Reciprocal Protection of Investment, with Annex, signed at Washington on September 29, 1999. I transmit also, for the information of the Senate, the report of the Department of State with respect to this Treaty. The bilateral investment treaty (BIT) with Bahrain is the third such treaty between the United States and a Middle Eastern country. The Treaty will protect U.S. investment and assist Bahrain in its efforts to develop its economy by creating conditions more favorable for U.S. private investment and thus strengthen the development of its private sector.

The Treaty is fully consistent with U.S. policy toward international and domestic investment. A specific tenet of U.S. policy, reflected in this Treaty, is that U.S. investment abroad and foreign investment in the United States should receive national treatment. Under this Treaty, the Parties also agree to customary international law standards for expropriation. The Treaty includes detailed provisions regarding the computation and payment of prompt, adequate, and effective compensation for expropriation; free transfer of funds related to investments; freedom of investments from specified performance requirements; fair, equitable, and most-favored-nation treatment; and the investor's freedom to choose to resolve disputes with the host government through international arbitration.

I recommend that the Senate consider this Treaty as soon as possible, and give its advice and consent to ratification of the Treaty at an early date.

WILLIAM J. CLINTON

LETTER OF SUBMITTAL

* * * * * *

Department of State,
Washington, April 24, 2000.

The President,
The White House.

The President: I have the honor to submit to you the Treaty Between the Government of the United States of America and the Government of the State of Bahrain Concerning the Encouragement and Reciprocal Protection of Investment, with Annex, signed at Washington on September 29, 1999. I recommend that this Treaty with Annex, be transmitted to the Senate for its advice and consent to ratification.

The bilateral investment treaty (BIT) with Bahrain is the first such treaty signed between the United States and a member of the Cooperation Council for the Arab States of the Gulf. The Treaty is based on the view that an open investment policy contributes to economic growth. This Treaty will assist Bahrain in its efforts to develop its economy by creating conditions more favorable for U.S. private investment and thereby strengthening the development of its private sector. It is U.S. policy, however, to advise potential treaty partners during BIT negotiations that conclusion of such a treaty does not necessarily result in increases in private U.S. investment flows.

To date, 31 BITs are in force for the United States – with Albania, Argentina, Armenia, Bangladesh, Bulgaria, Cameroon, the Republic of the Congo, the Democratic Republic of the Congo (formerly Zaire), the Czech Republic, Ecuador, Egypt, Estonia, Georgia, Grenada, Jamaica, Kazakhstan, Kyrgyzstan, Latvia, Moldova, Mongolia, Morocco, Panama, Poland, Romania, Senegal, Slovakia, Sri Lanka, Trinidad & Tobago, Tunisia, Turkey, and Ukraine. In addition to the Treaty with Bahrain, the United States has signed, but not yet brought into force, BITS with Azerbaijan, Belarus, Bolivia, Croatia, El Salvador, Honduras, Jordan, Lithuania, Mozambique, Nicaragua, Russia, and Uzbekistan.

The Office of the United States Trade Representative and the Department of State jointly led this BIT negotiation, with assistance from the Departments of Commerce, Treasury, and Energy.

The U.S.-Bahrain Treaty

The Treaty with Bahrain is based on the 1994 U.S. prototype BIT and satisfies the U.S. principal objectives in bilateral investment treaty negotiations:

- All forms of U.S. investment in the territory of Bahrain are covered.
- Covered investments receive the better of national treatment or most-favored-nation (MFN) treatment both while they are being established and thereafter, subject to certain specified exceptions.
- Specified performance requirements may not be imposed upon or enforced against covered investments.
- Expropriation is permitted only in accordance with customary international law standards.
- Parties are obligated to permit the transfer, in a freely usable currency, of all funds related to a covered investment, subject to exceptions for specified purposes.
- Investment disputes with the host government may be brought by investors, or by their covered investments, to binding international arbitration as an alternative to domestic courts.

These elements are further described in the following article- by-article analysis of the provisions of the Treaty:

Title and Preamble

The Title and Preamble state the goals of the Treaty. Foremost is the encouragement and protection of investment. Other goals include economic cooperation on investment issues; the stimulation of economic development; higher living standards; promotion of respect for internationally-recognized worker rights; and maintenance of health, safety, and environmental measures. While the Preamble does not impose binding obligations, its statement of goals may assist in interpreting the Treaty and in defining the scope of Party-to- Party consultations pursuant to Article 8.

Article 1 (Definitions)

Article 1 defines terms used throughout the Treaty.

Company, Company of a Party

The definition of "company" is broad, covering all types of legal entities constituted or organized under applicable law, and includes corporations, trusts, partnerships, sole proprietorships, branches, joint ventures, and associations. The definition explicitly covers not-for-profit entities, as well as entities that are owned or controlled by the state. "Company of a Party" is defined as a company constituted or organized under the laws of that Party.

National

The Treaty defines "national" as a natural person who is a national of a Party under its own laws. Under U.S. law, the term "national" is broader than the term "citizen." For example, a native of American Samoa is a national of the United States, but not a citizen.

Investment, Covered Investment

The Treaty's definition of investment is broad, recognizing that investment can take a wide variety of forms. Every kind of investment is specifically incorporated in the definition; moreover, it is explicitly noted that investment may consist or take the form of any of a number of interests, claims, and rights.

The Treaty provides an illustrative list of the forms an investment may take. Establishing a subsidiary is a common way of making an investment. Other forms that an investment might take include equity and debt interests in a company; contractual rights; movable, immovable, intangible, and intellectual property; and rights conferred pursuant to law, such as licenses and permits. Investment as defined by the Treaty generally excludes claims arising solely from trade transactions, such as a sale of goods across a border that does not otherwise involve an investment.

The Treaty defines "covered investment" as an investment of a national or company of a Party in the territory of the other Party. An investment of a national or company is one that the national or company owns or controls, either directly or indirectly. Indirect ownership or control could be through other, intermediate companies or persons, including those of third countries. Control is not specifically defined in the Treaty; ownership of over 50 percent of the voting stock of a company would normally convey control, but in many cases the requirement could be satisfied by less than that proportion, or by other arrangements.

The broad nature of the definitions of "investment," "company," and "company of a Party" means that investments can be covered by the Treaty even if ultimate control lies with non-Party nationals. A Party may, however, deny the benefits of the Treaty in the limited circumstances described in Article 12.

State Enterprise, Investment Authorization, Investment Agreement

The Treaty defines "state enterprise" as a company owned, or controlled through ownership interests, by a Party. Purely regulatory control over a company does not qualify it as a state enterprise.

The Treaty defines an "investment authorization" as an authorization granted by the foreign investment authority of a Party to a covered investment or a national or company of the other Party.

The Treaty defines an "investment agreement" as a written agreement between the national authorities of a Party and a covered investment or a national or company of the other Party that (1) grants rights with respect to natural resources or other assets controlled by the national authorities and (2) the investment, national, or company relies upon in establishing or acquiring a covered investment. this definition thus excludes agreements with subnational authorities (including U.S. States) as well as agreements arising from various types of regulatory activities of the national government, including, in the tax area, rulings, closing agreements, and advance pricing agreements.

ICSID Convention, Centre, UNCITRAL Arbitration Rules

The "ICSID Convention," "Centre," and "UNCITRAL Arbitration Rules" are explicitly defined to make the text brief and clear.

Article 2 (Treatment of Investment)

Article 2 contains the Treaty's major obligations with respect to the treatment of covered investments.

Paragraph 1 generally ensures the better of national or MFN treatment in both the entry and post-entry phases of investment. It thus prohibits, outside of exceptions listed in the Annex, "screening" on the basis of nationality during the investment process, as well as nationality-based post-establishment measures. For purposes of the Treaty, "national treatment" means treatment no less favorable than that which a Party accords, in like situations, to investments in its territory of its own nationals or companies. For purposes of the Treaty, "MFN treatment" means treatment no less favorable than that which a Party accords, in like situations, to investments in its territory of nationals or companies of a third country. The Treaty obliges each Party to provide whichever of national treatment or MFN treatment is the most favorable. This is defined by the Treaty as "national and MFN treatment." Paragraph 1 explicitly states that the national and MFN treatment obligation will extend to state enterprises in their provision of goods and services to covered investments.

Paragraph 2 states that each Party may adopt or maintain exceptions to the national and MFN treatment standard with respect to the sectors or matters specified in the Annex. Further restrictive measures are permitted in each sector. (The specific exceptions are discussed in the section entitled "Annex" below.) In the Annex, Parties may take exceptions only to the obligation to provide national and MFN treatment; there are no sectoral exceptions to the rest of the Treaty's obligations. Finally, in adopting any exception under this provision, a Party may not require the divestment of a preexisting covered investment.

Paragraph 2 also states that a Party is not required to extend to covered investments national and MFN treatment with respect to procedures provided for in multilateral agreements concluded under the auspices of the World Intellectual Property Organization relating to the acquisition or maintenance of intellectual property rights. This provision clarifies that certain procedural preferences granted under intellectual property conventions, such as the Patent Cooperation Treaty, fall outside the BIT. This exception parallels those in the Uruguay Round's Agreement on Trade-Related Aspects of Intellectual Property Rights (TRIPS) and the North American Free Trade Agreement (NAFTA).

Paragraph 3 sets out a minimum standard of treatment based on standards found in customary international law. The obligations to accord "fair and equitable treatment" and "full protection and security" are explicitly cited, as is each Party's obligation not to impair, through unreasonable and discriminatory means, the management, conduct, operation, and sale or other disposition of covered investments. The general reference to international law also implicitly incorporates other fundamental rules of customary international law regarding the treatment of foreign investment. However, this provision does not incorporate obligations based on other international agreements.

Paragraph 4 requires that each Party provide effective means of asserting claims and enforcing rights with respect to covered investments.

Paragraph 5 ensures that transparency of each Party's regulation of covered investments.

Article 3 (Expropriation)

Article 3 incorporates into the Treaty customary international law standards for expropriation. Article 3 also includes detailed provisions regarding the computation and payment of prompt, adequate, and effective compensation. Paragraph 1 describes the obligations of the Parties with respect to expropriation and nationalization of a covered investment. These obligations apply to both direct expropriation and indirect expropriation through measures "tantamount to expropriation or nationalization" and thus apply to "creeping expropriations" – a series of measures that effectively amounts to an expropriation of a covered investment without taking title.

Paragraph 1 further bars all expropriations or nationalizations except those that are for a public purpose; carried out in a non-discriminatory manner; in accordance with due process of law; in accordance with the general principles of treatment provided in Article 3(3); and subject to "prompt, adequate and effective compensation." Paragraphs 2, 3, and 4 more fully describe the meaning of "prompt, adequate and effective compensation." The guiding principle is that the investor should be made whole.

Article 4 (Compensation for Damages Due to War and Similar Events)

Paragraph 1 entitles investments covered by the Treaty to national and MFN treatment with respect to any measure relating to losses suffered to a party's territory owing to war or other armed conflict, civil disturbances, or similar events. Paragraph 2, by contrast, creates an unconditional obligation to pay compensation for such losses when the losses result from requisitioning or from destruction not required by the necessity of the situation.

Article 5 (Transfers)

Article 5 protects investors from certain government exchange controls that limit current and capital account transfers, as well as limits on inward transfers made by screening authorities and, in certain circumstances, limits on returns in kind.

In paragraph 1, each Party agrees to "permit all transfers relating to a covered investment to be made freely and without delay into and out of its territory." Paragraph 1 also provides a list of transfers that must be allowed. The list is non-exclusive, and is intended to protect flows to both affiliated and non-affiliated entities.

Paragraph 2 provides that each Party must permit transfers to be made in a "freely usable currency" at the market rate of exchange prevailing on the date of transfer. "Freely usable" is a term used by the International Monetary Fund; at present there are five "freely usable" currencies: the U.S. dollar, Japanese yen, German mark, French franc, and British pound sterling.

In paragraph 3, each Party agrees to permit returns in kind to be made where such returns have been authorized by an investment authorization or written agreement between a Party and a covered investment or a national or company of the other Party. Paragraph 4 recognizes that, notwithstanding the obligations of paragraphs 1 through 3, a Party may prevent a transfer through the equitable, non-discriminatory, and good faith application of laws relating to bankruptcy, insolvency, or the protection of the rights of creditors; securities; criminal or penal offenses; or ensuring compliance with orders or judgments in adjudicatory proceedings.

Article 6 (Performance Requirements)

Article 6 prohibits either Party from mandating or enforcing specified performance requirements as a condition for the establishment, acquisition, expansion, management, conduct, or operation of a covered investment. This prohibition includes, but is not limited to, imposition of any of the specified performance requirements by means of a commitment or undertaking in connection with the receipt of a governmental permission or authorization. The list of prohibited requirements is exhaustive and covers domestic content requirements and domestic purchase preferences, the "balancing" of imports or sales in relation to exports or foreign exchange earnings, requirements to export products or services, technology transfer requirements, and requirements relating to the conduct of research and development in the host country. Such requirements are major burdens on investors and impair their competitiveness.

The last sentence of Article 6 makes clear that a Party may, however, impose conditions for the receipt or continued receipt of benefits and incentives.

Article 7 (Entry, Sojourn, and Employment of Aliens)

Paragraph 1 requires each Party to allow, subject to its laws relating to the entry and sojourn of aliens, the entry into its territory of the other Party's nationals for certain purposes related to a covered investment and involving the commitment of a "substantial amount of capital." This paragraph serves to render nationals of Bahrain eligible for treaty-investor visas under U.S. immigration law. It also affords similar treatment for U.S. nationals entering Bahrain. The requirement to commit a "substantial amount of capital" is intended to prevent abuse of treaty-investor status; it parallels the requirements of U.S. immigration law.

In addition, paragraph 1(b) prohibits labor certification requirements and numerical restrictions on the entry of treaty-investors.

Paragraph 2 requires that each Party allow covered investments to engage top managerial personnel of their choice, regardless of nationality. This provision does not require that such personnel be granted entry into a Party's territory. Such persons must independently qualify for an appropriate visa for entry into the territory of the other party. Nor does this provision create an exception to U.S. equal employment opportunity laws.

Article 8 (State-State Consultations)

Article 8 provides for prompt consultation between the Parties, at either Party's request, on any matter relating to the interpretation or application of the Treaty or to the realization of the Treaty's objectives. A Party may thus request consultations for any matter reasonably related to the encouragement or protection of covered investment, whether or not a Party is alleging a violation of the Treaty.

Article 9 (Settlement of Disputes Between One Party and a National or Company of the Other Party)

Article 9 sets forth several means by which disputes brought against a Party by an investor (specifically, a national or company of the other Party) may be resolved. Article 9 procedures apply to an "investment dispute," which is any dispute arising out of or relating to an investment authorization, an investment agreement, or an alleged breach of rights conferred, created, or recognized by the Treaty with respect to a covered investment.

In the event that an investment dispute cannot be settled amicably, paragraph 2 gives an investor an exclusive (with the exception in paragraph 3(b) concerning injunctive relief, explained below) choice among three options to settle the dispute. These three options are: (1) submitting the dispute or the courts or administrative tribunals of the Party that is a party to the dispute; (2) invoking dispute–resolution procedures previously agreed upon by the national or company and the host country government; or (3) invoking the dispute- resolution mechanisms identified in paragraph 3 of Article 9.

Under paragraph 3(a), the investor can submit an investment dispute to binding arbitration 90 days after the dispute arises, provided that the investor has not submitted the claim to a court or administrative tribunal of the Party or invoked a dispute resolution procedure previously agreed upon. The investor may choose among the International Centre for Settlement of Investment Disputes (ICSID) (Convention Arbitration), the Additional Facility of ICSID (if Convention Arbitration is not available), ad hoc arbitration using the Arbitration Rules of the United Nations Commission on International Trade Law (UNCITRAL), or any other arbitral institution or rules agreed upon by both parties to the dispute.

Before or during such arbitral proceedings, however, paragraph 3(b) provides that an investor may seek, without affecting its right to pursue arbitration under this Treaty, interim injunctive relief not involving the payment of damages from local courts or administrative tribunals of the Party that is a party to the dispute for the preservation of its rights and interests. This paragraph does not alter the power of the arbitral tribunals to recommend or order interim measures they may deem appropriate.

Paragraph 4 constitutes each Party's consent to the submission of investment disputes to binding arbitration in accordance with the choice of the investor.

Paragraph 5 provides that any non-ICSID Convention arbitration shall take place in a country that is a party to the United Nations Convention on the Recognition and Enforcement of Arbitral Awards. This provision facilitates enforcement of arbitral awards.

In addition, in paragraph 6, each Party commits to enforcing arbitral awards rendered pursuant to this Article.

The Federal Arbitration Act (9 U.S.C. 1 et seq.) satisfies the requirement for the enforcement of non-ICSID Convention awards in the United States. The Convention on the Settlement of Investment Disputes Act of 1966 (22 U.S.C. 1650-1650a) provides for the enforcement of ICSID awards.

Paragraph 7 ensures that a Party may not assert as a defense, or for any other reason, that the investor involved in the investment dispute has received or will receive reimbursement for the same damages under an insurance or guarantee contract. Paragraph 8 provides that, for the purposes of this article, the nationality of a company in the host country will be determined by ownership or control, rather than by place of incorporation. This provision allows a company that is a covered investment to bring a claim in its own name.

Article 10 (Settlement of Disputes Between the Parties)

Article 10 provides for binding arbitration of Disputes between the United States and Bahrain concerning the interpretation or application of the Treaty that are not resolved through consultations or other diplomatic channels. The article specifies various procedural aspects of such arbitration proceedings, including time periods, selection of arbitrators, and distribution of arbitration costs between the Parties. The article constitutes each Party's prior consent to such arbitration.

Article 11 (Preservation of Rights)

Article 11 clarifies that the Treaty does not derogate from any obligation a Party might have to provide better treatment to the covered investment than is specified in the Treaty. Thus, the Treaty establishes a floor for the treatment of covered investments. A covered investment may be entitled to more favorable treatment through domestic legislation, other international legal obligations, or a specific obligation (e.g., to provide a tax holiday) assumed by a Party with respect to that covered investment.

Article 12 (Denial of Benefits)

Article 12(a) preserves the right of each Party to deny the benefits of the Treaty to a company owned or controlled by nationals of a non-Party country with which the denying Party does not have normal economic relations, e.g., a country to which it is applying economic sanctions. For example, at this time the United States does not maintain normal economic relations with, among other countries, Cuba and Libya.

Article 12(b) permits each Party to deny the benefits of the Treaty to a company of the other Party if the company is owned or controlled by non-Party nationals and if the company has no substantial business activities in the Party where it is established. Thus, the United States could deny benefits to a company that is a subsidiary of a shell company organized under the laws of Bahrain if controlled by nationals of a third country. However, this provision would not generally permit the United States to deny benefits to a company of Bahrain that maintains its central administration or principal place of business in the territory of, or has a real and continuous link with, Bahrain.

Article 13 (Taxation)

Article 13 excludes tax matters generally from the coverage of the BIT, on the basis that tax matters should be dealt with in bilateral tax treaties. However, Article 13 does not preclude a national or company from bringing claims under Article 9 that taxation provisions in an investment agreement or authorization have been violated. In addition, the dispute settlement provisions of Articles 9 and 10 apply to tax matters in relation to alleged violations of the BIT's expropriation article.

Under paragraph 2, a national or company that asserts in a dispute that a tax matter involves expropriation may submit that dispute to arbitration pursuant to Article 9(3) only if (1) the investor has first referred to the competent tax authorities of both Parties the issue of whether the tax matter involves an expropriation, and (2) the tax authorities have not both determined, within 9 months from the time of referral, that the matter does not involve an expropriation. The "competent tax authority" of the United States is the Assistant Secretary of the Treasury for Tax Policy, who will make such a determination only after consultation with the Inter-Agency Staff Coordinating Group on Expropriations.

Article 14 (Measures Not Precluded)

The first paragraph of Article 14 reserves the right of a Party to take measures that it considers necessary for the fulfillment of its international obligations with respect to maintenance or restoration of international peace or security, as well as those measures it regards as necessary for the protection of its own essential security interests.

International obligations with respect to maintenance or restoration of peace or security would include, for example, obligations arising out of Chapter VII of the United Nations Charter. Measures permitted by the provision on the protection of a Party's essential security interests would include security-related actions taken in time of war or national emergency. Actions not arising from a state of war or national emergency must have a clear and direct relationship to the essential security interests of the Party involved. This Treaty makes explicit the implicit understanding that measures to protect a Party's essential security interests are self-judging in nature, although each Party would expect the provisions to be applied by the other in good faith.

The second paragraph permits a Party to prescribe special formalities in connection with covered investments, provided that these formalities do not impair the substance of any Treaty rights. Such formalities could include reporting requirements for covered investments or for transfers of funds, or incorporation requirements.

Article 15 (Application to Political Subdivisions and State Enterprises of the Parties)

Paragraph 1(a) makes clear that the obligations of the Treaty are applicable to all political subdivisions of the Parties, such as provincial, State, and local governments.

Paragraph 1(b) recognizes that under the U.S. federal system, States of the United States may, in some instances, treat out-of-State residents and corporations in a different manner than they treat in-State residents and corporations. The Treaty provides that the national treatment commitment, with respect to the States, means treatment no less favorable than that provided by a State to U.S. out-of-State residents and corporations.

Paragraph 2 extends a Party's obligations under the Treaty to its state enterprises in the exercise of any delegated governmental authority. This paragraph is designed to clarify that the exercise of governmental authority by a state enterprise must be consistent with a Party's obligations under the Treaty.

Article 16 (Entry Into Force, Duration, and Termination)

Paragraph 1 stipulates that the Treaty enters into force 30 days after exchange of instruments of ratification. The Treaty remains in force for a period of 10 years and continues in force thereafter unless terminated by either Party as provided in paragraph 2. Paragraph 2 permits a Party to terminate the Treaty at the end of the initial 10 year period, or at any later time, by giving 1 year's written notice to the other Party. Paragraph 1 also provides that the Treaty applies to covered investments existing at the time of entry into force as well as to those established or acquired thereafter. The Treaty does not state an intention by the Parties to apply the Treaty's provisions retroactively. Thus, under customary international law, the Treaty does not apply to disputes with respect to acts or facts which took place before the Treaty came into force or to any situation which ceased to exist before the date of entry into force of the Treaty.

Paragraph 3 provides that, if the Treaty is terminated, all investments that qualified as covered investments on the date of termination (i.e., 1 year after the date of written notice of termination) continue to be protected under the Treaty for 10 years from that date as long as these investments qualify as covered investments. A Party's obligations with respect to the establishment and acquisition of investments would lapse immediately upon the date of termination of the Treaty.

Paragraph 4 stipulates that the Annex shall form an integral part of the Treaty. Paragraph 5 states that all dates and periods mentioned in the Treaty are reckoned according to the Gregorian calendar. The final clause of the Treaty provides that the English and Arabic language texts are each authentic; however, in the event of divergence, the English text will prevail. Bahrain requested that the English text prevail in the event of divergence, in recognition of the widespread use of the English language in international commercial transactions in Bahrain.

Annex

U.S. bilateral investment treaties allow for exceptions to national and MFN treatment, where the Parties' domestic regimes do not afford national and MFN treatment, or where treatment in certain sectors or matters is negotiated in and governed by other agreements. Future derogations from the national treatment obligations of the Treaty are generally permitted only in the sectors or matters listed in the Annex, pursuant to Article 2(2), and must be made on an MFN basis unless otherwise specified therein.

Under a number of statutes, many of which have a long historical background, the U.S. federal government or States may not necessarily treat investments of nationals or companies of Bahrain as they do U.S. investments or investments from a third country. Paragraphs 1 and 2 of the Annex list the sectors or matters subject to U.S. exceptions.

The U.S. exceptions from its national treatment obligation are: atomic energy; custom-house brokers; licenses for broadcast, common carrier, or aeronautical radio stations; COMSAT; subsidies or grants, including but not limited to, government-supported loans, guarantees, and insurance; State and local measures exempt from Article 1102 of the North American Free Trade Agreement pursuant to Article 1108 thereof; and landing of submarine cables.

The U.S. exceptions from its national and MFN treatment obligations are: fisheries; air and maritime transport, and related activities; banking, insurance, securities, and other financial services; and one-way satellite transmissions of Direct-to-Home (DTH) and Direct Broadcasting Satellite (DBS) television services and of digital audio services.

Paragraph 3 of the Annex lists Bahrain's exceptions from its national treatment obligation, which are: ownership or control of television and radio broadcasting and other forms of mass media; fisheries; and initial privatization of exploration or drilling for crude oil.

Paragraph 4 of the Annex lists Bahrain's exceptions from its national and MFN treatment obligation, which are: air transportation; purchase or ownership of land; and until January 1, 2005, purchase or ownership of shares quoted on the Bahrain Stock Exchange.

Paragraph 5 of the Annex ensures that national treatment is granted by each Party in all leasing of minerals or pipeline rights-of-way on government lands. In so doing, this provision affects the implementation of the Minerals Lands Leasing Act (MLLA) (30 U.S.C. 181 et seq.) and 10 U.S.C. 7435, regarding Naval Petroleum Reserves, with respect to nationals and companies of Bahrain. The Treaty provides for resort to binding international arbitration to resolve disputes, rather than denial of mineral rights or rights to naval petroleum shares to investors of the other Party, as is the current process under the statute. U.S. domestic remedies, would, however, remain available for use in conjunction with the Treaty's provisions.

The MLLA and 10 U.S.C. 7435 direct that a foreign investor be denied access to leases for minerals on on-shore federal lands, leases of land within the Naval Petroleum and Oil Shale

Reserves, and rights-of-way for oil or gas pipelines across on- shore federal lands, if U.S. investors are denied access to similar or like privileges in the foreign country.

Bahrain's extension of national treatment in these sectors will fully meet the objectives of the MLLA and 10 U.S.C. 7435. Bahrain was informed during negotiations that, were it to include this sector in its list of treatment exemptions, the United States would (consistent with the MLLA and 10 U.S.C. 7435) exclude the leasing of minerals or pipeline rights-of-way on Government lands from the national and MFN treatment obligations of this Treaty.

The listing of a sector or matter in the Annex does not necessarily signify that domestic laws have entirely reserved it for nationals. And, pursuant to Article 2(2), any additional restrictions or limitations that a Party may adopt with respect to listed sectors or matters may not compel the divestiture of existing covered investments.

Finally, listing a sector or matter in the Annex exempts a Party only from the obligation to accord national or MFN treatment. Both parties are obligated to accord to covered investments in all sectors–even those listed in the Annex–all other rights conferred by the Treaty.

The other U.S. Government agencies that participated in negotiating the Treaty join me in recommending that it be transmitted to the Senate at an early date.

Respectfully submitted,

MADELEINE ALBRIGHT.

TREATY BETWEEN
THE GOVERNMENT OF THE UNITED STATES OF AMERICA
AND THE GOVERNMENT OF THE STATE OF BAHRAIN
CONCERNING THE ENCOURAGEMENT
AND RECIPROCAL PROTECTION OF INVESTMENT

The Government of the United States of America and the Government of the State of Bahrain (hereinafter the "Parties");

Desiring to promote greater economic cooperation between them, with respect to investment by nationals and companies of one Party in the territory of the other Party;

Recognizing that agreement upon the treatment to be accorded such investment will stimulate the flow of private capital and the economic development of the Parties;

Agreeing that a stable framework for investment will maximize effective utilization of economic resources and improve living standards;

Recognizing that the development of economic and business ties can promote respect for internationally recognized worker rights;

Agreeing that these objectives can be achieved without relaxing health, safety and environmental measures of general application; and

Having resolved to conclude a Treaty concerning the encouragement and reciprocal protection of investment;

Have agreed as follows:

ARTICLE I

For the purposes of this Treaty,

(a) "company" means any entity constituted or organized under applicable law, whether or not for profit, and whether privately or governmentally owned or controlled, and includes, but is not limited to, a corporation, trust, partnership, sole proprietorship, branch, joint venture, association, or other organization;

(b) "company of a Party" means a company constituted or organized under the laws of that Party;

(c) "national" of a Party means a natural person who is a national of that Party under its applicable law;

(d) "investment" of a national or company means every kind of investment owned or controlled directly or indirectly by that national or company, and includes, but is not limited to, investment consisting or taking the form of:

(1) a company;

(2) shares, stock, and other forms of equity participation, and bonds, debentures, and other forms of debt interests, in a company;

(3) contractual rights, such as under turnkey, construction or management contracts, production or revenue-sharing contracts, concessions, or other similar contracts;

(4) moveable and immovable property; and intangible property, including, but not limited to, rights, such as leases, mortgages, liens and pledges;

(5) intellectual property, including, but not limited to:
copyrights and related rights, patents, rights in plant varieties, industrial designs, rights in semiconductor layout designs, trade secrets, including, but not limited to, know-how and confidential business information, trade and service marks, and trade names; and

(6) rights conferred pursuant to law, such as licenses and permits;

(e) "covered investment" means an investment of a national or company of a Party in the territory of the other Party;

(f) "state enterprise" means a company owned, or controlled through ownership interests, by a Party;

(g) "investment authorization" means an authorization granted by the foreign investment authority of a Party to a covered investment or a national or company of the other Party;

(h) "investment agreement" means a written agreement between the national authorities of a Party and a covered investment or a national or company of the other Party that (1) grants rights with respect to natural resources or other assets controlled by the national authorities and (2) the investment, national or company relies upon in establishing or acquiring a covered investment;

(i) "ICSID Convention" means the Convention on the Settlement of Investment Disputes between States and Nationals of Other States, done at Washington, March 18, 1965;

(j) "Centre" means the International Centre for Settlement of Investment Disputes Established by the ICSID Convention; and

(k) "UNCITRAL Arbitration Rules" means the arbitration rules of the United Nations Commission on International Trade Law.

ARTICLE 2

1. With respect to the establishment, acquisition, expansion, management, conduct, operation and sale or other disposition of covered investments, each Party shall accord treatment no less favorable than that it accords, in like situations, to investments in its territory of its own nationals or companies (hereinafter "national treatment") or to investments in its territory of nationals or companies of a third country (hereinafter "most favored nation treatment"), whichever is most favorable (hereinafter "national and most favored nation treatment"). Each Party shall ensure that its state enterprises, in the provision of their goods or services, accord national and most favored nation treatment to covered investments.

2. (a) A Party may adopt or maintain exceptions to the obligations of paragraph 1 in the sectors or with respect to the matters specified in the Annex to this Treaty. In adopting such an exception, a Party may not require the divestment, in whole or in part, of covered investments existing at the time the exception becomes effective.

(b) The obligations of paragraph 1 do not apply to procedures provided in multilateral agreements concluded under the auspices of the World Intellectual Property Organization relating to the acquisition or maintenance of intellectual property rights.

3. (a) Each Party shall at all times accord to covered investments fair and equitable treatment and full protection and security, and shall in no case accord treatment less favorable than that required by international law.

(b) Neither Party shall in any way impair by unreasonable and discriminatory measures the management, conduct, operation, and sale or other disposition of covered investments.

4. Each Party shall provide effective means of asserting claims and enforcing rights with respect to covered investments.

5. Each Party shall ensure that its laws, regulations, administrative practices and procedures of general application, and adjudicatory decisions, that pertain to or affect covered investments are promptly published or otherwise made publicly available.

ARTICLE 3

1. Neither Party shall expropriate or nationalize a covered investment either directly or indirectly through measures tantamount to expropriation or nationalization ("expropriation") except for a public purpose; in a non-discriminatory manner; upon payment of prompt, adequate and effective compensation; and in accordance with due process of law and the general principles of treatment provided for in Article 2, paragraph 3.

2. Compensation shall be paid without delay; be equivalent to the fair market value of the expropriated investment immediately before the expropriatory action was taken ("the date of expropriation"); and be fully realizable and freely transferable. The fair market value shall not reflect any change in value occurring because the expropriatory action had become known before the date of expropriation.

3. If the fair market value is denominated in a freely usable currency, the compensation paid shall be no less than the fair market value on the date of expropriation, plus interest at a commercially reasonable rate for that currency, accrued from the date of expropriation until the date of payment.

4. If the fair market value is denominated in a currency that is not freely usable, the compensation paid–converted into the currency of payment at the market rate of exchange prevailing on the date of payment–shall be no less than:

(a) the fair market value on the date of expropriation, converted into a freely usable currency at the market rate of exchange prevailing on that date, plus

(b) interest, at a commercially reasonable rate for that freely usable currency, accrued from the date of expropriation until the date of payment.

ARTICLE 4

1. Each Party shall accord national and most favored nation treatment to covered investments as regards any measure relating to losses that investments suffer in its territory owing to war or other armed conflict, revolution, state of national emergency, insurrection, civil disturbance, or similar events.

2. Each Party shall accord restitution, or pay compensation in accordance with paragraphs 2 through 4 of Article 3, in the event that covered investments suffer losses in its territory, owing to war or other armed conflict, revolution, state of national emergency, insurrection, civil disturbance, or similar events, that result from:

(a) requisitioning of all or part of such investments by the Party's forces or authorities, or

(b) destruction of all or part of such investments by the Party's forces or authorities that was not required by the necessity of the situation.

ARTICLE 5

1. Each Party shall permit all transfers relating to a covered investment to be made freely and without delay into and out of its territory. Such transfers include, but are not limited to:

(a) contributions to capital;

(b) profits, dividends, capital gains, and proceeds from the sale of all or any part of the investment or from the partial or complete liquidation of the investment;

(c) interest, royalty payments, management fees, and technical assistance and other fees;

(d) payments made under a contract, including, but not limited to, a loan agreement; and

(e) compensation pursuant to Articles 3 and 4, and payments arising out of an investment dispute.

2. Each Party shall permit transfers to be made in a freely usable currency at the market rate of exchange prevailing on the date of transfer.

3. Each Party shall permit returns in kind to be made as authorized or specified in an investment authorization, investment agreement, or other written agreement between the Party and a covered investment or a national or company of the other Party.

4. Notwithstanding paragraphs 1 through 3, a Party may prevent a transfer through the equitable, non-discriminatory and good faith application of its laws relating to:

(a) bankruptcy, insolvency or the protection of the rights of creditors;

(b) issuing, trading or dealing in securities;

(c) criminal or penal offenses; or

(d) ensuring compliance with orders or judgments in adjudicatory proceedings.

ARTICLE 6

Neither Party shall mandate or enforce, as a condition for the establishment, acquisition, expansion, management, conduct or operation of a covered investment, any requirement (including, but not limited to, any commitment or undertaking in connection with the receipt of a governmental permission or authorization):

(a) to achieve a particular level or percentage of local content, or to purchase, use or otherwise give a preference to products or services of domestic origin or from any domestic source;

(b) to limit imports by the investment of products or services in relation to a particular volume or value of production, exports or foreign exchange earnings;

(c) to export a particular type, level or percentage of products or services, either generally or to a specific market region;

(d) to limit sales by the investment of products or services in the Party's territory in relation to a particular volume or value of production, exports or foreign exchange earnings;

(e) to transfer technology, a production process or other proprietary knowledge to a national or company in the Party's territory, except pursuant to an order, commitment or undertaking that is enforced by a court, administrative tribunal or competition authority to remedy an alleged or adjudicated violation of competition laws; or

(f) to carry out a particular type, level or percentage of research and development in the Party's territory.

Such requirements do not include conditions for the receipt or continued receipt of an advantage.

ARTICLE 7

1. (a) Subject to its laws relating to the entry and sojourn of aliens, each Party shall permit to enter and to remain in its territory nationals of the other Party for the purpose of establishing, developing, administering or advising on the operation of an investment to which they, or a company of the other Party that employs them, have committed or are in the process of committing a substantial amount of capital or other resources.

(b) Neither Party shall, in granting entry under paragraph 1 (a), require a labor certification test or other procedures of similar effect, or apply any numerical restriction.

2. Each Party shall permit covered investments to engage top managerial personnel of their choice, regardless of nationality.

ARTICLE 8

The Parties agree to consult promptly, on the request of either, to resolve any disputes in connection with the Treaty, or to discuss any matter relating to the interpretation or application of the Treaty or to the realization of the objectives of the Treaty.

ARTICLE 9

1. For purposes of this Treaty, an investment dispute is a dispute between a Party and a

national or company of the other Party arising out of or relating to an investment authorization, an investment agreement or an alleged breach of any right conferred, created or recognized by this Treaty with respect to a covered investment.

2. A national or company that is a party to an investment dispute may submit the dispute for resolution under one of the following alternatives:

(a) to the courts or administrative tribunals of the Party that is a party to the dispute; or

(b) in accordance with any applicable, previously agreed dispute-settlement procedures; or

(c) in accordance with the terms of paragraph 3.

3. (a) Provided that the national or company concerned has not submitted the dispute for resolution under paragraph 2 (a) or (b), and that ninety days have elapsed from the date on which the dispute arose, the national or company concerned may submit the dispute for settlement by binding arbitration:

(1) to the Centre, if the Centre is available; or

(2) to the Additional Facility of the Centre, if the Centre is not available; or

(3) in accordance with the UNCITRAL Arbitration Rules; or

(4) if agreed by both parties to the dispute, to any other arbitration institution or in accordance with any other arbitration rules.

(b) A national or company, notwithstanding that it may have submitted a dispute to binding arbitration under paragraph 3 (a), may seek interim injunctive relief, not involving the payment of damages, before the judicial or administrative tribunals of the Party that is a party to the dispute, prior to the institution of the arbitral proceeding or during the proceeding, for the preservation of its rights and interests.

4. Each Party hereby consents to the submission of any investment dispute for settlement by binding arbitration in accordance with the choice of the national or company under paragraph 3 (a) (1), (2), and (3) or the mutual agreement of both parties to the dispute under paragraph 3 (a) (4). This consent and the submission of the dispute by a national or company under paragraph 3 (a) shall satisfy the requirement of:

(a) Chapter II of the ICSID Convention (Jurisdiction of the Centre) and the Additional Facility Rules for written consent of the parties to the dispute; and

(b) Article II of the United Nations Convention on the Recognition and Enforcement of Foreign Arbitral Awards, done at New York, June 10, 1958, for an "agreement in writing."

5. Any arbitration under paragraph 3 (a) (2), (3) or (4) shall be held in a state that is a party to the United Nations Convention on the Recognition and Enforcement of Foreign Arbitral Awards, done at New York, June 10, 1958.

6. Any arbitral award rendered pursuant to this Article shall be final and binding on the parties to the dispute. Each Party shall carry out without delay the provisions of any such award and provide in its territory for the enforcement of such award.

7. In any proceeding involving an investment dispute, a Party shall not assert, as a defense, counterclaim, right of set-off or for any other reason, that indemnification or other compensation for all or part of the alleged damages has been received or will be received pursuant to an insurance or guarantee contract.

8. For purposes of Article 25 (2) (b) of the ICSID Convention and this Article, a company of a Party that, immediately before the occurrence of the event or events giving rise to an

investment dispute, was a covered investment, shall be treated as a company of the other Party.

ARTICLE 10

1. Any dispute between the Parties concerning the interpretation or application of the Treaty, that is not resolved through consultations or other diplomatic channels, shall be submitted upon the request of either Party to an arbitral tribunal for binding decision in accordance with the applicable rules of international law. In the absence of an agreement by the Parties to the contrary, the UNCITRAL Arbitration Rules shall govern, except to the extent these rules are (a) modified by the Parties or (b) modified by the arbitrators unless either Party objects to the proposed modification.

2. Within two months of receipt of a request, each Party shall appoint an arbitrator. The two arbitrators shall select a third arbitrator as chairman, who shall be a national of a third state. The UNCITRAL Arbitration Rules applicable to appointing members of three-member panels shall apply *mutatis mutandis* to the appointment of the arbitral panel except that the appointing authority referenced in those rules shall be the Secretary General of the Centre.

3. Unless otherwise agreed, all submissions shall be made and all hearings shall be completed within six months of the date of selection of the third arbitrator, and the arbitral panel shall render its decisions within two months of the date of the final submissions or the date of the closing of the hearings, whichever is later.

4. Expenses incurred by the Chairman and other arbitrators, and other costs of the proceedings, shall be paid for equally by the Parties. However, the arbitral panel may, at its discretion, direct that a higher proportion of the costs be paid by one of the Parties.

ARTICLE 11

This Treaty shall not derogate from any of the following that entitle covered investments to treatment more favorable than that accorded by this Treaty:

    (a) laws and regulations, administrative practices or procedures, or administrative or adjudicatory decisions of a Party;
    (b) international legal obligations; or
    (c) obligations assumed by a Party, including, but not limited to, those contained in an investment authorization or an investment agreement.

ARTICLE 12

Each Party reserves the right to deny to a company of the other Party the benefits of this Treaty if nationals of a third country own or control the company and

    (a) the denying Party does not maintain normal economic relations with the third country; or
    (b) the company has no substantial business activities in the territory of the Party under whose laws it is constituted or organized.

ARTICLE 13

1. No provision of this Treaty shall impose obligations with respect to tax matters, except that:

(a) Articles 3, 9 and 10 will apply with respect to expropriation; and
(b) Article 9 will apply with respect to an investment agreement or an investment authorization.

2. With respect to the application of Article 3, an investor that asserts that a tax measure involves an expropriation may submit that dispute to arbitration pursuant to Article 9, paragraph 3, provided that the investor concerned has first referred to the competent tax authorities of both Parties the issue of whether that tax measure involves an expropriation.

3. However, the investor cannot submit the dispute to arbitration if, within nine months after the date of referral, the competent tax authorities of both Parties determine that the tax measure does not involve an expropriation.

ARTICLE 14

1. This Treaty shall not preclude a Party from applying measures which it considers necessary for the fulfillment of its obligations with respect to the maintenance or restoration of international peace or security, or the protection of its own essential security interests.

2. This Treaty shall not preclude a Party from prescribing special formalities in connection with covered investments, such as a requirement that such investments be legally constituted under the laws and regulations of that Party, or a requirement that transfers of currency or other monetary instruments be reported, provided that such formalities shall not impair the substance of any of the rights set forth in this Treaty.

ARTICLE 15

1. (a) The obligations of this Treaty shall apply to the political subdivisions of the Parties.

(b) With respect to the treatment accorded by a State, Territory or possession of the United States of America, national treatment means treatment no less favorable than the treatment accorded thereby, in like situations, to investments of nationals of the United States of America resident in, and companies legally constituted under the laws and regulations of, other States, Territories or possessions of the United States of America.

2. A Party's obligations under this Treaty shall apply to a state enterprise in the exercise of any regulatory, administrative or other governmental authority delegated to it by that Party.

ARTICLE 16

1. This Treaty shall enter into force thirty days after the date of exchange of instruments of ratification. It shall remain in force for a period of ten years and shall continue in force unless terminated in accordance with paragraph 2. It shall apply to covered investments existing at the time of entry into force as well as to those established or acquired thereafter.

2. A Party may terminate this Treaty at the end of the initial ten year period or at any time thereafter by giving one year's written notice to the other Party.

3. For ten years from the date of termination, all other Articles shall continue to apply to covered investments established or acquired prior to the date of termination, except insofar as those Articles extend to the establishment or acquisition of covered investments.

4. The Annex shall form an integral part of the Treaty.

5. All dates and periods mentioned in this Treaty shall be reckoned according to the Gregorian calendar.

IN WITNESS WHEREOF, the respective plenipotentiaries have signed this Treaty.

DONE at Washington, this twenty-ninth day of September, 1999, in duplicate in the English and Arabic languages, each text being authentic; however, in the case of divergence, the English text shall prevail.

FOR THE GOVERNMENT OF THE
UNITED STATES
OF AMERICA:

FOR THE GOVERNMENT OF
THE STATE
OF BAHRAIN:

_____

_____

[signature]

[signature]

APPENDICES:

ANNEX

1. The Government of the United States of America may adopt or maintain exceptions to the obligation to accord national treatment to covered investments in the sectors or with respect to the matters specified below:

> atomic energy; customhouse brokers; licenses for broadcast, common carrier, or aeronautical radio stations; COMSAT; subsidies or grants, including, but not limited to, government-supported loans, guarantees and insurance; state and local measures exempt from Article 1102 of the North American Free Trade Agreement pursuant to Article 1108 thereof; and landing of submarine cables.

Most favored nation treatment shall be accorded in the sectors and matters indicated above.

2. The Government of the United States of America may adopt or maintain exceptions to the obligation to accord national and most favored nation treatment to covered investments in the sectors or with respect to the matters specified below:

> fisheries; air and maritime transport, and related activities; banking, insurance, securities, and other financial services; and one-way satellite transmissions of direct-to-home (DTH) and direct broadcast satellite (DBS) television services and of digital audio services.

3. The Government of the State of Bahrain may adopt or maintain exceptions to the obligation to accord national treatment to covered investments in the sectors or with respect to the matters specified below:

ownership or control of television and radio broadcasting and other forms of mass media; fisheries; initial privatization of exploration or drilling for crude oil.

Most favored nation treatment shall be accorded in the sectors and matters indicated above.
4. The Government of the State of Bahrain may adopt or maintain exceptions to the obligation to accord national and most favored nation treatment to covered investments in the sectors or with respect to the matters specified below:

air transportation; purchase or ownership of land; and until 1 January 2005, purchase or ownership of shares quoted on the Bahrain Stock Exchange.

5. Each Party agrees to accord national treatment to covered investments in the following sectors:

leasing of minerals and pipeline rights-of-way on government lands.

NORTH AMERICAN FREE TRADE AGREEMENT

PART FIVE

INVESTMENT, SERVICES AND RELATED MATTERS

Chapter Eleven: Investment

Section A – Investment

Article 1101: Scope and Coverage

1. This Chapter applies to measures adopted or maintained by a Party relating to:

   (a) investors of another Party;

   (b) investments of investors of another Party in the territory of the Party; and

   (c) with respect to Articles 1106 and 1114, all investments in the territory of the Party

2. A Party has the right to perform exclusively the economic activities set out in Annex III and to refuse to permit the establishment of investment in such activities.

3. This Chapter does not apply to measures adopted or maintained by a Party to the extent that they are covered by Chapter Fourteen (Financial Services).

4. Nothing in this Chapter shall be construed to prevent a Party from providing a service or performing a function such as law enforcement, correctional services, income security or insurance, social security or insurance, social welfare, public education, public training, health, and child care, in a manner that is not inconsistent with this Chapter.

Article 1102: National Treatment

1. Each Party shall accord to investors of another Party treatment no less favorable than that it accords, in like circumstances, to its own investors with respect to the establishment, acquisition, expansion, management, conduct, operation, and sale or other disposition of investments.

2. Each Party shall accord to investments of investors of another Party treatment no less favorable than that it accords, in like circumstances, to investments of its own investors with respect to the establishment, acquisition, expansion, management, conduct, operation, and sale or other disposition of investments.

3. The treatment accorded by a Party under paragraphs 1 and 2 means, with respect to a state or province, treatment no less favorable than the most favorable treatment accorded, in like circumstances, by that state or province to investors, and to investments of investors, of the Party of which it forms a part.

4. For greater certainty, no Party may:

(a) impose on an investor of another Party a requirement that a minimum level of equity in an enterprise in the territory of the Party be held by its nationals, other than nominal qualifying shares for directors or incorporators of corporations; or

(b) require an investor of another Party, by reason of its nationality, to sell or otherwise dispose of an investment in the territory of the Party.

Article 1103: Most-Favored-Nation Treatment

1. Each Party shall accord to investors of another Party treatment no less favorable than that it accords, in like circumstances, to investors of any other Party or of a non-Party with respect to the establishment, acquisition, expansion, management, conduct, operation, and sale or other disposition of investments.

2. Each Party shall accord to investments of investors of another Party treatment no less favorable than that it accords, in like circumstances, to investments of investors of any other Party or of a non-Party with respect to the establishment, acquisition, expansion, management, conduct, operation, and sale or other disposition of investments.

Article 1104: Standard of Treatment

Each Party shall accord to investors of another Party and to investments of investors of another Party the better of the treatment required by Articles 1102 and 1103.

Article 1105: Minimum Standard of Treatment

1. Each Party shall accord to investments of investors of another Party treatment in accordance with international law, including fair and equitable treatment and full protection and security.

2. Without prejudice to paragraph 1 and notwithstanding Article 1108(7)(b), each Party shall accord to investors of another Party, and to investments of investors of another Party, non-discriminatory treatment with respect to measures it adopts or maintains relating to losses suffered by investments in its territory owing to armed conflict or civil strife.

3. Paragraph 2 does not apply to existing measures relating to subsidies or grants that would be inconsistent with Article 1102 but for Article 1108(7)(b).

Article 1106: Performance Requirements

1. No Party may impose or enforce any of the following requirements, or enforce any commitment or undertaking, in connection with the establishment, acquisition, expansion, management, conduct or operation of an investment of an investor of a Party or of a non-Party in its territory:

(a) to export a given level or percentage of goods or services;

(b) to achieve a given level or percentage of domestic content;

(c) to purchase, use or accord a preference to goods produced or services provided in its territory, or to purchase goods or services from persons in its territory;

(d) to relate in any way the volume or value of imports to the volume or value of exports or to the amount of foreign exchange inflows associated with such investment;

(e) to restrict sales of goods or services in its territory that such investment produces or provides by relating such sales in any way to the volume or value of its exports or foreign exchange earnings;

(f) to transfer technology, a production process or other proprietary knowledge to a person in its territory, except when the requirement is imposed or the commitment or undertaking is enforced by a court, administrative tribunal or competition authority to remedy an alleged violation of competition laws or to act in a manner not inconsistent with other provisions of this Agreement; or

(g) to act as the exclusive supplier of the goods it produces or services it provides to a specific region or world market.

2. A measure that requires an investment to use a technology to meet generally applicable health, safety or environmental requirements shall not be construed to be inconsistent with paragraph 1(f). For greater certainty, Articles 1102 and 1103 apply to the measure.

3. No Party may condition the receipt or continued receipt of an advantage, in connection with an investment in its territory of an investor of a Party or of a non-Party, on compliance with any of the following requirements:

(a) to achieve a given level or percentage of domestic content;

(b) to purchase, use or accord a preference to goods produced in its territory, or to purchase goods from producers in its territory;

(c) to relate in any way the volume or value of imports to the volume or value of exports or to the amount of foreign exchange inflows associated with such investment; or

(d) to restrict sales of goods or services in its territory that such investment produces or provides by relating such sales in any way to the volume or value of its exports or foreign exchange earnings.

4. Nothing in paragraph 3 shall be construed to prevent a Party from conditioning the receipt or continued receipt of an advantage, in connection with an investment in its territory of an investor of a Party or of a non-Party, on compliance with a requirement to locate production, provide a service, train or employ workers, construct or expand particular facilities, or carry out research and development, in its territory.

5. Paragraphs 1 and 3 do not apply to any requirement other than the requirements set out in those paragraphs.

6. Provided that such measures are not applied in an arbitrary or unjustifiable manner, or do not constitute a disguised restriction on international trade or investment, nothing in paragraph 1(b) or (c) or 3(a) or (b) shall be construed to prevent any Party from adopting or maintaining measures, including environmental measures:

(a) necessary to secure compliance with laws and regulations that are not inconsistent with the provisions of this Agreement;

(b) necessary to protect human, animal or plant life or health; or

(c) necessary for the conservation of living or non-living exhaustible natural resources.

Article 1107: Senior Management and Boards of Directors

1. No Party may require that an enterprise of that Party that is an investment of an investor of another Party appoint to senior management positions individuals of any particular nationality.

2. A Party may require that a majority of the board of directors, or any committee thereof, of an enterprise of that Party that is an investment of an investor of another Party, be of a particular nationality, or resident in the territory of the Party, provided that the requirement does not materially impair the ability of the investor to exercise control over its investment.

Article 1108: Reservations and Exceptions

1. Articles 1102, 1103, 1106 and 1107 do not apply to:

  (a) any existing non-conforming measure that is maintained by
      (i)   a Party at the federal level, as set out in its Schedule to Annex I or III,
      (ii) a state or province, for two years after the date of entry into force of this Agreement, and thereafter as set out by a Party in its Schedule to Annex I in accordance with paragraph 2, or
      (iii) a local government;
  (b) the continuation or prompt renewal of any non-conforming measure referred to in subparagraph (a); or
  (c) an amendment to any non-conforming measure referred to in subparagraph (a) to the extent that the amendment does not decrease the conformity of the measure, as it existed immediately before the amendment, with Articles 1102, 1103, 1106 and 1107.

2. Each Party may set out in its Schedule to Annex I, within two years of the date of entry into force of this Agreement, any existing nonconforming measure maintained by a state or province, not including a local government.

3. Articles 1102, 1103, 1106 and 1107 do not apply to any measure that a Party adopts or maintains with respect to sectors, subsectors or activities, as set out in its Schedule to Annex II.

4. No Party may, under any measure adopted after the date of entry into force of this Agreement and covered by its Schedule to Annex II, require an investor of another Party, by reason of its nationality, to sell or otherwise dispose of an investment existing at the time the measure becomes effective.

5. Articles 1102 and 1103 do not apply to any measure that is an exception to, or derogation from, the obligations under Article 1703 (Intellectual Property National Treatment) as specifically provided for in that Article.

6. Article 1103 does not apply to treatment accorded by a Party pursuant to agreements, or with respect to sectors, set out in its Schedule to Annex IV.

7. Articles 1102, 1103 and 1107 do not apply to:

  (a) procurement by a Party or a state enterprise; or
  (b) subsidies or grants provided by a Party or a state enterprise, including government supported loans, guarantees and insurance.

8. The provisions of:

  (a) Article 1106(1)(a), (b) and (c), and (3)(a) and (b) do not apply to qualification requirements for goods or services with respect to export promotion and foreign aid programs;
  (b) Article 1106(1)(b), (c), (f) and (g), and (3)(a) and (b) do not apply to procurement by a Party or a state enterprise; and
  (c) Article 1106(3)(a) and (b) do not apply to requirements imposed by an importing Party relating to the content of goods necessary to qualify for preferential tariffs or preferential quotas.

Article 1109: Transfers

1. Each Party shall permit all transfers relating to an investment of an investor of another Party in the territory of the Party to be made freely and without delay. Such transfers include:

    (a) profits, dividends, interest, capital gains, royalty payments, management fees, technical assistance and other fees, returns in kind and other amounts derived from the investment;

    (b) proceeds from the sale of all or any part of the investment or from the partial or complete liquidation of the investment;

    (c) payments made under a contract entered into by the investor, or its investment, including payments made pursuant to a loan agreement;

    (d) payments made pursuant to Article 1110; and

    (e) payments arising under Section B.

2. Each Party shall permit transfers to be made in a freely usable currency at the market rate of exchange prevailing on the date of transfer with respect to spot transactions in the currency to be transferred.

3. No Party may require its investors to transfer, or penalize its investors that fail to transfer, the income, earnings, profits or other amounts derived from, or attributable to, investments in the territory of another Party.

4. Notwithstanding paragraphs 1 and 2, a Party may prevent a transfer through the equitable, non-discriminatory and good faith application of its laws relating to:

    (a) bankruptcy, insolvency or the protection of the rights of creditors;

    (b) issuing, trading or dealing in securities;

    (c) criminal or penal offenses;

    (d) reports of transfers of currency or other monetary instruments; or

    (e) ensuring the satisfaction of judgments in adjudicatory proceedings.

5. Paragraph 3 shall not be construed to prevent a Party from imposing any measure through the equitable, non-discriminatory and good faith application of its laws relating to the matters set out in subparagraphs (a) through (e) of paragraph 4.

6. Notwithstanding paragraph 1, a Party may restrict transfers of returns in kind in circumstances where it could otherwise restrict such transfers under this Agreement, including as set out in paragraph 4.

Article 1110: Expropriation and Compensation

1. No Party may directly or indirectly nationalize or expropriate an investment of an investor of another Party in its territory or take a measure tantamount to nationalization or expropriation of such an investment ("expropriation"), except:

    (a) for a public purpose;

    (b) on a non-discriminatory basis;

    (c) in accordance with due process of law and Article 1105(1); and

    (d) on payment of compensation in accordance with paragraphs 2 through 6.

2. Compensation shall be equivalent to the fair market value of the expropriated investment immediately before the expropriation took place ("date of expropriation"), and shall not

reflect any change in value occurring because the intended expropriation had become known earlier. Valuation criteria shall include going concern value, asset value including declared tax value of tangible property, and other criteria, as appropriate, to determine fair market value.

3. Compensation shall be paid without delay and be fully realizable.

4. If payment is made in a G7 currency, compensation shall include interest at a commercially reasonable rate for that currency from the date of expropriation until the date of actual payment.

5. If a Party elects to pay in a currency other than a G7 currency, the amount paid on the date of payment, if converted into a G7 currency at the market rate of exchange prevailing on that date, shall be no less than if the amount of compensation owed on the date of expropriation had been converted into that G7 currency at the market rate of exchange prevailing on that date, and interest had accrued at a commercially reasonable rate for that G7 currency from the date of expropriation until the date of payment.

6. On payment, compensation shall be freely transferable as provided in Article 1109.

7. This Article does not apply to the issuance of compulsory licenses granted in relation to intellectual property rights, or to the revocation, limitation or creation of intellectual property rights, to the extent that such issuance, revocation, limitation or creation is consistent with Chapter Seventeen (Intellectual Property).

8. For purposes of this Article and for greater certainty, a non-discriminatory measure of general application shall not be considered a measure tantamount to an expropriation of a debt security or loan covered by this Chapter solely on the ground that the measure imposes costs on the debtor that cause it to default on the debt.

Article 1111: Special Formalities and Information Requirements

1. Nothing in Article 1102 shall be construed to prevent a Party from adopting or maintaining a measure that prescribes special formalities in connection with the establishment of investments by investors of another Party, such as a requirement that investors be residents of the Party or that investments be legally constituted under the laws or regulations of the Party, provided that such formalities do not materially impair the protections afforded by a Party to investors of another Party and investments of investors of another Party pursuant to this Chapter.

2. Notwithstanding Articles 1102 or 1103, a Party may require an investor of another Party, or its investment in its territory, to provide routine information concerning that investment solely for informational or statistical purposes. The Party shall protect such business information that is confidential from any disclosure that would prejudice the competitive position of the investor or the investment. Nothing in this paragraph shall be construed to prevent a Party from otherwise obtaining or disclosing information in connection with the equitable and good faith application of its law.

Article 1112: Relation to Other Chapters

1. In the event of any inconsistency between this Chapter and another Chapter, the other Chapter shall prevail to the extent of the inconsistency.

2. A requirement by a Party that a service provider of another Party post a bond or other form of financial security as a condition of providing a service into its territory does not of itself make this Chapter applicable to the provision of that crossborder service. This Chapter applies to that Party's treatment of the posted bond or financial security.

Article 1113: Denial of Benefits

1. A Party may deny the benefits of this Chapter to an investor of another Party that is an enterprise of such Party and to investments of such investor if investors of a non-Party own or control the enterprise and the denying Party:

(a) does not maintain diplomatic relations with the non-Party; or

(b) adopts or maintains measures with respect to the non-Party that prohibit transactions with the enterprise or that would be violated or circumvented if the benefits of this Chapter were accorded to the enterprise or to its investments.

2. Subject to prior notification and consultation in accordance with Articles 1803 (Notification and Provision of Information) and 2006 (Consultations), a Party may deny the benefits of this Chapter to an investor of another Party that is an enterprise of such Party and to investments of such investors if investors of a non-Party own or control the enterprise and the enterprise has no substantial business activities in the territory of the Party under whose law it is constituted or organized.

Article 1114: Environmental Measures

1. Nothing in this Chapter shall be construed to prevent a Party from adopting, maintaining or enforcing any measure otherwise consistent with this Chapter that it considers appropriate to ensure that investment activity in its territory is undertaken in a manner sensitive to environmental concerns.

2. The Parties recognize that it is inappropriate to encourage investment by relaxing domestic health, safety or environmental measures. Accordingly, a Party should not waive or otherwise derogate from, or offer to waive or otherwise derogate from, such measures as an encouragement for the establishment, acquisition, expansion or retention in its territory of an investment of an investor. If a Party considers that another Party has offered such an encouragement, it may request consultations with the other Party and the two Parties shall consult with a view to avoiding any such encouragement.

Section B – Settlement of Disputes between a Party and an Investor of Another Party

Article 1115: Purpose

Without prejudice to the rights and obligations of the Parties under Chapter Twenty (Institutional Arrangements and Dispute Settlement Procedures), this Section establishes a mechanism for the settlement of investment disputes that assures both equal treatment among investors of the Parties in accordance with the principle of international reciprocity and due process before an impartial tribunal.

Article 1116: Claim by an Investor of a Party on Its Own Behalf

1. An investor of a Party may submit to arbitration under this Section a claim that another Party has breached an obligation under:

(a) Section A or Article 1503(2) (State Enterprises), or

(b) Article 1502(3)(a) (Monopolies and State Enterprises) where the monopoly has acted in a manner inconsistent with the Party's obligations under Section A,

and that the investor has incurred loss or damage by reason of, or arising out of, that breach. 2. An investor may not make a claim if more than three years have elapsed from the date on which the investor first acquired, or should have first acquired, knowledge of the alleged breach and knowledge that the investor has incurred loss or damage.

Article 1117: Claim by an Investor of a Party on Behalf of an Enterprise

1. An investor of a Party, on behalf of an enterprise of another Party that is a juridical person that the investor owns or controls directly or indirectly, may submit to arbitration under this Section a claim that the other Party has breached an obligation under:

(a) Section A or Article 1503(2) (State Enterprises), or
(b) Article 1502(3)(a) (Monopolies and State Enterprises) where the monopoly has acted in a manner inconsistent with the Party's obligations under Section A, and that the enterprise has incurred loss or damage by reason of, or arising out of, that breach.

2. An investor may not make a claim on behalf of an enterprise described in paragraph 1 if more than three years have elapsed from the date on which the enterprise first acquired, or should have first acquired, knowledge of the alleged breach and knowledge that the enterprise has incurred loss or damage.
3. Where an investor makes a claim under this Article and the investor or a non-controlling investor in the enterprise makes a claim under Article 1116 arising out of the same events that gave rise to the claim under this Article, and two or more of the claims are submitted to arbitration under Article 1120, the claims should be heard together by a Tribunal established under Article 1126, unless the Tribunal finds that the interests of a disputing party would be prejudiced thereby.
4. An investment may not make a claim under this Section.

Article 1118: Settlement of a Claim through Consultation and Negotiation

The disputing parties should first attempt to settle a claim through consultation or negotiation.

Article 1119: Notice of Intent to Submit a Claim to Arbitration

The disputing investor shall deliver to the disputing Party written notice of its intention to submit a claim to arbitration at least 90 days before the claim is submitted, which notice shall specify:

(a) the name and address of the disputing investor and, where a claim is made under Article 1117, the name and address of the enterprise;
(b) the provisions of this Agreement alleged to have been breached and any other relevant provisions;
(c) the issues and the factual basis for the claim; and
(d) the relief sought and the approximate amount of damages claimed.

Article 1120: Submission of a Claim to Arbitration

1. Except as provided in Annex 1120.1, and provided that six months have elapsed since the events giving rise to a claim, a disputing investor may submit the claim to arbitration under:

    (a) the ICSID Convention, provided that both the disputing Party and the Party of the investor are parties to the Convention;

    (b) the Additional Facility Rules of ICSID, provided that either the disputing Party or the Party of the investor, but not both, is a party to the ICSID Convention; or

    (c) the UNCITRAL Arbitration Rules.

2. The applicable arbitration rules shall govern the arbitration except to the extent modified by this Section.

Article 1121: Conditions Precedent to Submission of a Claim to Arbitration

1. A disputing investor may submit a claim under Article 1116 to arbitration only if:

    (a) the investor consents to arbitration in accordance with the procedures set out in this Agreement; and

    (b) the investor and, where the claim is for loss or damage to an interest in an enterprise of another Party that is a juridical person that the investor owns or controls directly or indirectly, the enterprise, waive their right to initiate or continue before any administrative tribunal or court under the law of any Party, or other dispute settlement procedures, any proceedings with respect to the measure of the disputing Party that is alleged to be a breach referred to in Article 1116, except for proceedings for injunctive, declaratory or other extraordinary relief, not involving the payment of damages, before an administrative tribunal or court under the law of the disputing Party.

2. A disputing investor may submit a claim under Article 1117 to arbitration only if both the investor and the enterprise:

    (a) consent to arbitration in accordance with the procedures set out in this Agreement; and

    (b) waive their right to initiate or continue before any administrative tribunal or court under the law of any Party, or other dispute settlement procedures, any proceedings with respect to the measure of the disputing Party that is alleged to be a breach referred to in Article 1117, except for proceedings for injunctive, declaratory or other extraordinary relief, not involving the payment of damages, before an administrative tribunal or court under the law of the disputing Party.

3. A consent and waiver required by this Article shall be in writing, shall be delivered to the disputing Party and shall be included in the submission of a claim to arbitration.

4. Only where a disputing Party has deprived a disputing investor of control of an enterprise:

    (a) a waiver from the enterprise under paragraph 1(b) or 2(b) shall not be required; and

    (b) Annex 1120.1(b) shall not apply.

Article 1122: Consent to Arbitration

1. Each Party consents to the submission of a claim to arbitration in accordance with the procedures set out in this Agreement.

2. The consent given by paragraph 1 and the submission by a disputing investor of a claim to arbitration shall satisfy the requirement of:

(a) Chapter II of the ICSID Convention (Jurisdiction of the Centre) and the Additional Facility Rules for written consent of the parties;
(b) Article II of the New York Convention for an agreement in writing; and
(c) Article I of the InterAmerican Convention for an agreement.

Article 1123: Number of Arbitrators and Method of Appointment

Except in respect of a Tribunal established under Article 1126, and unless the disputing parties otherwise agree, the Tribunal shall comprise three arbitrators, one arbitrator appointed by each of the disputing parties and the third, who shall be the presiding arbitrator, appointed by agreement of the disputing parties.

Article 1124: Constitution of a Tribunal When a Party Fails to Appoint an Arbitrator or the Disputing Parties Are Unable to Agree on a Presiding Arbitrator

1. The Secretary-General shall serve as appointing authority for an arbitration under this Section.
2. If a Tribunal, other than a Tribunal established under Article 1126, has not been constituted within 90 days from the date that a claim is submitted to arbitration, the Secretary-General, on the request of either disputing party, shall appoint, in his discretion, the arbitrator or arbitrators not yet appointed, except that the presiding arbitrator shall be appointed in accordance with paragraph 3.
3. The Secretary-General shall appoint the presiding arbitrator from the roster of presiding arbitrators referred to in paragraph 4, provided that the presiding arbitrator shall not be a national of the disputing Party or a national of the Party of the disputing investor. In the event that no such presiding arbitrator is available to serve, the Secretary-General shall appoint, from the ICSID Panel of Arbitrators, a presiding arbitrator who is not a national of any of the Parties.
4. On the date of entry into force of this Agreement, the Parties shall establish, and thereafter maintain, a roster of 45 presiding arbitrators meeting the qualifications of the Convention and rules referred to in Article 1120 and experienced in international law and investment matters. The roster members shall be appointed by consensus and without regard to nationality.

Article 1125: Agreement to Appointment of Arbitrators

For purposes of Article 39 of the ICSID Convention and Article 7 of Schedule C to the ICSID Additional Facility Rules, and without prejudice to an objection to an arbitrator based on Article 1124(3) or on a ground other than nationality:

(a) the disputing Party agrees to the appointment of each individual member of a Tribunal established under the ICSID Convention or the ICSID Additional Facility Rules;
(b) a disputing investor referred to in Article 1116 may submit a claim to arbitration, or continue a claim, under the ICSID Convention or the ICSID Additional Facility Rules, only on condition that the disputing investor agrees in writing to the appointment of each individual member of the Tribunal; and
(c) a disputing investor referred to in Article 1117(1) may submit a claim to arbitration, or

continue a claim, under the ICSID Convention or the ICSID Additional Facility Rules, only on condition that the disputing investor and the enterprise agree in writing to the appointment of each individual member of the Tribunal.

Article 1126: Consolidation

1. A Tribunal established under this Article shall be established under the UNCITRAL Arbitration Rules and shall conduct its proceedings in accordance with those Rules, except as modified by this Section.
2. Where a Tribunal established under this Article is satisfied that claims have been submitted to arbitration under Article 1120 that have a question of law or fact in common, the Tribunal may, in the interests of fair and efficient resolution of the claims, and after hearing the disputing parties, by order:

   (a) assume jurisdiction over, and hear and determine together, all or part of the claims; or
   (b) assume jurisdiction over, and hear and determine one or more of the claims, the determination of which it believes would assist in the resolution of the others.

3. A disputing party that seeks an order under paragraph 2 shall request the Secretary-General to establish a Tribunal and shall specify in the request:

   (a) the name of the disputing Party or disputing investors against which the order is sought;
   (b) the nature of the order sought; and
   (c) the grounds on which the order is sought.

4. The disputing party shall deliver to the disputing Party or disputing investors against which the order is sought a copy of the request.
5. Within 60 days of receipt of the request, the Secretary-General shall establish a Tribunal comprising three arbitrators. The Secretary-General shall appoint the presiding arbitrator from the roster referred to in Article 1124(4). In the event that no such presiding arbitrator is available to serve, the Secretary-General shall appoint, from the ICSID Panel of Arbitrators, a presiding arbitrator who is not a national of any of the Parties. The Secretary-General shall appoint the two other members from the roster referred to in Article 1124(4), and to the extent not available from that roster, from the ICSID Panel of Arbitrators, and to the extent not available from that Panel, in the discretion of the Secretary-General. One member shall be a national of the disputing Party and one member shall be a national of a Party of the disputing investors.
6. Where a Tribunal has been established under this Article, a disputing investor that has submitted a claim to arbitration under Article 1116 or 1117 and that has not been named in a request made under paragraph 3 may make a written request to the Tribunal that it be included in an order made under paragraph 2, and shall specify in the request:

   (a) the name and address of the disputing investor;
   (b) the nature of the order sought; and
   (c) the grounds on which the order is sought.

7. A disputing investor referred to in paragraph 6 shall deliver a copy of its request to the disputing parties named in a request made under paragraph 3.
8. A Tribunal established under Article 1120 shall not have jurisdiction to decide a claim, or a part of a claim, over which a Tribunal established under this Article has assumed jurisdiction.

9. On application of a disputing party, a Tribunal established under this Article, pending its decision under paragraph 2, may order that the proceedings of a Tribunal established under Article 1120 be stayed, unless the latter Tribunal has already adjourned its proceedings.

10. A disputing Party shall deliver to the Secretariat, within 15 days of receipt by the disputing Party, a copy of:

(a) a request for arbitration made under paragraph (1) of Article 36 of the ICSID Convention;

(b) a notice of arbitration made under Article 2 of Schedule C of the ICSID Additional Facility Rules; or

(c) a notice of arbitration given under the UNCITRAL Arbitration Rules.

11. A disputing Party shall deliver to the Secretariat a copy of a request made under paragraph 3:

(a) within 15 days of receipt of the request, in the case of a request made by a disputing investor;

(b) within 15 days of making the request, in the case of a request made by the disputing Party.

12. A disputing Party shall deliver to the Secretariat a copy of a request made under paragraph 6 within 15 days of receipt of the request.

13. The Secretariat shall maintain a public register of the documents referred to in paragraphs 10, 11 and 12.

Article 1127: Notice

A disputing Party shall deliver to the other Parties:

(a) written notice of a claim that has been submitted to arbitration no later than 30 days after the date that the claim is submitted; and

(b) copies of all pleadings filed in the arbitration.

Article 1128: Participation by a Party

On written notice to the disputing parties, a Party may make submissions to a Tribunal on a question of interpretation of this Agreement.

Article 1129: Documents

1. A Party shall be entitled to receive from the disputing Party, at the cost of the requesting Party a copy of:

(a) the evidence that has been tendered to the Tribunal; and

(b) the written argument of the disputing parties.

2. A Party receiving information pursuant to paragraph 1 shall treat the information as if it were a disputing Party.

Article 1130: Place of Arbitration

Unless the disputing parties agree otherwise, a Tribunal shall hold an arbitration in the territory of a Party that is a party to the New York Convention, selected in accordance with:

(a) the ICSID Additional Facility Rules if the arbitration is under those Rules or the ICSID Convention; or
(b) the UNCITRAL Arbitration Rules if the arbitration is under those Rules.

Article 1131: Governing Law

1. A Tribunal established under this Section shall decide the issues in dispute in accordance with this Agreement and applicable rules of international law.
2. An interpretation by the Commission of a provision of this Agreement shall be binding on a Tribunal established under this Section.

Article 1132: Interpretation of Annexes

1. Where a disputing Party asserts as a defense that the measure alleged to be a breach is within the scope of a reservation or exception set out in Annex I, Annex II, Annex III or Annex IV, on request of the disputing Party, the Tribunal shall request the interpretation of the Commission on the issue. The Commission, within 60 days of delivery of the request, shall submit in writing its interpretation to the Tribunal.
2. Further to Article 1131(2), a Commission interpretation submitted under paragraph 1 shall be binding on the Tribunal. If the Commission fails to submit an interpretation within 60 days, the Tribunal shall decide the issue.

Article 1133: Expert Reports

Without prejudice to the appointment of other kinds of experts where authorized by the applicable arbitration rules, a Tribunal, at the request of a disputing party or, unless the disputing parties disapprove, on its own initiative, may appoint one or more experts to report to it in writing on any factual issue concerning environmental, health, safety or other scientific matters raised by a disputing party in a proceeding, subject to such terms and conditions as the disputing parties may agree.

Article 1134: Interim Measures of Protection

A Tribunal may order an interim measure of protection to preserve the rights of a disputing party, or to ensure that the Tribunal's jurisdiction is made fully effective, including an order to preserve evidence in the possession or control of a disputing party or to protect the Tribunal's jurisdiction. A Tribunal may not order attachment or enjoin the application of the measure alleged to constitute a breach referred to in Article 1116 or 1117. For purposes of this paragraph, an order includes a recommendation.

Article 1135: Final Award

1. Where a Tribunal makes a final award against a Party, the Tribunal may award, separately or in combination, only:

(a) monetary damages and any applicable interest;

(b) restitution of property, in which case the award shall provide that the disputing Party may pay monetary damages and any applicable interest in lieu of restitution.

A tribunal may also award costs in accordance with the applicable arbitration rules.

2. Subject to paragraph 1, where a claim is made under Article 1117(1):

(a) an award of restitution of property shall provide that restitution be made to the enterprise;

(b) an award of monetary damages and any applicable interest shall provide that the sum be paid to the enterprise; and

(c) the award shall provide that it is made without prejudice to any right that any person may have in the relief under applicable domestic law.

3. A Tribunal may not order a Party to pay punitive damages.

Article 1136: Finality and Enforcement of an Award

1. An award made by a Tribunal shall have no binding force except between the disputing parties and in respect of the particular case.

2. Subject to paragraph 3 and the applicable review procedure for an interim award, a disputing party shall abide by and comply with an award without delay.

3. A disputing party may not seek enforcement of a final award until:

(a) in the case of a final award made under the ICSID Convention

    (i)   120 days have elapsed from the date the award was rendered and no disputing party has requested revision or annulment of the award, or

    (ii) revision or annulment proceedings have been completed; and

(b) in the case of a final award under the ICSID Additional Facility Rules or the UNCITRAL Arbitration Rules

    (i)   three months have elapsed from the date the award was rendered and no disputing party has commenced a proceeding to revise, set aside or annul the award, or

    (ii) a court has dismissed or allowed an application to revise, set aside or annul the award and there is no further appeal.

4. Each Party shall provide for the enforcement of an award in its territory.

5. If a disputing Party fails to abide by or comply with a final award, the Commission, on delivery of a request by a Party whose investor was a party to the arbitration, shall establish a panel under Article 2008 (Request for an Arbitral Panel). The requesting Party may seek in such proceedings:

(a) a determination that the failure to abide by or comply with the final award is inconsistent with the obligations of this Agreement; and

(b) a recommendation that the Party abide by or comply with the final award.

6. A disputing investor may seek enforcement of an arbitration award under the ICSID Convention, the New York Convention or the InterAmerican Convention regardless of whether proceedings have been taken under paragraph 5.

7. A claim that is submitted to arbitration under this Section shall be considered to arise out of a commercial relationship or transaction for purposes of Article I of the New York Convention and Article I of the InterAmerican Convention.

Article 1137: General

Time when a Claim is Submitted to Arbitration

1. A claim is submitted to arbitration under this Section when:

   (a) the request for arbitration under paragraph (1) of Article 36 of the ICSID Convention has been received by the Secretary-General;

   (b) the notice of arbitration under Article 2 of Schedule C of the ICSID Additional Facility Rules has been received by the Secretary-General; or

   (c) the notice of arbitration given under the UNCITRAL Arbitration Rules is received by the disputing Party.

Service of Documents

2. Delivery of notice and other documents on a Party shall be made to the place named for that Party in Annex 1137.2.

Receipts under Insurance or Guarantee Contracts

3. In an arbitration under this Section, a Party shall not assert, as a defense, counterclaim, right of setoff or otherwise, that the disputing investor has received or will receive, pursuant to an insurance or guarantee contract, indemnification or other compensation for all or part of its alleged damages.

Publication of an Award

4. Annex 1137.4 applies to the Parties specified in that Annex with respect to publication of an award.

Article 1138: Exclusions

1. Without prejudice to the applicability or non-applicability of the dispute settlement provisions of this Section or of Chapter Twenty (Institutional Arrangements and Dispute Settlement Procedures) to other actions taken by a Party pursuant to Article 2102 (National Security), a decision by a Party to prohibit or restrict the acquisition of an investment in its territory by an investor of another Party, or its investment, pursuant to that Article shall not be subject to such provisions.

2. The dispute settlement provisions of this Section and of Chapter Twenty shall not apply to the matters referred to in Annex 1138.2.

Section C – Definitions

Article 1139: Definitions

For purposes of this Chapter:

   disputing investor means an investor that makes a claim under Section B;
   disputing parties means the disputing investor and the disputing Party;
   disputing party means the disputing investor or the disputing Party;

disputing Party means a Party against which a claim is made under Section B;

enterprise means an "enterprise" as defined in Article 201 (Definitions of General Application), and a branch of an enterprise;

enterprise of a Party means an enterprise constituted or organized under the law of a Party, and a branch located in the territory of a Party and carrying out business activities there.

equity or debt securities includes voting and non-voting shares, bonds, convertible debentures, stock options and warrants;

G7 Currency means the currency of Canada, France, Germany, Italy, Japan, the United Kingdom of Great Britain and Northern Ireland or the United States;

ICSID means the International Centre for Settlement of Investment Disputes;

ICSID Convention means the *Convention on the Settlement of Investment Disputes between States and Nationals of other States*, done at Washington, March 18, 1965;

InterAmerican Convention means the *InterAmerican Convention on International Commercial Arbitration*, done at Panama, January 30, 1975;

investment means:

(a) an enterprise;

(b) an equity security of an enterprise;

(c) a debt security of an enterprise
  (i) where the enterprise is an affiliate of the investor, or
  (ii) where the original maturity of the debt security is at least three years, but does not include a debt security, regardless of original maturity, of a state enterprise;

(d) a loan to an enterprise
  (i) where the enterprise is an affiliate of the investor, or
  (ii) where the original maturity of the loan is at least three years, but does not include a loan, regardless of original maturity, to a state enterprise;

(e) an interest in an enterprise that entitles the owner to share in income or profits of the enterprise;

(f) an interest in an enterprise that entitles the owner to share in the assets of that enterprise on dissolution, other than a debt security or a loan excluded from subparagraph (c) or (d);

(g) real estate or other property, tangible or intangible, acquired in the expectation or used for the purpose of economic benefit or other business purposes; and

(h) interests arising from the commitment of capital or other resources in the territory of a Party to economic activity in such territory, such as under
  (i) contracts involving the presence of an investor's property in the territory of the Party, including turnkey or construction contracts, or concessions, or
  (ii) contracts where remuneration depends substantially on the production, revenues or profits of an enterprise;

but investment does not mean,

(i) claims to money that arise solely from
  (i) commercial contracts for the sale of goods or services by a national or enterprise in the territory of a Party to an enterprise in the territory of another Party, or
  (ii) the extension of credit in connection with a commercial transaction, such as trade financing, other than a loan covered by subparagraph (d); or

(j) any other claims to money,

that do not involve the kinds of interests set out in subparagraphs (a) through (h);

investment of an investor of a Party means an investment owned or controlled directly or indirectly by an investor of such Party;

investor of a Party means a Party or state enterprise thereof, or a national or an enterprise of such Party, that seeks to make, is making or has made an investment;

investor of a non-Party means an investor other than an investor of a Party, that seeks to make, is making or has made an investment;

New York Convention means the *United Nations Convention on the Recognition and Enforcement of Foreign Arbitral Awards*, done at New York, June 10, 1958;

Secretary-General means the Secretary-General of ICSID;

transfers means transfers and international payments;

Tribunal means an arbitration tribunal established under Article 1120 or 1126; and

UNCITRAL Arbitration Rules means the arbitration rules of the United Nations Commission on International Trade Law, approved by the United Nations General Assembly on December 15, 1976.

Annex 1120.1 Submission of a Claim to Arbitration

Mexico

With respect to the submission of a claim to arbitration:

(a) an investor of another Party may not allege that Mexico has breached an obligation under:
  (i) Section A or Article 1503(2) (State Enterprises), or
  (ii) Article 1502(3)(a) (Monopolies and State Enterprises) where the monopoly has acted in a manner inconsistent with the Party's obligations under Section A,
      both in an arbitration under this Section and in proceedings before a Mexican court or administrative tribunal; and
(b) where an enterprise of Mexico that is a juridical person that an investor of another Party owns or controls directly or indirectly alleges in proceedings before a Mexican court or administrative tribunal that Mexico has breached an obligation under:
  (i) Section A or Article 1503(2) (State Enterprises), or
  (ii) Article 1502(3)(a) (Monopolies and State Enterprises) where the monopoly has acted in a manner inconsistent with the Party's obligations under Section A,
  the investor may not allege the breach in an arbitration under this Section.

Annex 1137.2 Service of Documents on a Party Under Section B

Each Party shall set out in this Annex and publish in its official journal by January 1, 1994, the place for delivery of notice and other documents under this Section.

Annex 1137.4 Publication of an Award

Canada

Where Canada is the disputing Party, either Canada or a disputing investor that is a party to the arbitration may make an award public.

Mexico

Where Mexico is the disputing Party, the applicable arbitration rules apply to the publication of an award.

United States

Where the United States is the disputing Party, either the United States or a disputing investor that is a party to the arbitration may make an award public.

Annex 1138.2: Exclusions from Dispute Settlement

Canada

A decision by Canada following a review under the *Investment Canada Act*, with respect to whether or not to permit an acquisition that is subject to review, shall not be subject to the dispute settlement provisions of Section B or of Chapter Twenty (Institutional Arrangements and Dispute Settlement Procedures).

Mexico

A decision by the National Commission on Foreign Investment ("Comisión Nacional de Inversiones Extranjeras") following a review pursuant to Annex I, page IM4, with respect to whether or not to permit an acquisition that is subject to review, shall not be subject to the dispute settlement provisions of Section B or of Chapter Twenty (Institutional Arrangements and Dispute Settlement Procedures).

ANNEX 9

SELECTED BIBLIOGRAPHY

Books

Dolzer, R., Stevens, M., Bilateral Investment Treaties (1995).
Fouchard, Gaillard, Goldman, On International Commercial Arbitration (1999).
Schreuer, C., The ICSID Convention: A Commentary (2001).

Articles

Amerasinghe, C.F., Jurisdiction Ratione Personae under the Convention on the Settlement of Investment Disputes between States and Nationals of Other States, 47 British Year Book of International Law 227 (1974/75).

Amerasinghe, C.F., Interpretation of Article 25(2)(b) of the ICSID Convention, *in* International Arbitration in the 21st Century: Towards Judicialization and Uniformity? (*Lillich, R.B.* and *Brower, C.N. eds.*) 223 (1994).

Bagner, H., The Confidentiality Conundrum in International Commercial Arbitration, ICC Bulletin, Vol. 12, No.1 (2001), p. 18.

Bishop, R.D. and Russell, W.W., Survey of Arbitration Awards Under Chapter 11 of the North American Free Trade Agreement, 19(6) Journal of International Arbitration 505 (2002).

Broches, A., The Convention on the Settlement of Investment Disputes between States and Nationals of Other States, 136 Recueil des Cours 331, 351-364 (1972-II).

Broches, A., The 'Additional Facility' of the International Centre for Settlement of Investment Disputes (ICSID), 4 Yearbook Commercial Arbitration 373 (1979).

Broches, A., Observations on the Finality of ICSID Awards, 6 ICSID Review – FILJ 321 (1991).

Broches, A., Convention on the Settlement of Investment Disputes between States and Nationals of Other States of 1965, Explanatory Notes and Survey of its Application, 18 Yearbook Commercial Arbitration 627, 641-647 (1993).

Brower, C., The Initiation of Arbitration Proceedings: "Jack be Nimble, Jack be Quick ...!", 13 ICSID Review – FILJ 15 (1998).

Lalive, P., The First 'World Bank' Arbitration (*Holiday Inns v. Morocco*) – Some Legal Problems, 51 British Year Book of International Law 123 (1980).

Obadia, E., Current Issues in Investment Disputes, The Journal of World Investment, Vol. 2, No.1, p. 219.

Obadia, E., ICSID, Investment Treaties and Arbitration: Current and Emerging Issues, ICSID News, Vol. 18, No. 2, p. 4.

Parra, A.R., Provisions on the Settlement of Investment Disputes in Modern Investment Laws, Bilateral Investment Treaties and Multilateral Instruments on Investment, 12 ICSID Review – FILJ 287 (1997).

Parra, A., The Role of the ICSID Secretariat in the Administration of Arbitration Proceedings Under the ICSID Convention, 13 ICSID Review – FILJ 85 (1998).

Parra, A., The Limits of Party Autonomy in Arbitration Proceedings under the ICSID Convention, ICC Bulletin, Vol. 10, No.1 (1999), p. 27.

Paulsson, J., Arbitration Without Privity, 10 ICSID Review – FILJ 232 (1995).

Peters, P., Dispute Settlement Arrangements in Investment Treaties, 22 Netherlands Yearbook of International Law 91 (1991).

Schreuer, C., Access to ISCID Dispute Settlement for Locally Incorporated Companies, *in*; International Economic Law with a Human Face (*Weiss, F. ed*) 497 (1998).

Stevens, M., Confidentiality Revisited, ICSID News, Vol. 17, No. 1, p. 1.

Toriello, P., The Additional Facility of the International Centre for Settlement of Investment Disputes, 4 Italian Yearbook of International Law 59 (1978/79).

Townsend, J., The Initiation of Arbitration Proceedings: "My Story Had Been Longer", 13 ICSID Review – FILJ 21 (1998), at p. 24.

Tupman, W.M., Challenge and Disqualification of Arbitrators in International Commercial Arbitration, 38 International and Comparative Law Quarterly 26 (1989).

Websites

www.icsid.org

www.unctad.org

www.naftaclaims.com

ANNEX 10

Selective Chart of ICSID Contracting States Party to BITs as of 2003

Key: Dates in normal font = Date of signature
Dates in **bold font** = Date of entry into force

The chart is a matrix whose columns are the Industrialized States and whose rows are the Contracting States, with additional columns at right for Selected Industrialized States and the United States. Column headers (left to right): Albania, Australia, Austria, Belgium-Luxembourg, Denmark, Finland, France, Germany, Greece, Hungary, Ireland, Israel, Italy, Japan, Korea Republic of, Netherlands, New Zealand, Norway, Portugal, Singapore, Spain, Sweden, Switzerland, Turkey, United Kingdom, United States.

Contracting State	Australia	Austria	Belgium-Luxembourg	Denmark	Finland	France	Germany	Greece	Hungary	Ireland	Israel	Italy	Japan	Korea Rep.	Netherlands	New Zealand	Norway	Portugal	Singapore	Spain	Sweden	Switzerland	Turkey	United Kingdom	United States
1 Albania		01.08.95	18.09.82	05.09.95	20.02.99	16.06.96	18.08.95	04.01.95	01.04.98		18.02.97	29.01.96		01.09.96	01.09.96			11.06.99		17.01.96	01.04.96	30.04.93		30.08.95	04.01.90
2 Algeria	01.01.95	01.01.95	17.09.82	25.01.99	03.05.96	13.02.93	11.03.93	26.10.99	01.10.97			26.11.93		25.09.96	01.10.94		01.10.94	03.85.96		17.01.94	28.09.92	06.11.92	03.06.98	19.02.93	28.10.94
3 Argentina	11.01.97	01.01.98	20.05.94	02.02.95	03.05.93	03.03.93	08.11.93	26.10.99	01.10.97		to be ratified	14.10.93		25.09.96	01.10.94	27.08.99	01.10.94	03.85.96		28.09.92	28.09.92	06.11.92	21.03.98	11.07.96	29.03.96
4 Armenia	07.08.01		04.11.95		11.05.95	21.06.97	21.12.95	28.04.95	01.08.97			23.07.98			01.06.96					20.10.99	21.11.79	19.11.98	09.02.94		11.12.96	01.08.97
5 Azerbaijan	28.05.01		26.02.03		26.02.03	01.09.99	29.07.98					25.09.96									22.06.96		26.06.98	09.02.94		30.10.91	01.08.97
6 Bahrain	28.05.01		14.09.87			03.10.86										01.06.96						14.10.00	14.10.00		19.06.80	25.07.89
7 Bangladesh	01.06.02	14.09.87	14.09.87			03.10.86						20.09.94		06.10.88	06.10.88						22.12.95	22.12.95	22.12.95	20.02.97	19.06.80	25.07.89
8 Barbados	01.06.02	09.04.02	09.04.02			01.09.86	03.10.86							09.08.97	01.06.96						13.07.94	13.07.94	13.07.94	20.02.97	28.12.94	15.01.94
9 Belize	01.06.02	11.12.94			11.12.94	28.10.93	23.09.96	02.12.94			to be ratified	12.08.97			20.09.32						01.11.96	01.11.96	08.08.95	21.03.98	30.04.82	
10 Benin			18.05.01			18.07.85		23.09.96							13.12.21								06.18.73		27.11.87	
11 Bolivia	29.07.97	01.07.02	25.04.90	22.03.97		12.10.96	09.11.90				17.12.96	22.02.92	04.06.97	04.06.97	01.11.36					12.05.92	03.07.92	13.05.91	21.01.98	16.02.90	17.04.98
12 Bosnia and Herzegovina			08.12.81					01.11.90							01.01.30								26.06.98		02.11.02	
13 Brunei Darussalam						30.03.98	01.03.98								07.85.66								07.66.85	07.66.85		06.04.89
14 Bulgaria	01.11.97	01.11.97	29.09.98	20.05.95	16.04.99	01.05.90	18.05.98	29.04.95	07.09.95		17.12.96	01.11.97		06.09.94	01.05.81		07.09.94	20.11.00		22.04.98	31.04.95	26.10.93	19.09.97	24.06.97	02.06.94
15 Burkina Faso			18.05.01			22.10.96	22.10.96								10.11.80							21.11.79	15.09.69	20.02.97	13.09.90	
16 Burundi			12.09.93			15.02.87	09.12.87														13.09.96	12.09.30		21.03.98	13.09.90	
17 Cambodia							21.11.87							04.11.96								12.09.36		21.03.98	07.66.85	
18 Cameroon			01.11.81			13.08.60	21.11.63								07.85.66							66.04.64	66.04.64		07.06.85	06.04.89
19 Central African Republic						11.08.60	21.11.63															04.07.73	04.07.73		21.01.98	
20 Chad							21.01.68							11.06.69								31.18.67			09.11.96	
21 Chile	09.07.96	22.10.00	13.06.99	03.11.95	01.05.96	13.06.94	21.10.68	29.04.95	10.03.97		08.02.95	11.06.99	22.07.99	06.09.96	01.05.38	22.07.99	07.09.94	24.02.98		28.03.94	30.12.95	24.06.99	21.08.98	21.84.97	03.09.03
22 China	11.07.88	11.10.86	05.10.86	29.04.85	26.01.86	19.03.85	21.01.91		21.08.97		10.04.95	28.08.87	14.05.89	04.12.92	30.11.58	25.03.89	10.07.85	01.12.92	07.42.86	01.05.93	79.03.82	18.03.87	19.08.94	15.05.86	
23 Colombia	03.05.01					15.08.00			01.84.93			17.03.94		07.08.99	07.85.66			03.94		09.06.95			09.03.94		13.88.94	
24 Congo						15.08.60	14.18.67				14.03.85	17.03.94										11.07.64	11.07.64		28.07.89	
25 Congo, Democratic Republic of the		01.01.77	01.04.99		28.11.01	01.03.71	22.07.91	26.04.91			14.05.85	17.03.94	19.07.90		19.07.90	01.07.08			08.07.90		08.07.97		01.08.08	07.09.82	28.07.89
26 Costa Rica	01.04.99	01.04.99	01.04.99		28.11.01	01.03.71	23.07.69		15.05.96			12.06.96		10.03.93	08.89.66			03.94			29.10.99	29.10.99	18.11.62		99.10.97	13.07.96
27 Côte d'Ivoire		01.04.99	12.10.99		01.11.00	14.01.83	10.06.68		15.05.96				23.07.69		10.03.93	08.99.66			27.11.97			22.04.76	16.09.96	04.10.99	01.12.99	13.07.96
28 Croatia	03.05.01		08.04.98	21.03.97	01.11.00	61.10.75	21.11.00	21.10.97	21.08.97		23.05.95	27.11.97		01.05.95	01.83.01		15.86.92	23.12.00		26.04.99	01.09.79	01.09.79	16.89.96	04.10.99	24.02.76	10.03.99
29 Cyprus		19.02.97	12.10.99	01.11.00	01.11.00	65.03.98	12.11.92	01.82.97	15.05.96		13.10.98	12.06.98		16.03.95	01.83.01		15.86.92	23.12.00	08.48.84		17.09.08	08.01.93	07.08.91	03.06.97	16.04.98	13.07.96
30 Czech Republic	29.06.94	01.10.91	08.06.99	19.09.92	24.03.94	27.09.91	02.08.93	11.05.86	25.05.95		16.03.93	01.11.97		16.03.95	01.10.92	66.08.92		03.88.94	28.11.91		28.11.91	08.01.93	07.08.98	01.08.97	26.10.92	19.12.92
31 Dominican Republic	03.05.01	18.10.03	27.05.98		27.11.01	03.02.97	15.09.98		12.02.99		18.03.99	18.11.68		06.09.80	01.87.00		66.08.92				07.18.96	30.02.96			24.08.95	11.05.97
32 Ecuador	03.05.01	18.10.03	03.07.99		27.11.01	01.04.01	27.09.98	11.05.86	21.08.97		18.42.97	15.05.97		25.65.97	01.07.83			23.12.00		01.85.95	26.04.96	29.01.79	04.06.74		24.02.76	11.08.97
33 Egypt, Arab Republic of		28.02.99	28.02.99	06.01.95		01.10.75	22.07.78					25.56.98		07.07.98	01.87.91					26.04.96	29.01.79	16.89.93	04.10.99	24.02.76	27.06.92
34 El Salvador		01.10.95	12.10.99	01.11.00	20.02.03	01.10.75	21.11.00	21.08.97			20.03.97	20.03.97		07.07.98	01.83.01	15.86.92		23.12.00		20.02.96	29.01.79	16.89.95	03.06.97	10.03.99	10.03.99
35 Estonia	01.10.95	01.10.95	23.09.99	02.12.92		18.10.79	12.01.97				to be ratified	23.05.95		16.03.95	01.06.93		15.86.92	08.85.92			01.07.98	01.07.98	18.08.93	03.06.97	16.02.97	16.02.97
36 Ethiopia		23.09.99	27.05.98	02.12.92		18.10.77	15.09.98				to be ratified	18.11.68		26.12.96	11.06.79		15.86.92				02.03.95	07.12.98	18.10.72		62.07.02	
37 Gabon		27.05.98	27.05.98			12.02.74	15.09.98								11.06.79				08.04.96			30.03.94	30.03.94		09.09.02	
38 Gambia, The			03.05.96			27.05.98	15.09.98						18.11.68		03.02.98	01.87.91					02.03.95	02.03.95	18.10.72		62.07.02	
39 Georgia	18.10.01	18.10.01	03.07.99	06.01.95		03.02.97	27.09.98	11.05.86	21.08.97		18.42.97	15.05.97		16.03.95	03.02.98			23.12.00		20.02.98	29.07.93	18.10.72	31.10.98	15.02.95	17.08.97
40 Ghana		06.01.95		06.01.95		26.03.99	23.11.98	21.08.97				25.06.98		07.07.97	01.87.91		15.06.92	16.06.93			25.08.91	25.08.91	29.01.99	31.18.96	25.02.88	
41 Grenada	03.05.01					27.05.98									01.87.91		15.06.92			28.06.90	25.02.88	25.02.88			63.83.89	63.83.89
42 Guatemala	29.07.93	29.07.93	12.10.99	01.11.00		27.05.98	13.63.94		13.02.96			23.65.96		26.08.90	01.09.62					28.06.90	16.02.93	02.03.96	28.06.90	63.83.89	63.83.89
43 Guinea			17.06.72	17.06.72	62.67.68	07.05.97	19.04.71	13.02.96				25.86.95		10.63.94	01.99.82		26.08.90		28.86.90	12.02.97	18.02.93	21.11.91	25.02.02	14.85.87	07.83.97
44 Guinea-Bissau		23.01.01				18.10.79	27.05.88					21.07.96			11.09.95					20.10.99	20.10.99	02.03.77		24.04.80	
45 Guyana							13.04.94								01.07.90		15.06.92					20.77.66	20.77.66		11.04.90	
46 Haiti	29.07.93														31.16.86						14.10.99	14.10.99		27.83.95	13.12.83
47 Honduras	29.07.93		17.66.72	62.67.68		62.67.68	21.64.88						25.06.95	10.63.94	01.99.82		26.08.90	01.99.82		12.02.93	18.62.93	99.04.76	25.02.02	08.63.95	01.07.95
48 Indonesia		23.01.01	17.06.72			29.04.75	25.06.95		13.02.96			27.07.96		10.63.95	01.11.95			15.06.92		28.06.90	20.10.99	21.11.79	25.02.02	24.03.87	07.83.97
49 Jamaica		17.66.72	17.66.72			29.65.96							21.67.96		10.63.95	18.01.77			15.06.92	02.03.77	02.03.77	02.83.77		14.85.87	87.83.97
50 Jordan		62.87.68	62.87.68			18.10.79	13.48.97						19.42.97		26.12.96	11.06.79					20.10.99	02.03.77	02.03.77	25.02.02	24.04.80	13.06.03
51 Kazakhstan	23.01.01	06.02.01	06.02.01		14.02.98	63.02.98	10.65.95	03.05.96				12.67.96	26.12.96	18.01.77		01.88.94	02.03.95	22.06.95		20.10.99	13.85.98	13.85.98		23.11.95	12.01.94
52 Kenya	22.09.98		27.68.98				16.99.96						16.99.96	11.06.96	27.11.02						09.05.06		16.69.93	31.16.98	13.69.99
53 Kuwait	22.09.98		28.09.00	06.03.95		21.68.97	16.05.97	15.11.97	01.83.94			12.07.96	21.68.90	16.95.99	31.65.62		31.16.98		16.66.93		12.02.87	99.05.06	31.16.98	18.86.98	12.01.94
54 Kyrgyz Republic	81.05.96	04.84.99	04.84.99	18.11.94		07.12.92	81.10.94	06.09.99	10.06.96			02.03.99	02.83.99	26.11.94	81.84.95				81.12.92	18.63.99	14.83.97	66.21.92	16.84.33	15.82.95	26.13.96
55 Latvia	81.05.96	04.84.99	04.84.99	18.11.94		07.12.92	81.10.94	06.09.99	10.06.96			02.83.99		26.11.94	81.04.95					18.63.99	14.83.97	66.21.92	16.84.33	15.82.95	26.13.96

Selective Chart of ICSID Contracting States Party to BITs as of 2003

Key: Dates in normal font = Date of signature
Dates in **bold font** = Date of entry into force

Industrialized States	Australia	Austria	Belgium-Luxembourg	Denmark	Finland	France	Germany	Greece	Hungary	Ireland	Israel	Italy	Japan	Korea, Republic of	Netherlands	New Zealand	Norway	Portugal	Singapore	Spain	Sweden	Switzerland	Turkey	United Kingdom	United States	Selected Industrialized States
47 Lithuania	24.11.98	01.07.97 14.04.02	06.09.99 18.09.02	08.01.93	08.01.93 23.03.02	27.03.95 28.01.98	27.06.97 10.09.96	10.07.97	25.05.99		11.07.96	15.04.97		09.11.93	01.04.95	20.12.92	27.05.98		22.12.55	01.09.92 01.10.98	13.05.93 01.10.98	11.07.94 27.10.97	21.09.93	22.11.01	47 Lithuania
48 Macedonia		18.09.02		18.09.02	03.01.88	01.09.76	21.03.66								01.06.99	28.39.67				16.02.96 06.07.79	23.06.67	26.02.98	21.10.88		48 Macedonia
49 Madagascar		01.01.87	08.02.82	18.09.92	03.01.88	01.09.76	06.07.63		08.07.95			25.10.90		31.03.89 07.31.86	13.09.72					16.02.96 06.07.79	06.07.77				49 Madagascar
50 Malaysia						01.01.78	16.05.80								01.07.85						01.01.00		04.10.86		50 Malaysia
51 Mali			15.06.93				14.12.75				15.10.73														51 Mali
52 Mauritania			23.11.83			01.03.78	26.04.86																		52 Mauritania
53 Mauritius						01.03.74	27.08.73										03.01.99								53 Mauritius
54 Moldova	05.06.01	01.05.04	20.03.02	15.04.00	21.06.97	08.09.97	28.02.94	23.03.98	19.08.96		16.03.99	19.09.97		01.02.99	01.05.97					28.03.95	30.11.98	26.11.98	13.10.86	25.11.94	01.07.95	54 Moldova
55 Mongolia	01.05.84	15.04.00	02.04.96	62.04.96		22.12.93	23.06.96	23.03.98	29.08.95			19.09.95		30.04.91	01.06.96						27.05.99	29.11.96	30.07.98	01.01.97		55 Mongolia
56 Morocco	01.07.95	29.04.02		10.09.82		13.01.96	21.01.68	16.02.94	12.12.91		18.07.90	18.07.90	29.05.82	27.01.99	27.07.78 18.12.01	07.31.86	22.03.95 31.10.98		14.01.96	11.12.97		12.04.91 01.08.94	08.04.97	29.05.91		56 Morocco
57 Mozambique						25.06.98 13.06.02	21.12.97 07.07.88								26.11.02					26.09.90 29.11.02	27.05.99 01.08.94	30.11.98	30.10.90	01.12.98		57 Mozambique
58 Namibia						13.02.98																			58 Namibia
59 Nepal				26.01.96		19.08.91	10.01.66								01.01.03							30.11.98 17.11.62	02.03.93 04.12.96	01.07.95		59 Nepal
60 Nicaragua						04.07.96	04.02.86							01.02.99	01.02.94					28.03.95	27.05.99 18.04.02		11.12.90			60 Nicaragua
61 Niger	01.12.81				20.02.94	04.07.96	14.12.84					23.01.97 19.07.97		01.02.99 15.04.90	01.02.89 01.08.89					26.04.96 31.07.98	66.06.96 14.06.81	08.10.96 (16.03.95)	21.05.96 30.11.94			61 Niger
62 Nigeria	07.02.98		23.04.98	25.09.96		04.07.96 09.10.85	28.04.62					19.07.97	29.05.82		01.09.81		14.12.96	22.03.95 31.07.98	04.05.95	31.07.98	14.06.81	22.08.85	07.11.85	30.05.91		62 Oman
63 Pakistan	20.10.91					11.12.80 04.07.96	03.11.83 06.05.98	61.04.95				15.07.99	29.05.82				24.11.99 04.11.0				01.08.84 17.02.96	28.09.92 23.11.93	22.13.81 33.04.92	07.13.85		63 Pakistan
64 Papua New Guinea	02.02.97	01.01.00	06.12.80	19.84.98	14.06.96	04.07.96	11.02.98		01.04.95			18.10.95		20.04.94	01.08.84				23.01.99	17.02.96 21.09.94	01.08.84 17.08.99	23.04.94 30.07.94	23.04.94 17.84.96	10.01.96		64 Paraguay
65 Peru	08.12.95	14.01.98	01.06.80	24.08.95		13.06.96	06.05.96	21.10.92	06.05.96	26.08.92	26.08.92	04.11.93	27.05.00	25.09.96	01.10.67	9*.05.95	17.11.94		15.07.99	07.12.05	65.10.99	30.07.94 29.05.02	10.01.96 02.01.81	19.01.94		65 Philippines
66 Romania	22.84.94	01.07.97	13.10.91	26.08.96	06.01.93	21.06.96	12.11.98	23.02.97	29.05.96		14.01.77 06.01.97	14.01.77	27.05.00	30.12.94 10.07.91	01.10.87 28.07.51	23.03.92 2.05.98	17.11.94 21.07.94			28.11.91	29.03.02 07.06.96	26.08.91 15.10.63	10.01.96 15.12.97	17.06.92		66 Romania
67 Rwanda		01.09.91	01.08.85	15.08.91		09.04.96	05.08.91		29.05.86																	67 Rwanda
68 Saint Lucia	30.06.01						08.01.89																		68 Saint Lucia
69 Saint Vincent and the Grenadines						09.01.99				Date unknown																69 Saint Vincent and the Grenadines
70 Sao Tome & Principe						16.01.66						22.05.98					18.07.57								70 Sao Tome & Principe
71 Saudi Arabia	01.06.91						26.10.90 08.05.98							02.09.95 26.07.98	05.05.81					23.02.68	13.08.64		09.02.84	25.10.90		71 Saudi Arabia
72 Serbia & Montenegro						03.03.75	26.10.90		19.07.96		Date unknown	30.07.98		26.07.98	01.04.77						21.11.79		08.12.81			72 Serbia & Montenegro
73 Sierra Leone	01.10.91			20.05.96			10.12.66		15.10.96	13.05.98																73 Sierra Leone
74 Slovak Republic		01.02.99		03.05.00	11.02.98		18.07.98	29.05.97	03.12.96		30.07.98	30.07.98			01.10.92		15.05.99 04.05.00			26.02.98	01.01.93	20.03.97	26.10.92 12.05.99	19.12.92		74 Slovak Republic
75 Slovenia			12.05.99				15.02.85					30.07.98			01.08.98				25.01.99		01.01.93	21.01.97	12.05.99	16.11.96		75 Slovenia
76 Somalia	17.06.01			15.05.97	20.65.96	18.07.98	21.06.97			30.03.98		29.84.97								06.05.85	15.03.00	03.11.98				76 Somalia
77 Sri Lanka	03.09.01	18.88.81	23.84.99 17.04.98	21.03.02	25.10.97	19.84.82	23.05.98		01.07.92	03.03.98	18.02.97	02.03.98	07.08.82	15.07.80	01.05.85		63.11.99		15.07.99	66.85.94	30.04.82	12.02.82	18.12.80	61.05.93		77 Sri Lanka
78 Sudan		17.03.98			22.10.93	04.07.97	08.85.98				18.02.97	17.09.97	07.08.82	07.08.82	27.03.72		01.07.97			10.09.97	01.03.00	24.10.02	65.05.95			78 Sudan
79 Swaziland		03.02.00		30.10.02	16.18.98	12.87.68	15.06.96						07.08.95	18.12.98	31.07.01		11.08.95			85.01.98		16.09.65	19.08.96			79 Swaziland
80 Tanzania	12.06.02			18.05.96		19.07.91	10.84.65	18.10.91				05.06.90		30.09.89	01.03.73					09.09.97	23.03.60	16.09.69	19.08.96			80 Tanzania
81 Togo							21.12.64		12.10.99												23.11.00	17.11.97	11.08.79			81 Togo
Trinidad and Tobago		01.03.97	18.09.02	11.84.97		18.05.01 02.85.96	06.02.66 28.08.97	21.84.95				24.06.89		28.11.75 11.05.98		06.12.24				20.04.94	13.05.85	19.01.64 07.83.97	08.10.93 64.01.90	26.12.96 07.02.93		Trinidad and Tobago
82 Tunisia	01.06.91	18.09.92				18.01.99	19.08.68				18.02.97	12.12.97								20.46.94	13.05.85	07.02.93	49.02.95			82 Tunisia
83 Turkmenistan			27.07.01			62.85.96	19.08.68		19.07.96		18.02.97	12.09.97			01.01.83						13.83.97		24.84.98			83 Turkmenistan
84 Uganda	01.12.97	27.07.01	29.04.54	30.01.94		26.01.96	19.08.68	04.01.97	03.12.96		18.02.97			03.11.97	01.01.83				26.02.98	01.03.97	88.05.72		24.84.98	16.11.96		84 Uganda
85 Ukraine				15.05.97		10.84.95	21.06.97		03.12.96		18.02.97	12.09.97		03.11.97	01.01.83				26.02.98	01.03.97	21.01.97	21.85.98	10.02.93	16.11.96		85 Ukraine
86 United Arab Emirates	17.06.01					21.06.97	21.06.97					29.84.97			01.06.97					15.03.00 03.11.98		03.11.98	15.12.93		86 United Arab Emirates
87 Uruguay	18.88.81	23.84.99		21.03.02	84.07.97	29.06.90	23.05.98		01.07.92	30.03.98	18.02.97	29.84.97	62.03.98	15.07.80	01.07.97				66.85.94	01.10.99	22.84.91	01.08.97	24.11.93		87 Uruguay
88 Uzbekistan		17.04.98		22.10.93		15.86.96	23.85.98		01.07.92		18.02.97	17.09.97		20.11.93	01.07.97				10.09.97		85.01.98	09.11.94	24.11.93	6.12.94		88 Uzbekistan
89 Yemen, Republic		03.02.00	19.09.96			19.07.91	16.18.98							30.08.89	01.09.86		11.86.95				85.01.98	30.11.94	01.08.96			89 Yemen, Republic
90 Zambia		28.05.01				25.08.72	19.12.78					05.06.90											11.11.83			90 Zambia
91 Zimbabwe						29.09.95						16.04.99			01.05.98		05.05.94					07.83.95 15.08.96		01.05.95		91 Zimbabwe

Index by Subject

Table of Cases

Fedax N.V. v. Republic of Venezuela, ICSID Case No. ARB/96/3, Decision on Objections to Jurisdiction (11 July 1997), 5 *ICSID Reports* 183 (2002), p. **45**

Holiday Inns v. Morocco, p. **25, 27**

Klöckner Industrie-Anlagen GmbH and others v. United Republic of Cameroon and Société Camerounaise des Engrais, ICSID Case No. ARB/81/2, Award (21 October 1983), 2 *ICSID Reports* 9 (1994), p. **101, 102, 103**

Lauder v. Czech Republic (Final Award), *supra* note 79, at para. 187. *See also SGS v. Pakistan* (Decision on Jurisdiction), *supra* note 93; *Ethyl Corporation v. The Government of Canada*, Award on Jurisdiction (24 June 1998), 38 ILM 708, 724 (1999), p. **57**

Liberian Eastern Timber Corporation(LETCO) v. Republic of Liberia, ICSID Case No. ARB/83/2, Decision on Rectification (17 June 1986), 2 *ICSID Reports* 346 (1994), p. **18, 87, 108**

Maritime International Nominees Establishment (MINE) v. Republic of Guinea, ICSID Case ARB/84/4, Award (6 January 1988), 4 *ICSID Reports* 54 (1997), p. **102, 105**

Mihaly International Corporation v. Democratic Socialist Republic of Sri Lanka, ICSID Case No. ARB/00/2, Award (15 March 2002), 17 *ICSID Review*—FILJ 142 (2002), p. **15, 45, 46**

Phillipe Gruslin v. Malaysia, ICSID Case No. ARB/99/3, Award (27 November 2000), 5 *ICSID Reports* 484 (2002), p. **45, 103**

Pope & Talbot, Inc. v. Government of Canada, Award on the Merits of Phase 2 (10 April 2001), available at www.dfait-maeci.gc.ca/tna-nac/phases-en.asp#comm, p. **68**

SGS Société Générale de Surveillance S.A. v. Islamic Republic of Pakistan, ICSID Case No. ARB/01/13, Decision on Jurisdiction (6 August 2003), *ASIL International Law in Brief* (17 September 2003), p. **55, 60**

Société Ouest Africaine de Bétons Industriels (SOABI) v. State of Senegal, ICSID Case No. ARB/82/1, Decision on Jurisdiction (1 August 1984), 2 *ICSID Reports* 175, 204 (1994), p. **17, 108**

Southern Pacific Properties (Middle East) Ltd. and Southern Pacific Properties Ltd. (Hong Kong) v. Arab Republic of Egypt, Decision on Jurisdiction (27 November 1985), 3 *ICSID Reports* 112, 126 (1995), p. **37, 38, 97**

United Mexican States v. Metalclad Corporation, Judicial Review, Supreme Court of British Columbia (2001 BCSC 664), 5 *ICSID Review*—FILJ 236 (1990), p. **68**

Vacuum Salt Products Ltd. v. Republic of Ghana, ICSID Case No. ARB/92/1, Award (16 February 1994), 4 *ICSID Reports* 329 (1997), p. **18, 42**

Victor Pey Casado and Presidente Allende Foundation v. Republic of Chile, ICSID Case No. ARB/98/2, Decision on Provisional Measures (25 September 2001), 16 *ICSID Review*—FILJ 567 (2001), p. **86**

Waste Management, Inc. v. United Mexican States, ICSID Case No. ARB/98/2, Award (2 June 2000), 5 *ICSID Reports* 443(2002), p. **63**

Wena Hotels Ltd. v. Arab Republic of Egypt, ICSID Case No. ARB/98/4, Decision on Annulment (5 February 2002), 41 ILM 933 (2002), p. **103**